GLASGOW: THE REAL MEAN CITY

GLASGOW:
THE REAL MEAN CITY

True Crime and Punishment
in the Second City of the Empire

Malcolm Archibald

BLACK & WHITE PUBLISHING

First published 2013
by Black & White Publishing Ltd
29 Ocean Drive, Edinburgh EH6 6JL

1 3 5 7 9 10 8 6 4 2   13 14 15 16

ISBN: 978 1 84502 536 6

A CIP catalogue record for this book is available from the British Library.

Typeset by Ellipsis Digital Limited, Glasgow
Printed and bound by MPG Printgroup Ltd, Bodmin, Cornwall

FOR CATHY

Acknowledgements

I would like to thank the staff at the National Archives of Scotland; the Police Museum in Glasgow; and my wife, Cathy, for all their help and support in the writing of this book.

Contents

A great city with a strong leaven of scoundralism in its population.
—*Glasgow Herald*, 7 October 1850

Map of central Glasgow *c.* 1880

Preface

My grandfather, George Frederick Archibald, was a regular soldier. He joined the Royal Scots in 1897, aged 19, and left in 1919. During these twenty-two years, the world changed forever. He served in India, Burma and Ireland and throughout the First World War from Mons until the Armistice, and survived with a chest full of medals, lungs full of gas and a head full of stories with which he tantalised young grandchildren. Among the well-known tales such as 'The Angel of Mons', 'The Christmas of 1914', 'Ladies from Hell' and 'The Crucified Canadian' were many I have never seen written in any book about the Great War. Two of these involved regiments from Glasgow.

The first anecdote was of a time when a staff officer visited the trenches and saw a handful of Glasgow soldiers escorting a large number of German prisoners to the back areas. The officer was horrified to see that many of the Germans had broken noses and bruised faces. He accused the Glasgow men of abusing the Germans after capture. My grandfather, a CSM at the time, informed him gently that in hand-to-hand combat this partic-ular regiment sharpened the rim of their steel helmet and used it as a weapon: a trench-warfare Glasgow kiss. The second story was similar; he told me of having served alongside a regiment of Glasgow Bantams, men under five feet in height who had the reputation of having disposed of more of the enemy by the bayonet than by the bullet.

As a long-eared child with all a boy's interest in the gore and supposed glory of warfare, I lapped up these tales and often wondered what sort of men these Glaswegians were. I did not know then that Glasgow contributed an estimated 200,000 men to the British Army in that horrendous mass slaughter, or that in 1914 Glasgow reputedly built more ships than all of Germany or the United States of America. I was later to hear of the landlords who tried to evict women while their men were fighting in France, leading to the largest rent strike in British history and proving that Glaswegian women were every bit as formidable as their men. Much later, I read about Red Clydeside and a British government so afraid of supposed Glaswegian communism that it sent 10,000 English troops backed by tanks and artillery to the city, while confining the local Highland Light Infantry to barracks in case it joined the strikers. I heard of the police baton charge in George Square that was repelled by strikers who were campaigning purely for decent working conditions. I learned of Glasgow gangs that fought with bayonets, and of razor gangs a thousand strong battling it out in the streets. In time, I also knew about the Orange Marches and the bitter rivalry between Celtic and Rangers, two of the most famous football teams anywhere.

The stories and legends, true, half-true and pure fiction, all painted a picture of a city that resounded with verve and violence, yet when I visited I found forthright, cheerful and friendly people who were more than willing to share all they had. I had read of a city of bleak black tenements and foul slums, but although there were bad areas in Glasgow, as in every city, there were also splendid museums and beautiful parks, and some of the Victorian buildings were of such high quality they would be an asset anywhere. There are churches by 'Greek' Thomson, an Art School by Rennie Mackintosh, a City Chambers that would rival that of any city in the world and a number of quality universities. This city produced two British prime ministers and arguably Scotland's most controversial socialist in John Maclean; it built many of the Empire's railway locomotives and a huge proportion of the word's ships; it boasted the largest timber importing business in the world, as well as the artist Charles Rennie Mackintosh. Throughout the nineteenth century Glasgow was a beacon of progress, and there were probably more Gaelic speakers here than in any other city in the world . . . there were many sides to Glasgow. And yet the legends of crime and violence persisted. I wondered what had created this negative image of Glasgow and when it had earned its reputation as a grim dark place.

The answer does not lie very far back in time; it was the nineteenth century that saw Glasgow flourish as Scotland's largest city and fostered Glasgow's multi-faceted reputation for culture, progress, engineering and crime. This book will not attempt to write a history of Glasgow; far better qualified historians than I have done and will continue to do that. Instead, I will attempt to draw a picture of the criminal side of Glasgow in the nineteenth century – not only the obvious crimes of robbery, assault and brutal murders but also the more unusual, the fraudsters and child strippers and ship scuttlers, who all added to the overall pattern of crime.

The book starts with a brief explanation of the creation of industrial cities and the fear of crime they instigated, followed by a look at Glasgow itself. The bulk of the book consists of thematic chapters that cover the whole spread of the century. As it is impossible to cover even a fraction of the crime that occurred with a major city over this time period, what is mentioned is merely a representation of events, but hopefully enough to capture the atmosphere of Glasgow in the nineteenth century. Within these pages is the dark side of the city, but even here there are the bright splurges of humour, stern courage and undoubted humanity that help make Glasgow the great city it undoubtedly is.

1

Victorian Cities, Glasgow and Crime

When the English gentleman Edmund Burt visited Glasgow in 1730 he thought it 'the prettiest and most uniform town that I ever saw and I believe there is nothing like it in Britain'. In 1772 the Welsh naturalist Thomas Pennant thought Glasgow 'the best built of any second-rate city I ever saw'. These were only two of the travellers who gave favourable comments on Glasgow when the town had not yet mushroomed. Glasgow had been a quiet city that languished on the banks of the Clyde, always important but never quite central until eighteenth-century trade and nineteenth-century industry catapulted it into Scotland's largest city, the second largest city in Great Britain, the Second City of the Empire and the greatest shipbuilding centre the world had ever seen.

Glasgow's position on the West Coast of Scotland gave certain advantages with trade to North America during the troubled eighteenth century. It was distant from the main bases of the French privateers that wreaked havoc with English and East Coast Scottish shipping, and it was free of the tides and winds of what was then termed the British Channel, thus making the transatlantic passage less hazardous. Geography ensured the passage would take less time from the Clyde than either the Thames or the Severn. When the Glasgow merchants used these advantages and added kinship connections with the smaller tobacco plantations in North

America, they began to create vast commercial fortunes; history remembers them as the Tobacco Lords.

The tobacco trade between Scotland and the North American colonies had begun in the seventeenth century but escalated after 1707 when Scotland united her parliament with that of England to form Great Britain. Within a few decades Glasgow overtook Bristol and Liverpool in the transatlantic trade and used the wealth to create industries and deepen the Clyde so shipping could penetrate upriver as far as the Broomielaw. Although the American War of Independence severely damaged the tobacco trade, by then Glasgow's industry was well established and the city grew year on year. Glasgow was Scotland's boom town.

Of course, raw human material was required to fuel the constant expansion, and in the nineteenth century there was massive immigration into the city. Improvements to agriculture saw thousands of small farmers evicted throughout the country, to be replaced by modern techniques. Unemployed countrymen drifted to the new mills and factories of the towns. First from the Lowlands and then from the Highlands, where the Clearances destroyed a people in what was as sordid a display of cultural genocide as any in history, the dispossessed and unwanted found new homes and a new way of life in Glasgow. Then the Irish arrived. From at least the 1820s and perhaps particularly in the 1840s, so many Irish people immigrated into Glasgow that it had the second largest expatriate Irish community in the world, with only New York's being greater. In 1848 1,000 Irish arrived a week. They added to the cultural mix in Glasgow – not always amicably, as religious differences and poor housing combined to create tensions that could explode into violence. Glasgow became nearly ghettoised as different religions, backgrounds and levels of employment drove people into separate areas of the city.

These incomers were housed in hastily erected tenements containing houses of one and two rooms, and frequently lacking sanitation. The middle-class speculators minted money by cramming families into these hovels and charging rents that could sometimes only be afforded by sub-letting, leading to unhealthy overcrowding. In many ways, Glasgow was a microcosm of a procedure that occurred throughout the industrialising world as the land drained its people into the towns. The nineteenth century saw perhaps the greatest population shift in history, and Glasgow was a part of this phenomenon that created a plethora of new opportunities but also a raft of new difficulties and a greater awareness of crime and criminality than ever before.

As Asa Briggs stated in his *Victorian Cities*, the vast expansion of urban areas created a perception that industrial cities held new problems and a different lifestyle from older urban centres. This assumption may have owed its origin to the speed of growth, as the population of cities increased year on year, far more than their administrative or housing capacity to cope. Perhaps it was not surprising that this large influx of strangers into what had been relatively small and stable communities created insecurity, with some inhabitants of the towns scared of a perceived increase of crime. They were not alone.

The rise of industrial urbanism was a phenomenon that shook much of the nineteenth century establishment. These new types of towns seemed to be creating a sub-society about which they knew little and which they found hard to regulate. Large industrial cities were outwith the accepted social strata, which was still largely based on rural paternalism. Observers toured impoverished urban areas and created reports that castigated the poor as an inferior race with criminal habits. For example, in 1839 J. C. Symonds, Assistant Handloom Weaving Commissioner, wrote of Glasgow: 'I did not believe, until I visited the wynds of Glasgow, that so large amount of filth, crime, misery, and disease existed on one spot in any civilised country.' Symonds reported twenty people, male and female, clothed and unclothed, sleeping in a single room in a Glasgow lodging house, which suggested immorality to him.

As people crammed into the city, certain areas became notorious for congestion, disease and pestilence: the area south of the Trongate, Calton, the area west of the Saltmarket and the region near the old High Street contained housing that was amongst the worst in Europe. Here there were numbers of wynds and alleys, unlit, unventilated and occupied by the hopeless, the destitute and often the criminal.

For example, in 1871 the Laigh Kirk Close at 59 Trongate housed twenty brothels and three shebeens, illegal and unlicensed drinking houses. According to the Glasgow author and historian Jack House in his book *The Heart of Glasgow*, inside one-sixteenth of a square mile of central Glasgow there were 150 shebeens and 200 brothels. The best of the shebeens could hold up to forty dedicated drinkers; the worst saw the near destitute rub shoulders with prostitutes and thieves as they shared a dram of kill-me-deadly in some festering slum.

Arguably the best-known account of British poverty is Frederick Engels' *The Condition of the Working Class in England*, published in 1844. Engels' description of conditions in the poorer quarters of industrial cities include mind-shuddering gems, such as 'the streets are generally unpaved . . . filled with vegetable and animal refuse, without sewers or gutters . . . filth and tottering ruin . . . foul liquids emptied before the doors . . .' Even allowing for Engels' socialist agenda, the description argues for poor living conditions in industrial towns; this way of life both appalled and frightened observers from more favoured areas. In his *London Labour and the London Poor*, the journalist Henry Mayhew wrote of 'a prostitute . . . with her eye blackened, [who] stood by the bar. She was also well-attired, and ready to accompany them. Burglars of this class often have a woman to go before them, to carry their housebreaking tools . . .' Mayhew's description is a microcosm of contemporary observers who presented the life of the urban poor as intertwined with vice and crime; the worst areas were seen as a breeding ground of criminality, with drink a principal cause. Glasgow was no different from other large cities.

Although the middle and upper classes enjoyed their tipples as much as anybody, the temperance movement was still viewed as the engine of social advancement with tracts such as *Moral Statistics of Glasgow* (1849) and *Facts and Observations of the Sanitary State of Glasgow* (1844) intending to prove the connection between vice, drink and morality. These reports helped formulate perceptions of Glasgow and other cities as places where drink fed poverty, crime, begging and prostitution. Although most published comments were from middle-class observers with different backgrounds and values from their subjects, their judgements shared a general perception that reducing the alcohol consumption and raising the moral standards of the poor would reduce the crime rate. Crime, drink and poverty were seen as synonymous, and for much of the period the poor were blamed for their own misfortune.

In common with other Scottish urban centres, from 1833 in Glasgow, £10 householders, which meant those whose annual rent was woth £10 or more, elected councils, magistrates and the Commissioners of Police, who were responsible for much more than just the control of crime. They also governed water hygiene and public health. The town councils controlled much of the trade and used local Police Acts to regulate the conduct of the inhabitants and improve the physical environment. Therefore, although the bulk of the urban population were from the working classes, the middle classes ran the administration and created the townscape. Glasgow Police also gained the power to regulate lodging houses, so the poorest people were subject to some rigid social control with their homes liable to be legally raided and inspected at any hour of the day or night. It was understandable that the police were not always the most popular people in the world.

By the middle of the century, the middle classes generally regarded society as split between the respectable and the residuum. The respectable included that section of the working class who shared middle-class morality; the residuum was those who did not. The unemployed and unemployable, the drunken, the petty and not-so-petty criminals, the destitute, the vagrants, the travelling folk and anybody else who could not be adequately controlled, categorised or pigeonholed were not considered respectable. Living alongside these, mingling with them and often hiding in their ranks were what were thought of as an entire underclass: the criminal class. The perceptions of increasing crime in the early nineteenth century encouraged the growth of criminology, so in *The Criminal Man* Cesare Lombroso propounded the theory of this class of born criminals, and in 1851 Thomas Plint stated in his *Crime in England* that the criminal class were found amidst the 'operative class'. This perceived class apparently lived entirely from crime, and occupied a distinct society that lived alongside the respectable, but in what became known as 'the slums', which was originally a slang word for a room. Contemporary theories argued that crime could be eradicated if this class was either bred out of society or reformed by punishment or improved morality.

The judge Lord Cockburn was a believer in a criminal class. In *Circuit Journeys* he mentions the case of Mary Boyle, who was released from a long spell in Perth Penitentiary in November 1843, but in spring 1844 was back in the circuit court. Cockburn termed Perth Penitentiary the 'very school of penal virtue'. Boyle was believed to be reformed but after a few weeks she joined a group of men in a burglary at the house of Alexander Alison, an ironmaster of Sauchiehall Street. Immediately Cockburn sentenced her to ten years' transportation; she dropped her humble air that had nearly fooled the jury and, according to Cockburn, began 'cursing prosecutor, judges, jury, her own counsel and all concerned in the coarsest terms'. She gripped the iron bars that penned her in the dock and held on until she was literally dragged away. Mary Boyle was no older than sixteen and looked very gentle and demure. Cockburn gave the comment that 'crime . . . runs in families . . . and this lady belongs to a race of thieves. She has a father and mother and two brothers or sisters already in Australia.' Her two remaining siblings were also convicted thieves with one, John Boyle, being a member of an active criminal gang. Perhaps there was something to be said for the theory of criminal families, if not a criminal class.

Although the slums in Victorian Britain were probably larger than and just as repugnant as their Georgian counterparts, progress through the century diminished the fear of the mob erupting from the morass and overturning established order. Rather than the casual brutality of eighteenth-century justice, nineteenth-century authority was visible in the tall figure of the uniformed police, backed by an acceptance of discipline that started in the schoolroom and was reinforced by the churches. Yet although the possibility of revolution was virtually extinguished after the failure of the 1848 Chartist outbreak, the fear of crime persisted as the respectable Victorians shunned the areas where the poorest people lived. As with most ancient cities, many of Glasgow's worst slums were near the centre of town in areas that had once contained the elite.

As the towns became more industrialised, so the centre of population shifted as those who could afford it moved to spacious suburbs such as the fine terraces in Kelvinside and the villas south of the Clyde. The poor remained in the older parts or were confined in hastily constructed areas often surrounding the mills or factories where they worked. This vertical segregation often destroyed the old harmony of the towns and helped create a new consciousness of class. However, class in Glasgow was not a uniform concept; the time-served skilled workers of the shipyards were as proud of their status as any entrepreneur, and would look down on the unskilled labourers as an inferior breed. Although there was a general perception of urban degradation in many towns, there was no uniform acceptance of the cause, although many blamed industrialisation as the root of social, criminal and moral evil. The *Dublin Penny Journal* of 6 July 1833 put its case succinctly: 'The vice and misery which is the fearful accompaniment of the introduction of manufactures ... a process of phys-ical and moral deterioration is continually going forward.' From these areas, the criminals or the desperate slithered into the more fortunate quarters of Glasgow to see what they could steal.

Such was the fascination of the perception of a criminal class that police detectives published their memoirs, and authors such as Dickens intro-duced criminals as characters in their novels. During the course of the century a new genre of literature – the detective novel – appeared and became firmly ensconced as a favourite in libraries and bookshops. The forerunners of these books – chapbooks, broadsheets and accounts such as the *Newgate Calendar* – had often been produced to show the degradation and immorality of crime, but in some cases there grew a sneaking admiration for the clever thief, such as the Viscount Georges de Fontenoy, who operated in Glasgow in the 1870s. For the respectable, however, the thief was beyond the pale and was literally kept at bay by barred windows, high stone walls topped with broken glass and an array of laws with sometimes brutal punishments.

Although Scotland had a Poor Law, able-bodied men were ineligible for relief and after the 1845 Poor Law Amendment (Scotland) Act, any claimant required five years' residency. This stipulation was probably intended to relieve the parish of the burden of providing for a host of unemployed incomers, but it also ensured that, without any safety net, the desperate had little choice but to turn criminal merely to eat. And many of the people who crowded into Glasgow were very desperate indeed; there are tales of men selling their only shirt to feed their family, so petty theft to fend off starvation was only a small step.

By the end of the nineteenth century, habitual criminals were regarded as products of racial decline created by industrialised urban life. To some, the perception of a criminal class was akin to Darwinian racism: the habitual criminal was a person from a lower species of humanity and therefore could be treated differently. There were theories that repeat offenders suffered from an innate condition and they were termed 'degenerate' or 'incorrigible'. Some blamed the demise of transportation in the 1860s for an apparent surge in violent crimes, and Hugh Miller spoke of 'a formidable class of wild beasts – the incorrigible criminals'. Today many criminologists agree that crime and poverty are linked, although others think an unbalanced society where great wealth exists side by side with real destitution is an even more important key. Nineteenth-century Glasgow was home to both extremes.

Before the advent of uniformed police, towns were regulated in a variety of ways, but in the event of serious disorder the army was called in. This fallback was understandable in the case of riots or civil unrest, but the army was not an option in the case of the much more common theft or assault. As the population of cities expanded, the authorities sought more efficient ways to control crime. Edinburgh had a uniformed City Guard but in 1779 it was Glasgow that was first to create a professional uniformed body of civilian police under Inspector James Buchanan. Although originally there were only eight men to control crime in the entire city, within two years lack of money led to the disbandment of the force. It was established again in 1788, but without a parliamentary bill to support it, there was a second collapse within two years. However, Glasgow is a persistent city, and tried a third time. In 1800 the Glasgow Police Act was passed. Funded by local taxes, the Act led to the formation of the City of Glasgow Police, the oldest in Great Britain and the forerunner of all other British uniformed police forces.

In common with the other Scottish forces, the Glasgow Police Force was only part of a holistic community, a force intended more to prevent crime than to enforce the law, although eventually it managed to do the latter very well indeed. David Barrie, in his *Police in the Age of Improvement: Police Development and the Civic Tradition in Scotland, 1775–1865*, suggests that the Scottish police were a development of the Scottish Enlightenment, created to secure the new wealth of the nation and voted for by a representative civic government. Nevertheless, as late as 1857 Glasgow dismissed 100 police officers out of a force of 700 men.

Glasgow was the most important Scottish port as well as a city of heavy industry. Trade increased exponentially after 1815 and shipbuilding, made easier by the coal and iron of Ayrshire, Stirlingshire and Lanarkshire, erupted. Native genius and skilled men ensured Glasgow became a world leader in engineering – ship, locomotive and civil. While work made it a magnet for inward migration, shipping ensured there was also a mobile population, both of seamen and people using Glasgow as a port of embarkation for further emigration. Many stayed – not always by choice, but steady immigration ensured a city whose population rose constantly throughout the century, while the shipping was also a magnet for crime.

*

By mid-century there were between 500 and 1,000 people to the acre in central Glasgow, with dilapidated housing and narrow streets. The middle classes and artisans had moved west so only the poorest remained, but because of the density of population, the accumulated rents made retention of run-down property profitable. Life in the worst areas was a lottery; if the population escaped crime, they still faced the probability of early death by disease. Cholera ravaged the city in 1832, and during the hungry 1840s the death rate reached an appalling annual 39.9 per 1,000. It fell thereafter, only to rise with a typhus epidemic in the early 1860s. Crime, naturally, continued throughout the period, with peaks and troughs that were of interest only to the statistician or the academic, the ordinary person who had to live with the reality rather than assess the theories.

The following chapters will look at some of these crimes that blighted what was undoubtedly one of the greatest cities of the nineteenth century.

2
Robbing the Paisley Union Bank

Bank robberies are not common things. Successful bank robberies are even less common. They are the epitome of the cracksman's art, for if banks are buildings that are virtually guaranteed to contain a great deal of money in a concentrated space, they are also by their very nature diffi-cult to rob. There were two main problems about robbing a bank: the first was getting into the vaults, and the second was getting away with the takings and not getting caught. The robbers of the Paisley Union Bank in 1811 faced both problems and were, to an extent, successful in both, at least for a while.

Five Hundred Guinea Reward

Most people learned of the robbery when the newspaper, the *Caledonian Mercury*, printed an indignant advertisement on 18 July 1811. After offering a reward for an astounding five hundred guineas, the proprietors of the bank gave some details of the robbery. They said that the 'office of the Paisley Union Bank Company at 49–51 Ingram Street Glasgow was this morning discovered to have been broken into since Saturday night'. The advertisement said that 'bank notes . . . to a very considerable amount' were stolen. To gain the reward, which was around ten years' wages for a skilled man, the informant had to give information that led to conviction of the thief and recovery of the money. If an accomplice of the thief were to convict his companions, then not only would he gain the reward but the bank proprietors would also apply for the royal Pardon. There was no guarantee that His Majesty would assent, however, so Mr John Likely, the cashier, and Mr Andrew Templeton, the chief manager of the bank, waited in vain for informers to queue up. Naturally, people were also requested to watch for the stolen banknotes.

The Paisley Union Bank was situated on the ground floor, with cellars beneath and rooms used as a warehouse above. John Thomson was the porter responsible for locking both the safe and the bank. On the evening of 13 July 1811, the bank had a box from Sir William Forbes and Company, a private banking company based in Edinburgh, who acted as the Paisley Bank's agents in the capital. The box held around £4,000 in notes, which Thomson counted before he locked the box, and then placed it in the iron safe, which was situated in the inner room of the two-room office. There were also a large number of banknotes, many of the Paisley Union Bank, together with a considerable amount of gold. After placing the box inside the safe, Thomson locked the safe, closed and secured the office door and took the keys to Mr Templeton in St Enoch Square. The key of the bank was placed in a box, which was also locked, and Thomson placed the box, as always, in a press in the lobby of Templeton's house.

Around half past seven on Monday morning Thomson returned to the bank; the safe was locked but the box from Forbes was lying on the floor, empty. When he opened the safe he saw the drawers had also been opened and the banknotes extracted. The robbers had not used any violence. They had used a skeleton key – then called a false key – to get into the bank on the Saturday night and had left without causing any fuss, without damaging a single lock or door or alerting anybody. They had lifted at least £20,000, although estimates varied to an astonishing £50,000, which was a sum equivalent to millions in today's currency, in probably as professional an operation as Glasgow had ever seen. Thomson raised the alarm and within a short time half the police in the city were searching for the bank robbers.

What Clacher Saw

However, it was sheer blind chance that gave the police their first big break and led to a chase that stretched the length of Britain. Early on the Sunday after the bank was robbed, an elderly wright named David Clacher was out walking. He lived nearby and he was heading toward the Stirling road. Dawn comes early in July, so he was well able to distinguish the three men he saw sitting on a wall, but wondered what they were up to at that time of day. He stood still and watched as they opened up a basket and divided up a pile of banknotes and some silver, and saw they had a foot-long bundle lying between them.

With the money divided, the men walked toward Sandy Leith's George Street coach yard, and were lost to sight. When Clacher heard of the bank robbery the next day he hurried to the bank and reported what he had seen. The bank immediately notified the police and the Glasgow force sprung into action to try and trace the movements of the three suspects.

When Sandy Leith was questioned he frankly admitted the men had hired a post chaise and headed for Airdrie. Two officials from the Paisley Bank hired another post chaise and traced the robbers from Airdrie across Scotland to Edinburgh. The robbers had chosen top-quality accommodation and the best wine on their journey, for which they paid with Paisley Bank notes. The bank officials had good descriptions of the wanted men. Two appeared like gentlemen; the first was about five foot ten, 'stoutly made and active with a full plump face and ruddy complexion'; he was marked by smallpox and could speak in both a Scots and an English accent. The second was five foot eight and slim, while the third was more like a tradesman, five foot nine, 'slender and ill made'.

Following the Trail

The robbers tipped the post boy, the driver of the chaise, so well that he remembered these 'kind liberal gentlemen', but once they left him in Princes Street they vanished. The Edinburgh Police checked the smacks from Leith to London, the mail coaches and the stagecoaches, but without success. They picked up the trail again in a small inn in Rose Street, where three supposed Englishmen had paid for a meal with a twenty-pound note of the Paisley Bank. With that clue, the police found that the suspects had hired a post chaise from Drysdale's Hotel and had driven on the Haddington road. The police then knocked on the magistrates' doors and obtained warrants for their arrest, and from there decided what was best to do.

Robert Walkinshaw, a Writer and one of the bank officials, together with John Likely, the cashier, decided not to sit idle and to follow the suspects, while a Glasgow Messenger-at-Arms, James McCrone, returned to Glasgow to search for information there. Picking up professional help in the person of Archibald Campbell, one of the Edinburgh city officers, Walkinshaw and Likely hired a post chaise and set off in pursuit.

Less than twenty miles away, Haddington was a bustling market town with a selection of inns. The suspects had called at the Blue Bell Inn, where they changed a ten-pound note of the Paisley Bank before moving on to the Press Inn, to change a twenty-pound note. Walkinshaw, Likely and Campbell followed the paper chase of notes to Berwick-upon-Tweed and the border with England. From the English frontier onward the suspects were able to swap their two-horse post chaise for a faster four-horse chaise, a type that was common in England but unusual in Scotland. A four-horse chaise was probably the fastest means of transport for long-distance travel on land, as a single horse would tire, while a post chaise could change horses at regular posting inns throughout the country.

The bankers and Campbell enquired at stables and inns as they traced the suspects further and further south until they left the Queen's Head in Durham and reached the Talbot Inn in Darlington. Here they met George Johnson, a helpful waiter who said the suspects had been at the inn just over a week before at about three in the afternoon. They had carried a large number of Scots and English notes and had tendered a Scottish twenty-pound note to pay for the hire of a chaise with some sherry and biscuits. Notes of that high a denomination were so rare that the landlord had to visit Hollingsworth's bank to obtain change and one of the suspects paid him 2/6d for the privilege. Not surprisingly, Johnson examined the men and claimed he would recognise them without difficulty.

The bankers and Campbell recruited this useful waiter and continued the pursuit. Johnson had also told them the suspects were travelling in a chaise and four. They drove southward and ever southward, following the trail of banknotes, hiring post boys who had already driven the suspects and knew exactly where they had been, and inevitably the trail led all the way to London.

Spreading the tale that the pursuers were highwaymen, the three men looked south as each innkeeper added his little bit of advice and help. At the White Hart Inn in Welwyn, Herefordshire, two stages north of London, a waiter named Henry Cumington had witnessed the suspects openly dividing banknotes. He said they had left a portmanteau and a coat to be sent on to a man named John Sculthorp at an address in Tottenham Court Road in London, with a further address in Coventry Street.

Bow Street Runners

When their post chaise rolled into London, Likely, Walkinshaw and Campbell drove straight to the Public Office at Bow Street and enlisted the help of the famous Bow Street Runners, a force of professional thief takers similar to the King's Messengers in Scotland. Funded by the government, they were attached to the Bow Street Magistrates' Court and could arrest criminals nationwide. It says much for the significance of the crime that three of the best came to help the search: John Vickery, Stephen Lavender and Harry Atkins. Together with Campbell, the Runners raided Sculthorp's house. Although they did not find the portmanteau, they did find a box with a selection of skeleton keys, pick locks and a number of other tools used in the art of housebreaking. The box had an address on top: Coventry Street.

That same night, Campbell and the Runners visited Sculthorp, a stove grate manufacturer, locksmith and the owner of the Coventry Street house. He lived in St George's Fields, but when they got there they also found a character by the name of Hufton, Henry or Houghton White. As soon as he saw the Runners, White made a dive for the window but he was held and hauled back inside the room.

Huffey White

There was no hesitation in arresting White. Better known as 'Huffey', White was one of the most notorious criminals in England. He had been sentenced to be transported for life but had escaped from the stinking Portsmouth hulks in which he had been penned prior to the long voyage south. The authorities had searched for him with no success, until now.

When the Runners arrested White they found a number of Bank of England notes and sixteen guineas in gold, but nothing from the Paisley Bank. There seemed no direct evidence connecting him with the Glasgow robbery, but White was undoubtedly an escaped convict, so the Runners took him to Bow Street, questioned him closely and locked him up for that instead. When Cumington was brought from Welwyn, he identified White right away, but there was still no concrete evidence. White was held in custody and examined again at the beginning of August, shortly afterward being prosecuted for escaping from transportation before his sentence had expired.

The wheels of justice ground on, slow, sure and inexorably ruthless. The perpetrators knew they could expect no mercy if they were caught. With property being the god of the authoritarian classes, the punishment for stealing such a sum would only be execution – but perhaps bribery would help. The thieves tried to ease White back into favour by anonymously handing back most of the money in the hope of reducing his inevitable death sentence. There appear to be two versions of what happened next. According to one, White was condemned once more, but escaped again that December, sliding off the *Retribution* hulk as she lay moored in the Thames off Woolwich. He did not go alone, but took three other convicts with him, and added the guard for good measure. The second account claims that when the sum of £11,000 was paid back to the bank, White, his wife and Sculthorp were all quietly released under a free pardon. Either way, by mid-December White was back at large, bitter after his incarceration and thirsting for success.

By that time the authorities knew the names of the other two robbers and sent placards around the country hunting for them. One was an English lock picker named Harry French, and the other was a Scotsman named James Moffat, alias McCoul. Neither Sculthorp nor White was literate, but Moffat was an educated man and so very useful in the thieving trade.

While the bankers had been busy in London, McCrone, the Messenger-at-Arms, and the Glasgow Police had not been idle. They had been making their own enquiries, which came out in a later trial. A man named James McCoul was arrested in London, and Archibald Campbell brought him to Glasgow by the mail coach, handcuffed by wrist and ankle. Moffat/McCoul remained in Glasgow jail for some time but was released due to lack of evidence and returned to London, thumbing his nose at authority.

Then in October 1812 Huffey White turned up again like a crooked penny. After his escape from the hulks, he had adopted the name Wallis and had roamed through Northamptonshire, Huntingdonshire and Cambridgeshire causing mayhem before he decided to become a highwayman. On the 26th he robbed the Leeds mail coach between Kettering and Higham Ferrers. The General Post Office immediately offered a £200 reward for his capture. They also issued a full description, saying he was a native Londoner, a cabinetmaker by trade in his mid-thirties, about five foot eight, upright and stoutish, with brown hair above a full forehead and a pale face with light grey eyes. This handsome, mild-mannered man was marred by the pockmarks of smallpox, he had a turned up nose and perhaps surprisingly, was described as having a 'squeaking voice', not quite what may be imagined in an expert thief, jail breaker and highwayman.

However, White's luck ran out as this time he was caught and after a trial that lasted over fourteen hours, he was found guilty and sentenced to death. This time there was no escape, and in October 1814 he was hanged at Northampton.

A Man of Many Aliases

Moffat was more professional than White. He was a man of many aliases, but most commonly travelled under the name of McCoul or Moffat, and was well known to the criminal fraternity and police of Edinburgh. He returned to Scotland in 1815 and lived in high style in Portobello with a woman he claimed was his wife. When he tried to pass over £1,800 in Paisley Bank notes in exchange for a banker's draft, the police were called. Moffat affected surprise that he should possess any stolen notes and promised to return home to Portobello and collect them. He left police custody and, not surprisingly, vanished.

However, Moffat was a bold man. He returned to London and legally demanded the return of 'his' £1,800, plus compensation for his time spent in Glasgow jail. The bank issued a counter claim for theft against him and the wheels of the law ground slowly on until they decided in the bank's favour. By that time the robbery of the Paisley Bank and the recovery of the remaining £8,000 slipped from the front of public thought, as other events became more important. There was war in India, the Navy was making heavy weather against the French in the Indian Ocean and Wellington was winning plaudits in the Peninsula; the robbery of a Glasgow bank was stale news.

The years rolled on. There was a war with the United States; Wellington defeated Bonaparte at Waterloo; there was trade depression in the Lowlands and the horror of the Clearances in the Highlands; the robbery of the Paisley Union Bank faded from public memory. One of the two remaining suspects, Harry or Henry French, was tried for murder, acquitted and then in 1818 tried for robbery at Middlesex and transported to Australia for seven years on the ship *Speke*, which sailed in December 1820. After that, French fades from history.

Then in June 1820, nearly nine years after the robbery, Moffat (alias McCoul, Martin or Wilson) came to trial in the High Court of Justiciary in Edinburgh. The charge was read out and Moffat pleaded not guilty. This time the prosecution had built up a formidable case against him. John Thomson, the porter, was the first witness and after detailing how he locked the safe and the office on the Friday and reopened on the Monday, he mentioned there was a note from the Renfrewshire Bank that had been torn and was fastened with a pin. That had also been stolen. The prosecution mentioned that John Likely had travelled to London to try and trace the missing money and when he returned a month later the torn Renfrew note was among the £600 or so he brought back.

Macauley's Evidence

Gradually the witnesses built up a story and the evidence against Moffat mounted. One significant lady was Margaret Macauley, who had lived in the Broomielaw in 1811. She spoke of Moffat and another two men who called themselves Downs and Stone lodging with her, initially for three weeks but staying much longer. The men had a trunk, a portmanteau and two greatcoats. When Macauley moved house, the men came as well, but they frequently remained out late, with Moffat claiming he was going to

Liverpool or Bristol. Macauley said that the other two men had clothes marked with initials that did not match their names and they were marked with smallpox; they also spoke with English accents.

Both Macauley and another witness, John Stewart, said that Moffat was waiting for a small parcel from the London mail coach. The three men also lodged with Stewart but left on 9 July, taking a large portmanteau with them. David Clacher, who had witnessed the three men dividing money beside the Stirling road, identified Moffat as one of the men. James Stirling had been the guard of the Telegraph Coach and porter of the George Street Coach Work in Glasgow; he recognised Moffat as one of three men who hired a chaise on 13 July. Moffat had carried a bundle under his arm and claimed to have a sick brother in Edinburgh. James Muir drove them to Airdrie, where they hired another chaise, paid for with silver. John McAusland, tavern keeper in Edinburgh's Rose Street, also recognised Moffat as having come to his house on 14 July in company with two others; they ate quickly and travelled to the east.

And so it continued; a succession of post chaise drivers, innkeepers and waiters all identified Moffat. Possibly the most significant single comment came from Alexander Livingston, a Leith merchant who knew Moffat personally. When he saw him in Leith Livingston remarked, 'Some storm is brewing as Moffat has come back to the country.'

Lavender and John Vickery of the Runners also recognised Moffat, and knew him as a thief with connections to Sculthorp, the stove grate manufacturer. Atkins, the third Runner, also knew Moffat's wife by the name of Mrs McCoul, while Mary, Huffey White's wife, confirmed that Moffat knew her husband. It was Mrs McCoul who bargained for White's life by handing back most of the proceeds of the robbery. There was talk of the remains of the money being buried in St Pancras Churchyard, or stored in the vault of a bank; talk of a man named Gibbons, a hackney coach master and bull baiter who acted as go-between with the banks, the Runners and White; but most of these conversations were speculative and none gave definite proof that Moffat was involved in the robbery, or that he was innocent.

William Gibbons hammered home the final nails in Moffat's coffin. He said he knew Moffat and knew he was in London in 1811. He detailed their meetings at the Black Horse and he detailed the amount of money Moffat had, including the denominations of the notes. He knew that Mrs McCoul kept the money stored at arm's length up the chimney in a back room and brought out around £14,000 for Mr Likely of the Paisley Bank.

Sculthorp was equally damning. He freely admitted that he made skeleton keys for White and Moffat; he spoke of letters ordering specific keys and signed by White, but as White was illiterate, Sculthorp thought Moffat had written the letters. The keys were sent to Glasgow, so presumably they were used to break into the Paisley Union Bank. The first keys he sent did not fit, so Moffat sent him a wooden model to work from; the second or third key was accepted. Sculthorp also mentioned that Moffat had promised him £5, but despite the money he had stolen, he was chary of actually paying anything out.

The jury did not have to deliberate long before they found Moffat guilty, and he was sentenced to be hanged in Edinburgh on 26 July 1820. Strangely, he seemed surprised and thoughtful at the sentence, as if he had expected to walk away.

There are many questions remaining in this case. Was the money paid by Mrs McCoul a bribe to the Runners or a sweetener to persuade the bank not to prosecute Huffey White? The figure of £14,000 counted out by Mrs McCoul did not correspond with the £11,000 brought back to Glasgow. Did that payment have anything to do with White's providential escape from the hulks? And what happened to the remaining £8,000? Is it still stashed in a chimney somewhere in London, or perhaps sitting in a bank vault waiting to be claimed, with interest, or even more intriguing, could it possibly be buried in St Pancras Graveyard, waiting for some hopeful adventurer with a shovel and a dark misty night?

3
Deadlier than the Male

The McMillan family were a bad bunch. The females of the breed had the nasty habit of presenting their charms to lonely men, inviting them to their house in the tenement known as the Rookery in Orr Street, knocking them down and robbing them blind. Their method was very simple: a nice smile, a wriggle of the hips, a brush of the hand and an invitation to stay the night. Immediately the unwary man stepped inside the house, and then the mother, Margaret McMillan, and the daughter, Elizabeth McMillan, together with Elizabeth's equally unpleasant sweetheart Joseph Mackie would fall on him. They would not only take his money and watch, but also most of his clothes, and leave him all but naked, battered, bruised and bemused. However, their luck ran out in February 1876 when Margaret's two young sons informed on them and they each were given thirty days in jail. The two boys were sent to an industrial school to protect them from their own mother.

As Kipling said, the female of the species is more deadly than the male, and there were occasions in Glasgow that seemed to prove the truth of that old adage. However, there was also one high profile murder case where a woman was the prime suspect, but which ended in dispute and confusion.

'She Cannae Answer the Door When She Was Dead'

All murders are sordid affairs, but the murder of Jessie McPherson was arguably the most brutal that Glasgow saw in the nineteenth century. McPherson was an attractive thirty-five-year-old and worked as maid-servant to eighty-seven-year-old James Fleming. They lived at 17 Sandyford Place, an elegant address close to Sauchiehall Street in the west end of the city. James had a son, John, who lived at the same address, but owned a second home at Dunoon, down the Clyde coast.

When John Fleming took his family away to Dunoon in July 1862, he was probably quite surprised to return to find the servant decapitated and her body sprawled bloodily on the floor of her locked bedroom. There were over forty shallow but ugly wounds on her. Fleming's surprise would heighten when his father informed him that McPherson had been away all weekend and he had not seen her.

Although old James Fleming was the first suspect as he had apparently been alone in the house with McPherson, the police were not totally convinced. They found that the bedroom floor and the kitchen next door had been partially, but not thoroughly, cleaned; they found that a chest in McPherson's room had been broken into and some items of her clothing stolen, together with some silver-plated forks, spoons and knives. They also found blood on the other clothes in the chest and in different parts of the house, including small and bloody footprints on the bedroom floor. As it was unlikely that Fleming had robbed his own house, and the footprints were certainly not his, the police widened their search; they concentrated on the stolen silverware.

It was normal for the police to check pawnbrokers for stolen goods, but this time the pawnbroker came to them while Fleming was still being questioned. The broker had heard of the murder and robbery and was a bit suspicious when a woman calling herself Mary McDonald handed in a small pile of silver-plated cutlery engraved with the letter 'F', which could stand for Fleming. The police followed the trail. The address the woman had given was false, and so, they reasoned, was her name. At first they had no clue as to the woman's identity, until helpful James Fleming suggested it might be a woman called Jessie McLachlan.

When the police realised that the pawnbroker's description of the mysterious Mary McDonald matched McLachlan perfectly, they traced and arrested her, together with her seaman husband. Mr McLachlan was soon released, as he had been at sea at the time, but McLachlan was held and closely questioned. McLachlan did not deny being at the house at Sandyford Place. She said she was a friend of McPherson's, as they had worked together as fellow servants in the house. She admitted visiting McPherson on the night she was murdered, but after that her story grew confused and implicated old James Fleming.

In fact, McLachlan gave several versions of events. In her first, she claimed that she, McPherson and old Mr Fleming had been drinking together; they had run out of whisky, but McLachlan ran out to fetch more supplies. She returned to find McPherson dead, half-naked and Fleming wielding a cleaver. McLachlan swore she would tell nobody, and pawned some of his items.

However, when the case came to trial, McLachlan was caught out on a few minor details. In another version of her story, she had claimed to be at home most of the night of the murder, while a witness, Mrs Campbell, had seen her go out in the evening and return the next morning, wearing a different dress. Some of McPherson's clothes had been found in her possession, but she claimed she had been given them to have them altered. The police found bloodied fragments of McLachlan's original dress in McPherson's room. The bloody footprints also matched McLachlan's shoes.

In her defence, McLachlan again tried to implicate James Fleming. The trial came down to a contest between these two. James Fleming said that McPherson had been missing all weekend, but he did not mention the absence of his servant on either of his two visits to the church. He swore he had heard a yell at about four in the morning and got up about nine, although the milk boy swore he had been fully dressed by half past seven when he answered the door. When he was asked why he answered the door in person rather than wait for his servant, James Fleming was said to have replied, 'She was dead, ye ken, she cannae answer the door when she was dead.'

James Fleming also denied knowing Jessie McPherson, although she had worked for him relatively recently. Either the old man's memory was failing or there was something a bit shady about him. The defence dug out all the dirt they could. They gave evidence that Fleming had appeared before the Kirk session for improper advances toward women and tried to prove he had also made moves toward McPherson. They came a bit unstuck when they said Fleming had asked McLachlan to pawn his silver, as Fleming was well off and had no need to pawn his own possessions.

McLachlan's closing statement was her fifth version of events. She now claimed that she had spent nearly the entire night drinking with McPherson and Fleming; she left to buy drink and returned to find McPherson lying on the ground with her head cut open. McLachlan said she had dressed the wounds and when she asked what had happened, McPherson told her that Fleming had made advances toward her and attacked her when she refused him. It seemed that Fleming had a habit of putting sexual suggestions to her. According to McLachlan's story, after a few moments Fleming regretted his actions and helped put McPherson to bed. It was when she was helping her friend that McLachlan's clothes had been smeared in blood.

During the night, McPherson's condition had deteriorated and McLachlan tried to go for a doctor but Fleming stopped her. She ran upstairs to look out of the window and came back down to see Fleming hacking at McPherson with a meat cleaver. Fleming told McLachlan that she was too deeply involved to escape and offered bribes for her compliance, so she helped him tidy up the body and make the murder scene look like a botched robbery by pawning some silverware and moving some of the clothes.

That was McLachlan's final story and there are elements that hint of the truth, but after her previous attempts, the jury was not inclined to believe her. Neither was the judge, Lord Deas, and his final summing up was nearly an accusation of guilt. Even before the jury reached their verdict fifteen minutes later, Lord Deas had his black cap, signifying the death penalty, ready. McLachlan was sentenced to death but reprieved after 50,000 Glaswegians petitioned for mercy. Instead she was imprisoned for life, being released in 1877 after she had served fifteen years in Perth. By that time her husband had vanished and after moving to Greenock, McLachlan eventually settled in the United States where she died in 1899.

Old James Fleming was never brought to trial, but the Glasgow public was against him and he had to leave the district. The truth will probably never be known, but it seems unlikely that James Fleming was completely innocent, or McLachlan completely guilty. In this case the female may not have been deadlier than the male, but she was certainly suspected of being so.

Other women were more obviously dangerous.

Honey Trap

On the night of 22 November 1843, Thomas McIntyre was walking along the High Street. He was a fruit merchant on his way home from work, and when an unknown woman smiled to him he responded. She came closer and asked him to come with her up a nearby close. Either very naive or very tired, McIntyre agreed, but no sooner had he arrived at a house in the close than he realised somebody was lying on the ground at his feet. He looked down, but the person grabbed his ankles and hauled forward so he fell backward. His head crashed against the paving stone. As he lay there, stunned, four women swarmed all over him. One smashed him in the teeth with a wooden club and the others punched and kicked him into submission before picking his pockets of a gold watch, guard, key and chain.

The police arrested Martha Doherty, Jean McKirdy, Elizabeth McInulty and Mary Thomson, who were all transported for fourteen years.

This type of assault was so common that it was surprising that any man in nineteenth-century Glasgow responded to a woman's smile with anything other than suspicion. Other women arguably had more justification for their actions.

A Vengeful Lover

Although many if not most of the crimes of the nineteenth century were no different from those committed today, there were some that were virtually period specific. One was the unpleasant habit of throwing vitriol – sulphuric acid – in the face of ex-lovers.

On Monday, 13 January 1868, Agnes McTaggart walked up to Thomas Hayes, a hammerman, in Paul's Close in Whitflat, Old Monkland, produced a phial of vitriol and threw the contents over him. Hayes screamed as the acid covered his face, burned through his lips and tongue, his right eye and dripped down his neck. When he lifted his hands to protect his face they were also burned, as were parts of his head. As a result, Hayes lost the sight of his right eye and his face was permanently mutilated.

Agnes McTaggart was no bitter old woman but an attractive youth of only eighteen. She had not attacked Hayes in a fit of rage, but after a period in which she had been deeply hurt and felt let down and betrayed. Thomas Hayes had been her sweetheart for over nine months and she had walked out with him in the full expectation of becoming his wife. Accordingly, they had slept together and she had become pregnant.

However, as soon as she announced her happy news to her intended, his attitude altered. Instead of hurrying the marriage arrangements forward as a respectable man should, he suggested she should have an abortion.

McTaggart refused point blank and carried on with the pregnancy and birth. When Hayes refused to help support the baby, McTaggart took him to court and obtained a decree. Her triumph did not last long though, for the agent said he would not pass it on to Hayes until the fees of £2 were paid, and McTaggart had no money at all. She tried to ask for help from her brother, with whom she lived, but he was already giving financial support to their mother and father, and instead of helping, threatened to throw her out of the house.

McTaggart had few places left to turn. She tried the Inspector of Poor, but he also turned her down, and finally, with her hope just about extinguished, she once again approached Thomas Hayes to ask for help in raising their child. She ran to his work and pleaded with him for money, but again he turned her down and this time he was nasty about it, saying she would regret asking him. They stepped into the close outside and there McTaggart pulled out her vitriol and threw it in his face.

However sympathetic the court may have been over McTaggart's predicament, the judge could not condone such a vicious assault and sentenced her to five years' penal servitude.

A Vengeful Wife

Margaret Broadly was not a happy woman. It was August 1882 and she was estranged from her husband James. Even worse, she knew he was seeing other women, getting drunk and generally enjoying himself, while she was living in utter misery. Not that he had been a good husband even at the best of times, as they had quarrelled incessantly and he liked his drink too much.

Margaret Broadly had taken to following him. She saw him laughing and carrying on; she saw him with another woman; and she nursed her wrath, keeping it warm with memories of better times. She visited a pharmacy and bought a bottle of vitriol, and waited for her opportunity. On 26 August she had her chance for revenge. James Broadly had been imbibing too freely again and was more than a little happy. He staggered out of a public house and into the court off Great Eastern Road where he lived, and there he collapsed, to sprawl on his back on the ground.

After months of pent up frustration and jealousy, Margaret had no thought of mercy. She adjusted her husband's clothing, took out her bottle of vitriol, and emptied the contents on him, from his navel to his thighs. The results can only be imagined. James Broadly was taken to the infirmary but he was permanently maimed. The judge, Lord Deas, was unsure what to do when Margaret Broadly pleaded guilty, but he decided that five years' penal servitude would be a fitting punishment. No doubt as she suffered in her cold cell, Margaret contemplated her actions, but there is no doubt that in her case, the female proved herself to be very dangerous to the male of the species.

4

Environs of the City

It was not only the centre of Glasgow that could be dangerous. In the nineteenth century the roads and seemingly idyllic fields that surrounded the town often hid sombre secrets.

Poachers in Pollokshaws

In the middle of the nineteenth century Glasgow was an expanding industrial city and areas that are now thought of as part of the city were then still rural. Among these areas was Pollokshaws, and although it was not densely populated, it had its own type of crime. Sir John Maxwell owned much of the land and his gamekeepers were hard pressed to keep the local poachers under control.

At around one in the morning of Friday, 2 January 1848, James Kirk and James Hutchison, two of Sir John's gamekeepers, were on patrol. It was a quiet night, with fair moonlight, and when they reached Cowglen they saw a small huddle of men on the private road to Laigh-Cowglen. There was no lawful reason for anybody to be there at that time of night, and when the keepers saw a dog trot across the adjacent field, they knew the men were poachers. Only a few months previously Hutchinson had been one of two keepers that poachers had attacked at nearby Drum-breck, so they were well aware of the danger. Perhaps for that reason Hutcheson had a six-barrelled revolver in his pocket.

Carrying their guns in the crooks of their arms, the keepers challenged the suspected poachers. Immediately as they did so, one of the poachers threw a dead hare over the hedge. When the dog ran onto the road toward them, Hutchinson lifted his gun, fired and wounded it. That seemed to be the signal for a general melee, for all three poachers drew weapons – two bludgeons and an iron poker – and attacked the keepers. After only a few seconds, Kirk broke and ran to the Laigh-Cowglen farmhouse for help, but Hutchinson was slower, so all three poachers concentrated on him. He tried to fight back with his now empty gun but the poachers stabbed him in the back and breast and smashed him over the head with the poker and a bludgeon. He fell to the ground, unconscious.

The poachers lifted the injured dog, rifled Hutchinson's prone body of the unused revolver and ran off. By the time Kirk returned there was nothing he could do but take care of his wounded companion. Hutcheson was badly bruised, but the stab wounds were superficial, while Kirk was bruised but still mobile. The keepers, however, had the last word. They had recognised all three poachers and had them arrested and put into jail in Pollokshaws.

Other encounters with poachers had more tragic outcomes.

Death of a Keeper

'Not Proven' is a verdict unique to the Scottish justice system. Sir Walter Scott termed it 'that bastard verdict, not proven'. It is not quite a 'not guilty', but means the accused is acquitted because the judge or jury has reasonable doubt. It is a logical statement where the jury is not quite sure if the accused has committed the crime, so does not want to put him or her in prison or on the scaffold.

In nineteenth-century Glasgow there were a number of cases where guilt was almost, but not quite, proven. One such was the killing of a gamekeeper near Cambuslang in September 1849.

Although evening was drawing in, it was still quite light at seven o'clock on 5 September 1849 when farmer's son, James Dick of Turnlaw, was riding his old horse from Greenlees, at the back of Cambuslang, to Stoneymeadow Toll. As he passed Crookedshield Road he met a young blacksmith named Andrew Forrest. The smith greeted Dick and walked on, with a double-barrelled shotgun balanced over his shoulder. The road was busy that evening, for about fifty yards further on, Dick met Joseph Kirkby, the gamekeeper at Gilberthall Castle, with his two dogs. He had one dark brown, rough-haired Newfoundland/bulldog cross on a leash, and a second smaller dog that trotted behind him. After another few minutes, Dick saw a boy pushing through the hedge that ran beside the road. Dick rode on to his destination about a mile further on, turned around and returned on the same road. Then he saw a body lying face down near a spot called The Beeches.

Only about twenty minutes had passed since Dick had seen Kirkby, but when he dismounted he realised the gamekeeper was dead. Kirkby's clothes were covered in blood, both dogs were with him and he still held the leash of the largest. Dick spurred on to Crookedshields farmhouse to tell his news, stabled his horse and returned to the scene. By that time there was a group of people gathered around the body, but the Newfoundland dog was snarling and showing his teeth if anybody came close to his master's body. A local man named Joseph Weir managed to remove the dogs and the crowd pressed closer. They saw that the blood had been spattered for a long way to the west of the body; Kirkby had been shot at close range.

The most obvious suspect was Andrew Forrest, the eighteen-year-old man who Dick had seen carrying a shotgun. He was a sickly young man who had come down from Glasgow to improve his health. He lived locally with his uncle, also Andrew, the miller at Bridge Mill. His cousin William, a youth of sixteen, told what he knew of Andrew Forrest's story. At about six on the evening of 5 September the two cousins had gone out shooting. They walked along the roads between Cambuslang and Crookedshields, with Andrew Forrest carrying his shotgun and William the shot bag and powder flask. The Duke of Hamilton owned the land on either side of the road. When Andrew Forrest saw a bevy of partridge rise from a park eastward of a copse of beeches he left the road, aimed his gun and fired. The sound of the shot was loud in the still air of the evening, the muzzle flare brilliant. Powder smoke drifted blue-white against the sombre green of the evening as a bird fell. William placed it inside his bag and listened to the sudden hush; the reverberations of the shot had killed the natural sounds of the night.

They returned to the road and strolled on toward Greenlees Toll when a call of nature took William Forrest to the shelter of the hedge that bordered the road. While there he saw Kirkby the gamekeeper sitting with his back to the hedge and his gun at one side. He had one small dog running loose and his Newfoundland securely held on a lead. As the boys were technically poaching, William Forrest was naturally unhappy to see the gamekeeper, who rose, left his gun and walked onto the road, following Andrew Forrest.

William Forrest heard Kirkby and Andrew Forrest speaking; their voices were raised. William left them to it, ducked back behind the hedge and threw away his shot bag and powder horn. He was running across the field when he heard the report of a shot and a man cry out in pain. Moments later Andrew Forrest approached at a run; he was spattered with blood and confessed he had shot Kirkby. The boys hurried across the fields to William Forrest's home in Bridge Mill and told his brother and cousin.

'How did you shoot Kirkby?' William Forrest asked.

Andrew Forrest explained that as he was talking to Kirkby, the Newfoundland had been snarling and growling at him. It either slipped free of the lead or Kirkby released it and it jumped at him, tearing his trousers and ripping open his thigh. Andrew Forrest was scared; he lifted the shotgun, intending to shoot the dog but the gun went off by accident and he shot Kirkby instead. The Newfoundland had a bad reputation locally. Its name was Bauldy, and it had already bitten at least two local men and was known to attack poachers. Nevertheless, Abraham Hamilton, Kirkby's assistant, thought Bauldy was under control, as he was usually muzzled. He claimed the dog was trained to knock down poachers and run around them until his master arrived.

Andrew Forrest did not stay long in Bridge Mill. He got changed and about half an hour later he made his way back to Glasgow, but the arm of the Law easily stretched that far. On 6 September, John Thomson, Messenger-at-Arms, knocked on his door, arrested him and escorted him to Hamilton Jail. Forrest was not a happy prisoner; he cried openly in his cell and was visibly disconsolate; he was anything but a hardened criminal. His trial took place at the High Court in Edinburgh in January 1850 and after hearing all the evidence, the jury found his case not proven and he walked free.

The environs of Glasgow were not only rife with poaching. The roads could be dangerous as well, with various types of highway robbers and footpads on the prowl.

'If You Say a Word I'll Blow Out Your Brains!'

Walking on a May evening in Scotland can be very pleasant – the nights are long and the weather is probably as good as it ever gets – so Robert McCulloch may have enjoyed his journey back from Glasgow to Paisley, at least until he was attacked.

McCulloch was a factory owner and he had been working in Glasgow until late. It was about ten o'clock on 19 May 1815 when he began the walk back to Paisley, with a full moon making the road nearly as clear as day. He was alone until he reached Cardonald Toll, but then two Irishmen joined him. One asked him the time and McCulloch checked his watch and told them before walking on, with the Irishmen falling into step at his side. Both Irishmen carried heavy sticks but they seemed friendly and for a while they passed the time in conversation. All that changed when they reached a quiet stretch of the road and the two men turned on

McCulloch. As the man on his left grabbed McCulloch's arm and held him tight, the man on the right gave an unequivocal warning: 'If you say a word I'll blow out your brains!'

The Irishmen knocked him down and held him on the ground, demanding his money. McCulloch tried to fight back, but one of his attackers threatened him with a large club, and the other stuffed a handkerchief in his mouth so he could not call for help. They took his silver watch and silk handkerchief, his hat and about eight shillings and seven pence in change.

'Hurry up!' one of the men said, and they ran off, leaving McCulloch bruised, shocked and bleeding on the ground. As they left, one of the attackers snatched McCulloch's handkerchief and grabbed McCulloch's hat, throwing down his own in contemptuous exchange.

After a few moments McCulloch staggered up and made his way into Paisley where he reported the robbery to Mr Brown, the Master of Police. Brown rode up to the scene and found the signs of a struggle, with churned up earth and flattened grass, as well as some small articles that obviously belonged to McCulloch. With the robbery proved, he set the police to searching for the robbers.

The police and city officers had a good description of both the attackers and the articles that had been stolen, and they scoured the known haunts of crime in the Glasgow area. On 31 May, three city officers, Alexander Calder, James Edmond and Hugh Ross, raided a known criminals' haunt in Bishopsbridge, owned by a man called McDonald. There were eight known thieves in the house. The first man they saw there was an Irishman called Barney Nilas, and round his neck was McCulloch's handkerchief. When Calder looked closer, he saw McCulloch's hat on Nilas' head as well, so promptly arrested him. They also brought in two other men, George Conner and John Sherry, and held a shoemaker named John Brown until he handed over McCulloch's watch that he had purchased in apparent good faith.

Nilas, Conner and Sherry were all charged with highway robbery, but the case against Conner was soon dropped through lack of witnesses, and Nilas turned King's Evidence against his old highwayman partner, which must have been frustrating for McCulloch.

Lords Meadowbank and Pitmilly presided over the trial at the Glasgow Circuit Court. John Sherry pleaded not guilty, but with Nilas giving evidence against him he had little chance to wriggle free. Nilas told the court the full story. He and John Sherry had met McCulloch on the road between Glasgow and Paisley. Nilas asked McCulloch the time and they walked together; after a while Sherry tried to knock McCulloch down but failed, so they followed and tried again, with Sherry using a stick. They robbed McCulloch of all they could and left him there.

Sherry spoke briefly to the court. He said he came from the county of Monaghan in Ireland but he was not guilty of the attack. The jury did not agree and found him guilty. The judge sentenced him to be hanged, but Sherry showed no emotion and accepted his fate.

Other would be highway robbers were equally unsuccessful.

Robbing an Ex-Soldier

There were occasions when footpads found they had caught a tiger by the tail and would have wished they had chosen an easier career. Such was the case when William Higgins and Thomas Harold tried their luck at highway robbery in the summer of 1814. Thomas Harold was from the north-east of England, although he lived in Carlisle. He claimed he had come to Glasgow to find work on a spinning loom. Higgins, a fair-haired man with bushy side-whiskers, seems to have been a local man.

It was around ten at night on Friday, 15 July 1814, the day of the Glasgow Fair, when Adam Wyllie was on the road gathering horse dung for his garden. Adam Wyllie was a weaver from Woodend, now about a mile from Tollcross but then deep in the country. As he gathered the dung he heard voices and three men came up to him. One man grabbed a handful of the dung, thrust it under Wyllie's nose and asked, 'What are you about?'

When Wyllie faced the three of them and replied he would do that to no man, they attacked him at once. Somebody punched him three times in the face and swore at him, while Harold pulled a pistol and Higgins drew a bayonet and said he would run him through. Bayonets seemed quite a common weapon at this period as the Napoleonic War reached its climax and the country was full of soldiers, returned soldiers and various bodies of men who liked to think of themselves as soldiers.

As Wyllie watched the bayonet, the third man knocked him to the ground. He called for help but Higgins shouted, 'Stop his mouth,' and one of the men began to throttle him, while Higgins stabbed him twice, once on the face and once on the buttock, then smacked him on the head with the flat of the blade.

'That will settle the bastard,' Higgins said, and without stopping to rob him, the attackers moved on to search for further prey. Wyllie lay still with his blood spreading over his face and onto the road.

When Peter Brown passed along the road he found Wyllie still prone on the ground. Brown helped him up and asked if he was fit to chase his attackers. When Wyllie said he was not, Brown said he would go himself. It took a few moments for Wyllie to recover, but he dragged himself upright and began to search for the men who had attacked him. As an ex-soldier and an ex-seaman, Wyllie was well able to take care of himself and he must have been annoyed at the treatment he had received. As it was the middle of summer, the night was still light and when he heard a woman shouting, 'Murder,' he hurried towards the sound and saw five men struggling on the road. The three men who had attacked him were now assaulting Thomas Anderson, a Bellshill cattle merchant and his servant, William Hare.

Anderson had come from the Glasgow Fair with a convoy of five carts and a group of four men and one woman. They had come out of Glasgow city and were at the milestone just past Tollcross, with William Hare driving the leading cart, when three men appeared. While one demanded money, Higgins drew his bayonet and stabbed Hare in the hip. As he slumped, wounded, Harold stole a book and a length of corduroy cloth from his cart – slim pickings. The men moved on. One seized the muzzle of Anderson's horse, thrust a pistol toward him and shouted for his money. Anderson, however, was not easily cowed, and tried to defend himself with a stick. There was a short, fierce scuffle, then the highwaymen shoved Anderson from the driving seat. As he fell on the road the cart continued, with one wheel driving right over his body.

Anderson lay on the ground, gasping in agony. Higgins leaned over him, pricked him with the bayonet and again demanded his money, but Anderson defied them, saying, 'You shall not get it if I can help it!' He heard the woman scream and the others in the convoy flee, except his own brother, who came to his aid.

Again Higgins demanded his money and threatened him with death, but Anderson's brother knocked him aside for the few moments necessary for Anderson to take his pocketbook from his pocket and throw it defiantly over the adjacent hedge. He had £78 in it, the proceeds of a successful day at Glasgow Fair, and he preferred it to be lost than to hand it to the highwaymen. Anderson was undoubtedly a brave man.

It was then that Wyllie arrived. He saw the three attackers haul Anderson along the ground, and Hare slumped on the driving seat of the cart, bleeding from a stab wound, and he hurried to help. As soon as Wyllie approached, Harold thrust his pistol against his chest and said, ludicrously, that he would blow out his brains. Somebody else, either Higgins or the unknown third man, shouted out, 'Stab the bastard!'

Wyllie was obviously a brave man, for rather than plead for mercy or try to run, he lunged at Higgins and grabbed hold of his wrists and tried to wrest the bayonet from him. Harold pressed the trigger of his pistol, but luckily it misfired so he dropped it, lifted a rock and crashed it against Wyllie instead. Wyllie staggered but kept his hold on Higgins until the bayonet clattered to the ground, whereupon he scooped it up. He noticed it was blunt, which in fact had probably saved his life.

By now more help had arrived, as a weaver called John Wilson and the local change-house keeper, William Figgins, hurried to their aid. Wyllie handed the bayonet to Wilson. With Higgins disarmed and Harold's pistol discarded, the attackers lost their aggression, and Wyllie, Figgins and Wilson were able to subdue them and take them to the police office in Glasgow.

Anderson was injured, but not fatally; he recovered in time for the trial, and at the Glasgow Circuit Court both Higgins and Harold pleaded not guilty. The jury did not see things their way, and both were condemned to be hanged on 19 October 1814.

Hanging seemed to be a habitual fate for highway robbers, but not all were as blatant as Harold and Higgins. George Gilchrist had quite different methods on his way from the highway to the Glasgow gallows.

The Greedy Highwayman

On 31 August 1831, George Gilchrist made history as the last man to be hanged for highway robbery in Scotland. He was not a typical highway robber, and had not followed the accepted procedure of riding up to the coach dressed in a black mask and wielding a pistol. Instead he had tried to be clever. Indeed, he was an undoubtedly intelligent man, but he was also greedy.

Gilchrist had once lived at Mid Calder, between Glasgow and Edinburgh, where he made a reputation as an honest horse dealer. However, honesty did not pay the bills, and Gilchrist was a twice-married family man whose finances were always pressing. Accordingly, he spent a few pounds in buying a stallion that was long past its prime, used all his expertise in making the horse look younger and fitter and took it to Edinburgh. He offered it for sale at a hundred pounds but nobody was fooled, and Gilchrist ended up out of pocket and with a useless old horse. Shortly after, a fire in Gilchrist's stable killed the poor beast, while a much more valuable horse seemed to have strayed into his courtyard. Gilchrist had insured the old stallion for 120 guineas.

Leaving Mid Calder, Gilchrist used his windfall to become the landlord of the inn at Airdrie and a partner in various companies that operated coaches between Glasgow and Edinburgh. He was still reckoned to be honest and his business became prosperous; his stables held around fifty quality horses and his wealth increased year on year. It was not until much later that it was realised Gilchrist was also dealing in forged banknotes. One of the coaches in which Gilchrist was a partner was the Prince Regent, but greed overcame any scruples he may have had, and he planned to rob his own coach.

The robbery was planned for 24 March 1831, and Gilchrist inveigled others to join him. A driver named John McDowall had control of the coach on the first stage of its journey from Glasgow to Edinburgh, and for most of the journey he had only a single outside passenger, a bank messenger named James Smith, who sat bundled up against the biting east wind. Smith had a battered but padlocked tin box that was chained in the front boot of the coach. However, despite the unprepossessing appearance of the box, it held £6,000 of the Commercial Bank's money that was being transferred from Glasgow to Edinburgh. Halfway through the journey McDowall was relieved by Jock McMillan, and the contents of the boot were checked at the changeover.

A handful of other passengers used the coach, with two labouring men joining at Coatbridge and disembarking at Bathgate, and a gentleman and a lady coming into the stuffy interior between Airdrie and the toll house at Armadale. The lady carried a white hand basket with two lugs and said very little. The coach stopped at Hillend to change horses, then clattered on to Uphall, where Smith asked McMillan to ensure his box was still safe in the boot, as that was his changeover point and another messenger would carry it the remainder of the journey.

McMillan opened the boot and both men stared in disbelief. The lining of the coach was torn, several parcels were scattered about, the padlock had been broken and the contents of the tin bank box stolen. 'Good God,' McMillan said, 'will the bank box be away?'

At first McMillan and Smith could not understand what had happened. The coach had hardly stopped and there had been no hold-up, so the only possible explanation was a robbery from inside the coach. They concluded that one of the inside passengers must have broken through the wall of the coach to get into the boot.

That was exactly what had happened. The woman had been Gilchrist in disguise. Brown was the lookout to ensure the coachman heard nothing, and Gilchrist had bought all the other inside seats to ensure there were no passengers other than his accomplices. He had closed the windows and curtains and bored through to the boot from inside the coach. With access secured he lifted out the tin box, opened it with a chisel, stole the money, replaced the lid so it looked much as it had before, and calmly disembarked with the money in his basket. Brown had held the door open and distracted the coachman with the offer of a half-crown tip. But that was not known, at first.

The bank proprietors and police began their investigation. They searched for the workmen and the two passengers, and took a number of people into custody. They arrested and questioned George Gilchrist and his brother William, as well as Thomas Campbell, a Mid Calder joiner, and James Brown, who had been the supposed labouring man who opened the door to allow the supposed gentleman and lady to enter the coach. The authorities found seventy sovereigns hidden in a fish basket in Brown's house.

When Gilchrist had been interrogated in the sheriff's chambers, he made a sudden dash for freedom, locked the door of the room so the sheriff officers could not catch him and scampered along Stockwell Street, roaring, 'Catch thief! Catch thief!' However, the sheriff officer opened the window and shouted a warning so that Gilchrist was again secured.

The bulk of the money was found in an attic in Falkirk, and in July William and George Gilchrist, together with James Brown, were tried for robbing the Prince Regent Coach. Only George Gilchrist was found guilty and sentenced to death. He was hanged in Edinburgh, a successful man whose greed led him to the gallows.

5
Bloody Assaults

Some crimes are common to every age and probably every culture. One is assault. In the nineteenth century every city in the country was plagued with assaults, some by stranger on stranger, others much more personal.

Three-Week Binge

Some households were not worth living in. That of William and Mary Muir was one. They lived at 127 Dumbarton Road, but the home was often in an uproar, particularly when one or the other of them had been drinking. Mary was not a quiet wife and from time to time had attacked William, once thumping him with a sugar bowl so he was in bed for weeks.

In the summer of 1890 matters came to a head when both decided to go on the batter. Mary Muir was first; she began to drink in late May and remained drunk for three weeks solid. On 14 June the two began to argue when William asked for his dinner but Mary confessed she had spent the food money on drink and said all he would get was the empty pan, which she lifted and threw at him.

It might have been the flying pan, or the fact Mary insulted his mother with a string of vituperation, or the mouthful of swear words she directed at him, but William grew angry. He was equally drunk and punched her in the face and kicked her around the house. The neighbours heard the row and called the police. Mary was still lying on the floor when Constable William McDonald arrived. Mary pointed to her husband and claimed, 'He has killed me,' whereupon William charmingly said that he would blow her brains out if she charged him with assault. Mary decided not to charge him, and the police left.

As they stood outside the Muirs' front door they heard cries of 'Murder' and 'Police' and returned inside to arrest William, who was eventually given five months for assault. Domestic violence was common at the period, but so was casual assault.

Glasgow Green

Glasgow was proud of its Green. It was a meeting place, a lung for the growing city, a place for sports and markets and an arena for political meetings. However, it was also a place that boasted more than its fair share of crime throughout the century. Sometimes the victims of crime were completely innocent, as happened in November 1804 when two young servant girls were drawing water from a well at the Green. The scene should have been idyllic: the girls in their ankle-length dresses carrying the pitchers, the swathe of the Green stretching into the November mist and the handsome young butcher's boy admiring them in the most natural manner.

But David Dalrymple was not there to admire the girls; he had an altogether more sinister object in mind. He was carrying a fully blown bladder, the early nineteenth-century equivalent of a football, with which he smacked the nearest girl in the face. Not surprisingly, she called him a blackguard, which annoyed him for he pulled a knife and thrust it through her side. It was not a lethal stroke but it did penetrate her bodice and leave a small wound. Dalrymple stabbed the second girl in the breast as she came to help, and then ran away.

Not being a particularly intelligent youth, Dalrymple walked about openly until he was identified and arrested. He spent the next year in jail for the knifings.

Trouble in the Green

Even crossing the Green could be hazardous. As it was located close to the city, it was a natural highway from the surrounding villages and therefore a natural gathering place for hopeful footpads.

On Friday, 18 October 1811, a gentleman made the unfortunate choice of walking across the Green from Hutchesontown to Glasgow at eleven o'clock at night. About halfway across, a youth ran up to him, punched him to the ground and began to search him for anything worth stealing. As the victim lay bleeding, roaring for help, his attacker nearly ripped the pantaloons off him in his desperation for loot. However, the victim's cries brought a watchman, who saw the attacker by the light of his lantern just as he ran off.

The early watchmen knew most of the desperadoes in their area and thought he recognised the attacker immediately, so he searched his known haunts in Calton and soon arrested him. The arrested man was a brass founder called James Ferguson, who had already been twice before the courts for assault and twice acquitted.

Ferguson was tried again at the Circuit Court, but once more there was a lack of evidence and he walked free. However, the police had not seen the last of him, for on 25 September 1812 he was arrested for robbing Thomas Inglis of £30 in the Old Wynd in Calton. This time his luck ran out, and the Circuit Court sentenced him to be hanged on Wednesday, 26 May.

Family Affair or Criminal Class?

Robbery and hangings around Glasgow Green could be quite a family affair. In an afternoon in late September 1814 a group of youths felt such a thirst that they could not wait to earn enough money to buy drink when there was a much easier alternative. They located a handy grocery shop in Tureen Street and worked out how to rob it while the owners were still inside. Tying the door closed with a length of rope, they smashed the window, helped themselves to all the bottles of whisky they could find and ran off. The shopkeepers eventually succeeded in untying the door and told the day patrol of police, who searched for the robbers.

When they found a group of youths sitting in the Green drinking from a number of bottles, the police moved in. The group scattered, but the police arrested three. One was a man named Menzies, whose brother had been recently hanged at Stirling; another was the sister of James Ferguson, the man who was known for attacking people in Glasgow Green and had been recently hanged for his exploits; the third was not known to the police and was arrested purely for choosing bad company. Notwithstanding their distinguished family backgrounds, all three were released for lack of evidence. Such families of criminals tended to reinforce the belief in the existence of a class of people born to crime.

But sometimes the human faults of the authorities helped the criminals.

The Flustered Messenger-at-Arms

There were many layers of law and justice in early nineteenth-century Scotland, with the police supported by a legal system that stretched back for hundreds of years. One major component of law enforcement was the force of Messengers-at-Arms, who were empowered to follow and arrest law-breakers across the country. Most would be honest hardworking men, who used their power with tact and discretion, but they were as human as anybody else.

Andrew Wilson was one such Messenger-at-Arms, and his job included handing out summonses and meeting people on legal business in Glasgow and elsewhere. He lived in the Saltmarket near the High Court, the centre of Glaswegian justice. However, Wilson had one small fault: like so many of his contemporaries in the early nineteenth century, he was overly fond of a drink.

On 28 October 1819, Wilson was ordered to serve papers on a man named William Stephen, with the meeting arranged in James Henderson's spirit shop in a close just off the Gallowgate. Stephen was not the first client of the day, and Wilson had already met three people in three different public houses. In each one he had shared a drink with his client, but he was not drunk when he approached Henderson's spirit shop late that night. In his own words, he was 'a little flustered'. He did not see the woman until she slipped out of a doorway on his left and said, 'Are you going to buy me a gill?' Although this seemed like an innocuous invitation to go for a drink, there was always the possibility that the lady was a prostitute seeking a client.

Not in the least surprised, for such requests were common at the time, Wilson turned her down, saying, 'I will do no such thing; my bawbees are no good.' He put the incident out of his mind and walked the twenty steps or so to the spirit shop, but a tall man sidled up and said, 'You had better buy the woman a gill.'

'I will not buy her nor you a gill,' Wilson said, 'but I am going into Henderson's, and I've no objection to build half-gable with you.' That meant drinking together as a threesome.

The interior of the shop had internal divisions where there was some privacy, and they found a vacant compartment. Wilson learned that the man was Alexander McDonald and the woman Margaret Smith. They bought whisky, although Smith did not partake, despite her initial approach to Wilson.

After a drink shared in friendship, Wilson said he had to leave on business, but McDonald insisted he should have another. Wilson agreed and brought in the whisky, although he argued that he should not pay for all three. However, he eventually paid up with the silver he held wrapped up in paper in his pocket. As he paid, he revealed he also had a couple of banknotes.

When he sat down again, Smith claimed he had a banknote as well. When Wilson denied it, she said, 'There it is,' and thrust her hand into Wilson's waistcoat pocket to try and get his money.

Wilson removed Smith's hand as both Henderson and the barmaid rebuked her. When McDonald tried the same thing, Wilson shoved him away in some anger as Smith tried to keep the peace by railing at McDonald at some length and then trying to alter the subject.

A few moments later, McDonald tried again, and again Wilson caught his hand and threw it away. It was obvious that McDonald was trouble, so Wilson left the table and stalked out of the shop. It was about quarter past twelve. Some Messengers-at-Arms may have tried to arrest McDonald, but Wilson was not forged from the mould of a hero and instead he fled across the street and right into the Old Crown Close.

He had barely gone a dozen steps when he heard the footsteps of two people behind him, and then he was attacked. Somebody cracked him hard across the left side of his forehead and he staggered and fell down. He did not know for how long he lay on the ground, but he knew he lost consciousness.

The lanterns were bobbing, casting long shadows on the ground, and there was the murmur of voices. Wilson sat up groggily and saw the watchmen around him, their faces quizzical, concerned and helpful. They asked him if he had been robbed; he checked his pockets and found them empty. All his money had gone: two twenty-shilling banknotes and eighteen shillings in change, as well as the papers he had come to serve. The watchmen helped him up and told him there were men chasing his attackers.

Wilson barely glanced at the two people the watchmen arrested; he was still concussed from the blow. It took ten days in bed for him to recover, but by then McDonald and Smith were both secure in custody. The case came to the High Court in March 1820, and Wilson immediately recognised the two prisoners as the man and woman he had met in Henderson's. He also admitted to having been arrested on a previous occasion for drinking in a public house after it was closed.

The jury listened to the evidence. Thomas Henderson, the publican, had locked up and left his pub only a few minutes after Wilson departed, closely followed by McDonald and Smith. He had only gone a few steps when McDonald and Smith exploded from the mouth of a close, running hard. Henderson heard the word 'Police' and saw a policeman stop the pair and ask what their business was. McDonald explained that he had just saved a woman from the evil designs of a man. He ran on, with Smith at his heels. They had only gone as far as Peacock Close, a short distance up the road, when the police closed in. They arrested McDonald there and then, but Smith slipped away, lifted her skirt and tried to escape up a flight of stairs. The police arrested her before she reached the top. Around Peacock Close they found a number of scattered papers.

There had been another witness to the attack in Old Crown Close. James Burnet was a shoemaker and was on his way home from escorting his girl-friend to her house when he heard a scream. In the darkness, he saw a man and woman crouching over the dim shape of Wilson lying on the ground, with papers spread all around. The crouching pair saw him watching, scooped up the papers and left hurriedly. Burnet saw that Wilson was injured, but as he moved to help, the police arrived and half carried him away. When the police surgeon, Dr Corkindale, examined Wilson, he found he had been thumped on the temple with a sharp implement and was feverish.

McDonald's version of events was completely different. He claimed that he was quietly walking along the Gallowgate when two men approached him. One was Andrew Wilson. The Messenger claimed he had a warrant for McDonald, which led to an argument, until Wilson agreed he had the wrong man. According to McDonald, they decided to settle their differences over a drink in Henderson's. When they left that pub, Wilson was drunk. They looked for another place of refreshment, joined by two men he did not know. As they were walking down Old Crown Close, Wilson fell down a flight of steps, to be helped by the watchmen.

Smith added some background details; she said she was married to McDonald in Edinburgh, but they had to leave there when, due to an unfortunate misunderstanding, her husband had been banished from the capital.

The jury had no difficulty in dismissing McDonald's story and the judge, Lord Pitmilly, sentenced McDonald and Smith to fourteen years' transportation.

Garrotters

Despite the monstrous crimes of Burke and Hare or Jack the Ripper, perhaps the most feared crime of the nineteenth century was garrotting, a particularly nasty form of mugging, or street assault, as it was known then. Garrotting usually involved two or more attackers and a lone, unwary victim. By the 1850s, garrotters stalked the streets of Glasgow.

One such predator struck late at night on Wednesday, 15 December 1852, as Robert William McLaren, a young shoemaker of Endrick Bank in Drymen, walked through the city. He had missed his last coach home and was hoping to spend the night with a relative in Hospital Street, but as he walked up the stair to their house, three men loomed out of the shadows. One seized him by the throat, one grabbed his arms and threw him to the ground and held him, while the third went through his pockets. They stole eighteen shillings and a few coppers, but the beat policeman heard McLaren yelling and came to investigate.

As the constable leaped up the stairs toward them, the three attackers tried to run, but the constable was in their way. They barged into him, and he managed to hold back two, while the third dashed to the stair window and jumped to freedom. When another constable arrived, the remaining two were arrested; they were James McKelvie and Bernard Leonard, a knife grinder with a string of convictions of assault.

The three men had been busy, for the previous night two of them had been suspected of attacking an engine driver named Mathew Harvey. When he was in King Street, one of the men pretended to know him and took him into a pub in Muirhead Street, Gorbals, near his home, where he bought them a dram. They parted as friends, but when Harvey stepped inside his own stair one of the men grabbed his throat and choked him until his nose bled. The men snapped the chain of his German silver watch and escaped. Harvey could not describe either of the men, but the broken chain was found in Leonard's pocket and the watch in his house, and that was enough evidence to convict him. McKelvie and Leonard were both jailed, but the third attacker escaped justice.

Harvey was a quiet countryman, but sometimes even men who had thrived in dangerous places could come to grief in the streets of Glasgow.

Robbing a Forty-Niner

The nineteenth century was a golden time for some, with gold strikes in California, South Africa, Canada and Australia. Tens of thousands of men sailed to the diggings in pursuit of wealth, much as people today hope to win the lottery. And like today, few were successful, but some did return with a modest fortune.

One such man arrived in Glasgow in February 1851, homeward bound to England from California. He had more than £700 in his pocket when he came ashore at the Broomielaw, but he fell in with a bold-eyed siren and was soon enjoying her company in her house in Stormont Street. Not surprisingly, she also relieved him of his money, and he ran complaining to the police, offering a substantial reward of £100 if his money was recovered.

Superintendent Mackay moved quickly and arrested all the women in the brothel, while asking his informants to tell him anything they knew. The police found the money buried in a sawpit at Anderston.

A Dangerous City

Glasgow in the 1850s was a dangerous place for lone men walking through the streets. In early October 1852 a gentleman was attacked in Richard Street, strangled unconscious and robbed of his watch. His wife found him at the foot of his own stairs, bleeding from his nose and mouth. A few nights later, Gavin Scott, a cloth lapper, was relieving himself near the Episcopal Chapel on Glasgow Green when three men loomed out of the dark. They grabbed him by the throat, punched him in the face and robbed him of all he possessed, a single shilling. In this case, a passing policeman intervened, called for help and arrested the ringleader, a labourer named William Brown. Brown had no previous convictions, so he may have turned to garrotting as an easy way of making money, or out of desperation.

On Monday, 25 July 1853, another gentleman entered his own close in Abbotsford Place when a well-dressed man stopped him and asked him some pointless questions. Thinking he was drunk, the gentleman fastened his coat tightly and walked on. He had only gone a few steps when the well-dressed man wrapped an arm around his throat and dragged him into the darkest part of the close, where a second man held his arms and a third punched him until he lost consciousness. However, a woman heard his shouts for help. Her window overlooked the close, and the attack was right outside her back door. Too sensible to leave her home, she banged loudly on her door and screamed at the garrotters to stop. The three attackers immediately scurried away, straight into two men at the entrance of the close. There was a brief struggle and one garrotter named Jeremiah Ritchie was captured right away and another, Alexander Taylor, was caught hiding in a stair nearby. Ritchie was a known thief with a history of garrotting, while Taylor was a blacksmith, who made and supplied all types of equipment for housebreakers.

Garrotting as a method of attack spread right across the country until parliament introduced more stringent punishments that included the lash. Nevertheless, garrotters continued to infest the streets until at least the 1880s.

The Garrotter That Disappeared

On Saturday evening 21 February 1880, Charles Rankin was returning home, walking up the stairway leading to his house at 18 Great Hamilton

Street. As he fumbled for his key, a young man loomed out of the shadows, threw his right arm around Rankin's throat and yanked back his head. As Rankin choked, the attacker grabbed his watch and chain, pulled it away and charged down the dark stairs.

'Thief!' Rankin roared. 'Police!'

He began to chase after the thief, with a few passers-by joining in. They ran along Great Hamilton Street and into a narrow close that led to a tall tenement. Then their quarry vanished. When the pursuers entered the stair, they found the staircase window open, and they peered out into the back court, which was equally empty, with the gate shut and locked. Baffled, the pursuers gave up, while Rankin reported the theft at the Eastern Police Office and expected to hear no more about it. However, Detective Campbell was on duty, and he was not a man to give up easily.

As soon as he heard about the theft, Campbell marched across to Great Hamilton Street and tried to trace the route of the thief. He looked at the stair, examined the window and decided that the thief had not left by that route. He knew that people could not disappear into nothingness, so there must have been a rational explanation. Campbell decided that, as the garrotter was obviously not hiding in the back court or in the stair, he must have been concealed inside one of the houses in the stair. Accordingly, he methodically knocked on each door in turn, asking the occupants if they had seen or given shelter to a stranger in the last couple of hours. All the answers were in the negative, until he reached the top floor, where an old lady invited him in.

The lady was very helpful. She told Detective Campbell that she had indeed had a young man come to her house and had let him in. Detective Campbell was very interested, and asked why. The lady explained that the young man had needed her help; he had been running from the notorious Muldoon band, a local gang, and had been terrified, so she had taken him in. Detective Campbell asked where the young man may be now, and the lady said he was still hiding inside.

Detective Campbell followed the lady into her bedroom, but it appeared empty. For a second Campbell thought the fugitive had slipped away again, but when he searched the room he found the man hiding under the bed. When Campbell did a body search, he found nothing, so searched the room and found Rankin's watch and chain under the mattress. The man was arrested.

Garrotting, however, was only one type of assault. There were many more – some entirely unexpected.

A Naked Attacker

Either in an attempt to prove their manhood, or as a show of contempt for authority, many young men sought to attack the police or private watchmen, especially after they had visited the local hostelries in the city. It was more normal for such events to occur when the men were fully dressed, but on New Year's Day of 1851, a naked man launched an attack on two watchmen on the south bank of the Clyde.

About five in the morning, the watchmen were walking along the Clyde directly opposite the Green when they saw Andrew Mitchell wearing only a coat and vest. Such sights were not entirely unexpected on that day, but the watchmen were not prepared for Mitchell to strip completely naked and suddenly attack one of them. Naturally, a naked, drunken man is at a severe disadvantage when fighting a fully dressed sober man armed with a staff, and Mitchell soon realised he was literally on a hiding to nothing. Breaking off his attack, he ran into the swollen river, but drunken men are not the best swimmers, and the current carried him away.

From being his adversary, the watchmen became Mitchell's rescuers. As he was swept past Wellington Place the watchmen, helped by a local boatman, plucked him out of the water and carried him to the house of the Humane Society. Although the term had not yet been coined,

Mitchell was suffering from hypothermia and it was six hours before he recovered.

An Unfortunate Returnee

Sometimes the perpetrator of an assault could become the victim.

When convicted prisoners were transported for a number of years, they did not always serve the full term of their sentence. There were different degrees of remission, from being allowed to leave the convict settlements to being permitted to live anywhere in the Australian colonies, or even allowed to settle anywhere in the world, except the British Empire.

Thomas Daily had been convicted of assault in 1853. In company with a man named Neil Higney, he had attacked a seaman in Goosedub Street, garrotted him and stolen two shillings. The attackers were unfortunate, as they were caught literally in the act. With no possible defence, they still pleaded not guilty, but the jury decided otherwise and were each transported for fourteen years, sailing on the ship *Adelaide*. While Higney disappeared into the dark maw of history, fate was not yet done with Daily.

Perhaps because he had no real option, he behaved himself in Western Australia and earned the approbation of the prison authorities. In 1856 he appeared to be so reformed that the authorities granted him a ticket of leave, which meant although he was still a convict, he was free to live and work anywhere in Australia, so long as he broke no laws. Two years later, his freedom was extended to anywhere in the world outside Queen Victoria's dominions, and Daily took ship for the west coast of South America.

His choice of location may not have been the wisest. In the nineteenth century there was a breed of predator called boarding masters, who preyed on unwary or inexperienced seamen. These people offered the seamen a bed for a single night or a week and kept them supplied with food, women and drink. Particularly drink. The prices were often inflated and the ultimate cost extreme, for as soon as the seaman's wages ran out, the boarding master gave them a spiked drink and they woke up on some hell ship bound for the ends of the earth with a bully mate and a flint-eyed Down East master, who paid the boarding master his blood money for the addition to his crew. The Pacific ports of the Americas were particularly noted for such practices, and Daily became just one more victim.

An American vessel was looking for hands just as Daily's wages came to an end, so he was drugged and bundled on board. With no choice in the matter, Daily had to obey orders when he was aboard, and when the ship docked in Liverpool in 1861 he was paid off and came ashore. Daily was quite aware of the terms of his ticket of leave, but now he was back in Britain he decided to take a chance and remain; so he came home to Glasgow. For the next year Daily worked diligently and honestly, but inevitably he was discovered and charged with returning from transportation before his term of transportation had expired, and once more he heard the clank of the prison door closing on his freedom.

Although garrotting was the most infamous type of assault in the century, it seldom ended in death. It was sometimes up to the judge to decide if a killing was murder or merely culpable homicide.

Was It a Murder?

There is a fine but definite degree of difference between murder and culpable homicide in Scottish law. Murder is a killing with intent: the murderer intended to end the life of his or her victim. Culpable homicide is killing by accident, but when the killer is to blame for the end of somebody's life.

Very early on Sunday, 30 December 1860, a crowd gathered at Glasgow Cross, cheering, roaring and encouraging two men who were pummelling each other in a fair fight. One man was William Clark, also known as Neil Coyle or sometimes Neil Kyle, but the name of the other man was never recorded. The men had met in a local shebeen, had drunk together, had argued and the verbal dispute had escalated into blows. It was a common sequence where alcohol and volatile, frustrated men combined. The combatants spilled out into the street and continued the dispute with fists and boots.

Thirty-year-old Coyle had a reputation as a hard man. In October 1859 he had been released from jail after a seven-year sentence for robbery and assault, and while inside had imposed his own authority on the inmates, but this time he was on the receiving end. Either the man he was facing was an adept pugilist or there was more than one opponent, but Coyle was taking so much of a battering that one of the watchers felt sorry for him. This man was John Gall, a twenty-three-year-old engine fitter with a kind heart.

As Coyle reeled back from an onslaught, Gall patted him on the shoulder, said the odds were against him, the fight was unfair and he should go home.

Obviously not a man softened by kindness, Coyle immediately turned on this well-wisher, grated, 'Gae oot, ye bastard!' and stabbed him in the groin.

Gall doubled up, clutching himself, and yelled, 'I am stabbed! For God's sake, go for a doctor!' and Coyle turned and ran.

'Hook it now!' somebody in the crowd shouted. 'You've done it at last!'

There was a moment's confusion as Coyle fled down the Saltmarket, and then the mob pursued him, baying for his blood in this unexpected twist in the night's entertainment.

A man named Charles Erskine was in the forefront of the pursuers as Coyle ran into number 18, Waverley Close. 'Come away, chaps,' Erskine said, 'and I'll catch him.' He landed a punch on Coyle, but the man kept running. Coyle ran in front but came up hard against a locked, eight-foot-high iron gate. He turned in defiance but was seized and held until constables Hugh MacPhail and John Hendry arrived.

In the meantime, Gall ran forward through the open arch of the steeple at the Cross, doubled-up and bleeding heavily. He grabbed hold of a lamppost, swung around it and slipped down to lie with his face to the ground. By the time the doctor reached him, it was too late. He died of loss of blood in the infirmary. He had been stabbed in the femoral artery. The police found Coyle's clasp knife on the ground in Waverley Close with the blade encrusted with blood.

Coyle appeared in the Circuit Court in April 1861. He pleaded not guilty of murder but was found guilty of culpable homicide and sentenced to penal servitude for the remainder of his natural life. But Coyle's case was not the only one where the citizens of Glasgow tried to help the police.

Citizens' Helping

In the early nineteenth century, even the most violent of footpads sometimes did not have things all their own way. At midnight on Wednesday, 10 July 1815, a seven-strong group of youths were passing Whitehill Porter Lodge, near present Dennistoun, on their return home to the country from the Glasgow Fair. They were raucous but happy, not causing anybody any trouble, when around twenty men showered them with stones, then launched a charge with staves and clubs.

The country people, including a young woman, fought back but, outnumbered more than two to one by armed and aggressive men, they were overpowered, beaten and robbed. However, once they took stock, they sorted themselves out and launched a counterattack. They did not recover their stolen property but managed to capture two of the attackers and wrestle them to a toll house on the Cumbernauld road before the remainder of the gang rallied. In a few moments, the tollhouse was under siege, but the countrymen gave a concerted roar of 'Murder', which alerted the locals.

When a crowd of people came to help, the gang retreated at great speed. On this occasion, the ordinary people of Glasgow managed to defeat the men of violence. At other times, criminals resorted to diabolical methods that escaped detection for some time.

Never Dilute Good Whisky with Lemonade

Glasgow criminals could always spring a surprise. In the 1850s they were possibly first to use the garrotting technique to immobilise their victims, and in the 1890s a pair of young, respectably dressed scoundrels devised a new method of rendering people helpless and ready to be robbed.

Alexander Houston and James Sutherland were extremely enterprising young men. To outward appearances, they were gentlemen, being well dressed, well spoken and good mannered, but beneath the facade they were calculating predators who stalked the streets in search of prey. They did not target helpless drunks, but looked for respectable men who may have some money or possessions worth stealing.

Around four in the afternoon of 31 August 1894, Houston saw Andrew Henderson, Inspector of Works in Partick, as he walked through Queen Street Station. Houston approached and said, 'Hello, Jimmy,' and said he came from Dumbarton and knew that Henderson was a grocer there. Although Henderson denied he was a Dumbarton man, he agreed to accompany Houston to a nearby spirit shop for a dram. Sutherland joined them in the pub.

Houston and Sutherland ordered lemonade, while Henderson had a half – a half-gill of whisky. They spoke about Dumbarton, with Henderson denying any connection, but he ordered another half for himself and more lemonade for his new companions. Henderson downed his half and then collapsed into unconsciousness. He woke up in the Western Police Office at half past eight with a raging throat, a buzzing head and no recollection of anything that had happened since he sipped at his second whisky, but he did realise that his watch and chain were missing, along with some stamps and £1 three shillings and nine pence. The sore throat and head continued for over a week.

However, there were two witnesses, Mrs Nicol and her son John, who had seen Houston and another man, presumably Sutherland, carrying

Henderson from a cab into a dark close in the Kent Road. Houston said that he had found Henderson drunk in the street. The beat constable found Henderson in the close and trundled him to the police office in a barrow. Henderson's watch turned up in a pawnshop later.

Two weeks after being robbed, Henderson met the thieves in Dundas Street, but Houston saw him watching. 'The old man has spotted us,' he said, and before Henderson could find a policeman, the pair had escaped.

Houston and Sutherland's next known victim was Claud Charles Lapsley. He was walking across George Square on 17 September when Sutherland rushed up to him with his hand outstretched in friendship. Lapsley, probably a little bemused, took the hand. Sutherland claimed to be an old friend of his called Smith, and invited him for a drink. Lapsley agreed, and they went into a pub in North Frederick Street, where Lapsley discovered they were both going to catch the same bus to Dennistoun. Sutherland bought Lapsley a half of whisky, while he ordered lemonade.

Sutherland was obviously a very friendly young man; he poured some of his lemonade into Lapsley's whisky. Lapsley knocked it back, and within a few moments he 'began to feel queer'. They left the pub, but Lapsley had hardly walked into George Square when he had to sit down on one of the benches. His memories of what happened next were hazy.

Lapsley knew that at some point a man had joined him on the bench and asked him where he lived. He remembered saying he lived at Cathcart, and the stranger said he did as well. He had vague memories being on the same train as the stranger, who left at Bridge Street, and when he arrived home he had been robbed of his watch. Once again, the watch appeared in a pawnshop, but this time the dealer identified Sutherland as the man who had pledged the pawn.

The third known victim was Henry Munro. As he was walking through Queen Street on the night of 22 September, Houston tapped him on the shoulder. Munro turned around and Houston immediately apologised, saying he thought Munro was his father, as they looked very alike. To show he was sincere, Houston offered to buy Munro a drink, and both men walked amicably into the nearest public house. Houston insisted on paying for two halves of what he called 'special' whisky and poured some lemonade into Munro's.

'That tastes a bit peculiar,' Munro said after tasting his drink.

'Oh, it's the strong lemonade that causes that,' Houston explained.

'It's more than that,' Munro said, but finished his whisky.

As soon as they left the pub, Munro began to feel dizzy. He managed to walk the length of Queen Street, but when he got into Cochrane Street, he collapsed. He woke up in the Central Police Office with his watch and chain missing, convinced that he had been drugged, but he was charged with being drunk and incapable and admonished before the Police Court. It was days before he fully recovered.

Houston and Sutherland were on a roll now. Their next known victim was John Armour, who went for a walk around Glasgow on 29 September. He was in Howard Street, a seagull's call from the Clyde, when Houston claimed to know him. Armour said that he must be mistaken and walked on, but Houston was persistent. He asked a second time, and insisted on buying Armour a drink. Armour agreed, and they walked into Scoular's pub, where he ordered a schooner of beer. The pub was quiet, but Sutherland joined the party, engaged in a private conversation with Houston, and bought Armour a second pint. Armour downed the pint, felt a strange tingling in his mouth and woke up in his own house with his money, watch and chain missing.

His wife informed him that a local man named Donald Ross had found him lying apparently drunk in the street and brought him home. It was eight days before Armour recovered. Houston pawned the watch.

The final known victim was a commission agent named Thomas Anderson. Houston's method was slightly more direct. He saw Anderson walking alone down Renfield Street at the back of seven on 3 October and asked if he would like a drink. Anderson politely refused and walked on, but Sutherland approached and asked if he had seen Mr Scott.

'Do you mean Mr Scott, the contractor in Greenock?' Anderson asked.

'That's the fellow,' Sutherland agreed.

'No, I have not,' Anderson said.

Instead of looking despondent, Sutherland invited Anderson for a drink, and this time he fell into the trap. They entered a pub in West Nile Street, where Houston joined them. While Sutherland and Anderson spoke about Greenock, Houston poured them all out some beer. Anderson drank his, saw Houston leave the pub and his next memory was waking up in the Southern Police Office sometime after five the next morning, bereft of twelve shillings and sixpence, and his watch and chain.

The only witness to the missing hours was a young girl called Margaret Robb, who saw two men bring him into a close in Eglinton Street. They gave her a penny and asked her to watch him until they returned, but they never came back. As with the others, Anderson was unwell for some days afterward.

It is not known if Houston and Sutherland carefully selected their victims, or chose random men, but in each case they gained a watch and a small amount of money. More interesting was the fact that the apparently drunk men were often helped by a well-disposed passer-by. Despite the crime, Glasgow's heartbeat was kindly, with people always willing to give help to a neighbour in need.

Strangely, it was not one of the victims who led the police to Houston and Sutherland, but a falling out between the thieves. At one in the morning of 4 October, Constable James McGown was on his beat in Parson Street when he heard the raised voices of an argument and the scuffling of a fight. The door of the house was locked and nobody answered his knocking, so he forced his way in. Houston was lying on top of a woman and holding her by the throat. She was fighting back, trying to kick him, while Sutherland lay on the bed, watching.

Constable McGown arrested all three for disorderly conduct, but as they left the house he saw Houston drop an Albert watch chain, so kindly picked it up and handed it back. McGown was intrigued when Houston threw it away again, so he reported the incident when he arrived back at the police office. His sergeant sent him back to search the house properly, where he found a number of curious things.

First there was a gold watch under the pillow where Sutherland had been lying. Then there were the bottles: four of them, two marked 'C', were in a drawer and two marked 'A' and 'D' were in the coal bunker. McGown thought they were rather odd, so took them back to the office, where Detective Skene questioned Houston and Sutherland about them.

Sutherland claimed he had never seen them before, but Houston said they contained his medicine. When Skene had the contents of the bottles analysed, he found that the bottles marked 'A' and 'D' held a solution of 120 grains of chloral hydrate, which could easily be mixed with lemonade, and if only twenty grains were ingested, would paralyse the nervous system. Whoever drank that would be unable to walk or think. It was not a substance that could be bought over the counter, and if too much was given it could kill. The bottles marked 'C' contained harmless syrup, which could be used to sweeten the chloral hydrate.

In November 1894, Houston and Sutherland were found guilty of having drugged and robbed five people. Houston, a young man with seven previous convictions, was given five years' penal servitude, while Sutherland, who had no record, was given three years.

6

Amazing Jewel Robberies

The 1840s was a significant decade in Glasgow. It was a decade of unemployment and political protest. It was a decade of immigration from the Highlands and Ireland, and then in 1848 came a surge of jewellery robberies in and around Argyle Street.

The First Robbery

The first was on the night of Thursday, 18 May 1848, when thieves robbed John Duncan's shop in the Argyll Arcade. As one of the oldest covered shopping arcades in Europe, the Argyll Arcade has been set in the very heart of Glasgow since it was built in 1827. John Baird, the Glaswegian builder, was influenced by French style but used the engineering skills that were making Glasgow famous throughout the world. The glass roof allowed light to permeate the thirty shops, as this short street slashes through tenement buildings between Buchanan Street and Argyle Street in a glittering L of jewellers and watchmakers. It is a ring hunter's paradise, but in the days of Queen Victoria that also made it a Mecca for jewel thieves.

That robbery created quite a stir in Glasgow. John Duncan was a hardware merchant as well as a jeweller, and was regarded as a kind and honest man. His business was about as secure as any jewellery shop in Glasgow could be. If he had been robbed, then nobody was safe. The Arcade had two gates, one opening into Argyle Street and one into Buchanan Street, but both were closed and locked at night and not opened until six in the morning. The beat policeman checked them regularly to ensure they were locked and the Arcade was secure. There was additional security with a watchman inside the Arcade. He had been on patrol all night but had seen nothing untoward the night Duncan was robbed, so the whole affair was a bit of a mystery.

The outside gates opened at six and the inside watchman stopped work at seven, and as Andrew Gray, the shop boy, did not open up until eight, there was a clear hour when the shop was unattended. Even so, at that time both Argyle Street and Buchanan Street would be bustling with people travelling to work. It was unlikely that a break-in would pass unnoticed. Despite these precautions, when Gray unlocked the door in the morning he found the shop had been very thoroughly robbed. It had not been a hurried job, for the thieves had been very selective in what they stole, with only the best quality and most valuable items being removed. What was more, neither of Duncan's two doors had been forced, so the thief either possessed the key to the shop or had made a false key. The thieves had got away with over fifty gold and silver watches, a large number of gold chains and rings and a selection of silver pencil cases. The total haul amounted to around £700, or around fourteen years' wages for a skilled man.

Naturally, suspicion fell on the watchman. The police put him under great pressure and interviewed him strongly, but he proved honest. He had not been involved in the robbery. There were no clues, and although the police kept a close eye on pawnshops and jewellers, none of the stolen jewellery turned up. Despite the network of police informers, nor were there any whispers about the thieves.

Duncan had two hundred bill posters made and pasted up all over Glasgow, with a £50 reward for any information about the robbery, but to no avail. The case was so mysterious that there were rumours that Duncan had never been robbed and the whole affair was a lie. There were whispers about Duncan's character, with people hinting it was all set up for the insurance, and eventually the slurs on his reputation began to affect his health. And then, nearly a year later, a curious coincidence helped the police unravel part of the story.

On Saturday, 17 March 1849, Duncan was working in his shop when a man named William Priestly arrived and asked for an Albert chain and key for his silver watch. Duncan examined the watch, recognised it as one that had been stolen the previous year and asked the man from where he had purchased it. 'From John Dougall, the watchmaker in Brunswick Street,' the man told him at once, and Duncan passed the information on to the police.

George McKay, the head of the Glasgow detectives, decided to take the case in person. His first call was at Dougall's shop. Dougall told him that Henry Gray, a gold-beater from Dunlop Street, had sold him the watches. McKay hunted down Gray and listened to a curious tale. Gray claimed he had bought twenty watches from a complete stranger in a pub in Dalmarnock Road.

McKay was sceptical and arrested him. With a little bit of questioning, McKay discovered that Gray did indeed know the seller, a blacksmith and bell hanger named Alexander Stewart, who lived in King Street. McKay also learned that a man named Archibald Leitch had tried to reset some. McKay knew nothing about Stewart; he could not arrest him on the unsupported word of Gray, so he checked out Stewart's friends and relations to see if there were any criminal connections. He struck gold when he found that Stewart knew a Mrs Walker, who kept a thief's den in Stockwell Street.

When McKay searched Walker's house he found a small leather case that held some of the stolen jewellery. His next stop was the home of Stewart's brother-in-law, Lawrence Anderson, in Oxford Street. Anderson's cellar yielded more of Duncan's jewellery, but rather than have him jailed, McKay turned him and used him as a witness.

Other customers remembered that Stewart had hawked a basket-load of watches around the pub. McKay asked more questions and traced Stewart to his favoured haunt of a local public house, where he arrested both him and his wife, Isabella. A search of Stewart's house located more of the stolen jewellery.

McKay found Leitch in the Trongate, escorted him to his shop and removed a parcel from his safe. Over a civilised glass of toddy in an Argyle Street tavern a few steps from the burgled shop, McKay opened the parcel and found seventeen silver watches.

As soon as he had the watches, Duncan compared their numbers with those that had been stolen. Only nine of Leitch's watches were his, but all the others had also been stolen from various places. A conscientious man, Duncan kept a watch stock book in which he recorded the numbers of all his watches. It was about now that the mystery of the robbery began to unravel. It had been months in the planning and had depended on very careful timing.

Stewart was a metalworker and had worked for an ironmonger named Liddell, who was the proprietor of a shop within the Argyll Arcade. In that position Stewart had worked in most of the shops and knew Duncan's business well. Sometime in this period he had access to Duncan's keys and made an impression on putty, so was able to create duplicate keys. Even so, he did not move right away but waited until every detail was known and in his favour.

The actual robbery was dependent on timing and a single trusted helper. Stewart knew that the shops were shut a short time before the gates of the Arcade were finally closed, to enable the last sauntering customers and the shop workers to get home. On the night of 18 May 1848, he slipped inside the Arcade just before the outer gates were locked, waited until the elbow of the Arcade prevented the watchman from seeing him and used his false key to get into Duncan's shop. He was inside before the watchman returned to close the Argyle Street gates, and all he had to do was ensure he was quiet and invisible until the gates were opened the next morning. Rather than alert the watchman by turning on the gas in the shop, Stewart had converted a lantern to throw a very slender pencil of light. He had the whole night to select whatever he wanted from the shop and only picked the best quality merchandise that he could easily transport from the shop. It must have been a long night – waiting for the gates to open, listening to the portentous pacing of the watchman and wondering if he would be caught.

At last the watchman unfastened the gates of the Arcade and Stewart prepared for the next stage of his plan. The first person to enter the Arcade was a woman with a mop and a tub, but rather than wash down the floor, she halted just outside Duncan's shop and gave a casual, quiet rap on the glass when she saw the watchman finish his shift and go home.

Stewart opened up the door and placed a packet of stolen jewellery in the bottom of the tub. The woman, his wife Isabella Stewart, covered the packet with her cloths and they left by different exits. It was only a few minutes later that the robbery was discovered.

McKay cast a wide net and arrested five people for the theft or for resetting the watches. As well as the Stewarts, there was Gray, Lawrence Anderson and the general dealer, Archibald Leitch. Anderson had been released, but in his place came a spirit dealer named James Dobbie.

McKay was not yet finished. He questioned his suspects one by one and found out that more of the stolen jewellery was scattered around west central Scotland, where the police gradually made a collection of most of the items.

In September 1849 the case came to trial in the Circuit Court. The Stewarts were charged with breaking into Duncan's shop by means of a false key or a lock pick and stealing a large quantity of items, including sixty-three watches, 216 rings, ninety pencil cases and ninety gold watch chains. Isabella Stewart was also charged with resetting the stolen goods. Leitch was charged with resetting eight watches, Gray with resetting twenty watches and Dobbie with resetting twenty-six rings. Gray and Dobbie absconded before the trial and were consequently outlawed, while a clerical error saw Leitch temporarily walk away free. The Stewarts were not so lucky and were sentenced to fourteen years' transportation.

A month later, Leitch was hauled back for trial, charged with resetting watches in the Crow Hotel in George Square and in John Robertson's chemist shop in Queen Street. After a trial where his defence depended on his previous good character, Leitch was found guilty and given eight months for his sins.

When everything was done and dusted, Duncan was immensely relieved. He did not recover all his stolen goods – only five of the thirty gold watches and fourteen of the silver – so he was down about £400, but that mattered less than having his good reputation restored. The rumours that he had staged the entire robbery were far worse to him than the loss of a few watches.

Not all robberies were as skilful as that of Duncan's shop. Sometimes they were so direct and blatant they indicate a man forced to desperation by poverty or constant frustration.

A Caricature of a Robbery

On Saturday, 26 August 1848, it was the turn of McLean's jewellery shop in Argyle Street. There was neither subtlety nor skill when George McDermott decided to become a shop breaker. He came to the front window at about eight in the evening when there were still scores of people in the street, raised his arms and smashed his elbows against the quarter-inch-thick plate glass. His actions were so blatant that people passing by did not pause to watch, but presumed he was one of McLean's employees working at the window. They huddled up against the pouring rain and hurried home.

Inside the shop, the workers heard the heavy banging against the glass, but did not know what it was or from where it originated. Instead of checking their window, which was well lit and sealed, they thought the noise came from the apartment above, and glanced to the ceiling. There was a second massive bang, and a third and then the crash and clatter of shattering glass. It was only then that the shop workers realised what was happening. They watched in astonishment as McDermott's hand thrust through the broken window and grabbed for the watches and jewellery on display.

At first McDermott grabbed a brass rod, from which hung half a dozen gold watches, but he had not realised the rod was bolted in to either side of the window and could not be easily removed. After a few moments' struggle, he transferred his attention to a single gold watch that lay on a tray. He snatched it and ran, but only managed a few steps before two men pounced on him. They had watched the whole comedy, worked out what was happening and decided to stop the robbery. As they grabbed him, McDermott dropped the watch, which fell down between the rungs of a street drain from where it was later recovered. The court gave McDermott fifteen months in jail to work out a better plan for his next attempt.

The Irish Connection

The third of this quartet of jewellery robberies is a story of mystery and betrayal that involves a pursuit by sea and investigations beyond Scotland. Walter Baird was mentioned as being a clockmaker in John Smith's book *Old Scottish Clockmakers 1453 to 1850*. His shop had a single window and a single door opening into Argyle Street, while there was a draper's shop next door. On Saturday night, 17 June 1848, Baird locked up as normal and walked home, quite confident his shop was secure, as he had augmented the police patrols and locks by having a security man in the premises all night.

John Ogle was an Irishman from County Monaghan. He had come to Scotland looking for work, had recommendations from a trio of utterly respectable people had worked for Walter Baird for some time. A swarthy, polite and modest man, Ogle was essential to Baird's business. While Ogle slept in a back room of the shop every night, separated from the shop itself by a wooden partition, his ferocious Newfoundland dog remained in the front. The combination of locks, watchful Irishman and large dog had kept the shop safe from thefts even during the turbulent decade of the Hungry Forties, until that fateful weekend.

Saturday night passed without incident and on the Sunday morning Ogle left the shop to go to church, returned later and continued to guard the shop. He was back in position on Sunday night, but when Baird opened up at seven on Monday morning, the shop had been thoroughly robbed. The thieves seemed to have used a simple technique: they had broken the lock off the back window of the muslin and lace shop next door and simply hacked a large hole in the connecting wall between the two shops. When the beat constable did his rounds he noted the muslin shop window was shut at half past five but open at quarter past six.

Ogle was distraught. He had been on duty all night and could not explain what had happened. He must have been very soundly asleep not to hear the noise as the robbers smashed through the wall, he said. He was more upset when the police suspected him of complicity, arrested him and subjected him to a rigorous questioning. However, Baird vouched for his honesty, and anyway, Baird argued, if he had been involved, he would have absconded with the jewellery. Twenty watches had been stolen, together with a collection of gold rings and sundry other articles, with a value of nearly £900.

Assistant Superintendent George McKay, the same man who had investigated the Duncan jewellery shop break-in, retained his suspicions about Ogle. He kept him in custody but did not charge him. Instead, he sent out his men to make enquiries and found out that Ogle's father, William, and one of his brothers had recently arrived in Glasgow on the Belfast boat. That information sent the alarm bells jangling in McKay's mind, and he checked out where William Ogle had stayed in Glasgow.

When he discovered that Ogle was booked into the next steamer for Belfast, McKay's suspicions grew even stronger, and he decided to arrest the elder Ogle to see what he had been up to in his brief visit that just happened to coincide with the robbery of the shop where his son worked. There was a choice of steamers between the Clyde and Belfast, with *Aurora* sailing direct from Glasgow and *Glow Worm* from Ardrossan, further down the coast.

Although McKay had never seen William Ogle in person, he obtained as good a description of him as he could and dashed to catch *Aurora*. He was too late, so caught the train to Ardrossan and boarded *Glow Worm* just as she left for Belfast. The journey was uneventful, save for an encounter with a distinguished gentleman who was collecting money for a destitute man. McKay handed over sixpence. He thought the charity collector was uncannily similar to his description of the elder Ogle, so kept him under surveillance, particularly as the gentleman was possessive of something he carried wrapped up in a handkerchief.

As *Glow Worm* came into Queen's Quay in Belfast in the early morning, McKay came up to the gentleman and asked what was inside the hand-kerchief.

'Watches,' the man said at once, and McKay had found his man. He arrested him there and then and took him to the Belfast Police Office to be searched. The handkerchief of watches was only the tip of the iceberg. The police took watches and jewellery from every pocket of his clothes, so within a few moments nearly £900 of stolen goods were piled on the desk.

With the older Ogle handcuffed securely, McKay returned to Glasgow on the Wednesday and resumed his pursuit of Henry, the third and final member of the family. The last Ogle, however, was innocent; he had taken steerage passage to the United States in a state of such poverty that it was obvious he had no connection with the robbery.

The police put together the final pieces of the jigsaw as they learned how John and William Ogle had committed the robbery. Their plan had been clever, but had neglected some basic security. The robbery had been planned for some time and father and son had gone over the details weeks before. Some three weeks earlier, Ogle's Newfoundland dog just happened to rip Baird's stock book to shreds. As the stock book contained a record of all the watches and their numbers, losing it would make later identification virtually impossible.

At four o'clock the next Tuesday morning they had met at the back window of Baird's shop, unfastened the lock of the shutters and discussed their plans. However, this window looked into a shared courtyard and the kitchen of the house opposite, where a servant was already hard at work on the weekly wash. The Ogles saw the servant and backed off quickly; they had to revise their ideas. They had intended a simple entrance by the back window of the shop, but their careless talking forced an alteration of the plan. McKay worked out what had happened. Although the next-door shop had its back window open and a hole punched through the wall, these were red herrings. The younger Ogle had casually selected the items he fancied from the stock and handed them to his father, who had come to the back window.

McKay did not immediately inform John Ogle his father had been arrested. Instead, with that flair for the dramatic that seemed normal at the time, he had Captain Miller bring him to the inside of the back window and had the shutters thrown open. McKay and William Ogle were in the courtyard outside, and both Ogles stared at each other through the glazed window. John Ogle was shocked for a second, but when he recovered he denied knowing his father was in Glasgow. Both Ogles were charged with the robbery; at the autumn Circuit Court both were transported to Australia for ten years.

The One-Legged Watchman

There was another epic attempt at robbing a jewellery shop in early October 1853. This time the target was D. C. Rait in Buchanan Street, the then largest jewellery business in the city. The robbery was very professional and had again been some time in the planning, but pure bad luck, or perhaps a slight inattention to detail, spoiled it.

On Saturday, 1 October 1853, two men waited in Buchanan Street until Rait's closed for the weekend. They knew the shop well, having visited as customers half a dozen times to purchase small items, while studying the layout and checking out the stock. They had timed the rounds of the beat policeman; they knew the surrounding streets; they thought they had covered every angle. Now they were ready to move in and glean the rewards.

The taller of the two called himself George Jackson, but the identity of the other is as mysterious today as it was then. Jackson was about twenty-eight years old, a gentleman by appearance, handsome as sin, dark-haired with a fine set of whiskers, clear steady eyes and an English accent, although if he was asked he would claim to be from Canada.

Carrying a bag full of tools and equipment, the two men slipped through the narrow passage into Prince's Court, which gave access to the back door of J & W Campbell's soft goods warehouse. A false key opened the locked gate that led to half a dozen different businesses in a common stair. The two men quietly shut the gate behind them and climbed up a flight of steps to the Counting House and warehouse of Campbell's. There were other premises above, but there was no need to go further.

They used another false key to open the door; Campbell's warehouse stretched right above Rait's shop, and they cut a square hole in the floor. This operation took them a few hours and ended in frustration. Rait's were well aware of the temptation their stock would be to the thieves of Glasgow, and they also knew that people often gained access by cutting through walls and ceilings. As a precaution, they had lined their ceiling with iron plates that proved invulnerable to the tools the burglars had brought.

Jackson and his companion were stumped for a moment, but they thought of a solution. Only a few years before there had been a robbery of Marshall's jewellers in Edinburgh. The thief there had gone in from the flat upstairs by removing the hearthstone. Perhaps these men remembered that event, or maybe they thought of that identical method themselves, but they moved to the fireplace and with great labour prised free the hearthstone. As they hoped, there were no iron plates beneath. It was the work of a few frantic minutes to saw through the timber joists and then kick through the plaster ceiling. There was a sizeable drop to the shop below, but the men had come prepared with a fine rope ladder, which again was the technique employed in the Edinburgh robbery. They swarmed down hand over hand to find the entire contents of Glasgow's largest jewellery shop open to them.

They were not greedy; they were selective. Rather than grabbing everything in sight, they chose only the most portable and most valuable. Using a cleverly adapted lantern that allowed only a glimmer of light, they chose diamond rings, gold bracelets, £800 worth of brooches of gold and pearl, plus gold chains, lockets and bracelets, all of which they packed neatly in the japanned leather travelling bag they had brought with them. The overall value was in the order of £3,000, which was a colossal amount for the time.

Once the bag was packed, the thieves waited until just after six on Sunday morning, slipped back down the rope ladder into Campbell's warehouse and out onto the stairs leading into Prince's Court. Quite confident that they had succeeded in a historic robbery, they walked down the stairs. And there they met the private watchman head on.

The shock for both parties must have been immense. Jackson had done his homework and knew that Hugh Carmichael, the watchman, knocked off at six, which is why he had waited until that hour before leaving Rait's premises. The next watchman was meant to take over at seven, allowing a one-hour-long window in which Jackson could escape. However, that morning the seven o'clock man had altered the system. He had been working the previous night and had asked Carmichael to stay longer.

Carmichael was elderly, wooden-legged and until then had never had any problems. He had the keys to all the external doors in the Court and checked all the premises assiduously; now he was confronted by two very respectable-looking men coming from the jeweller's at seven o'clock on a

Sunday morning. He had been on his rounds and had just checked the door of Griffin's Chemical Museum one flight further up and thought he heard a noise below. He returned down the stairs, his wooden leg clicking with each step, and now he was unsure what to make of these two well-dressed gentlemen on the landing.

If the thieves had both held their nerve all might have been well, but that did not happen.

Jackson remained calm. 'Could you open the door for us?' he asked, but before Carmichael had time to reply, the smaller man leapt on top of him, wrapped a hand around his throat and tried to cover his mouth so he could not make a noise.

The watchman jerked his head to one side and shouted, 'Murder! Thieves!' as loudly as he could, considering he had a hand clamped around his throat. It was fortunate for him, if not for the thieves, that Glasgow at seven on a Sunday morning was quiet, so his voice travelled. The beat policeman happened to hear his shouts and rushed to help.

The policeman thundered into the passageway, but the gate was shut so he could only watch in impotence through the iron bars as the two thieves scrambled upstairs away from the watchman. There was a small window six steps further up, and they wriggled through and jumped the fifteen feet or so to the court below, staggered and continued. They ran into Buchanan Street, and then separated, each man fleeing in a different direction. At that early hour there were no crowds to hide in, but equally there was nobody to help the police. The policeman could only follow one of the thieves, so he chose Jackson, and the smaller man vanished into the streets and wynds of the city.

As Jackson raced along Buchanan Street, he unfastened and dropped his greatcoat; the pursuing policeman let it lie and kept his eye on the main quarry as he turned into Queen Street. The policeman shouted and pounded after him, but Jackson did not look back and slipped into Tax Office Court; he hoped to escape in the narrow closes but instead he slammed into a closed gate. He stopped, looked around desperately for a way out, but there was none. The policeman grasped him, and Jackson knew he was under arrest. All that work, all the weeks of planning, had been ended by a one-legged watchman who should not have been there.

As the policeman hunted down his man, Carmichael dragged himself up from the ground, dusted himself down and found the leather bag the thieves had left behind in their mad scamper to escape.

Meanwhile, the police searched Jackson's discarded coat and the thief himself. In the coat they found a whole selection of false keys. They tried them on the door at the foot of the stairs and one opened it as smoothly as if it had been made for the purpose, which it had, of course. A small key in the pocket of Jackson's thief's waistcoat opened the leather bag and thousands of pounds' worth of stolen jewellery glinted up at the police. A luggage ticket led the police to a second bag in the station, in which was a fine selection of fashionable clothes and a number of books, including a French dictionary. Jackson also owned a pair of fine-legged callipers that were used for measuring locks preparatory to making false keys. There was great skill in the shop-breaking business.

By questioning and adroit detective work, the police backtracked Jackson's steps. They found out he had acted the part of a gentleman for some weeks as he studied his intended target. He had lived only a few rooms away from rooms occupied by the Circuit Judge in the Queen's Hotel, and had also spent time in the Royal Hotel and in lodgings in Renfrew Street. The police traced him further back, gradually unravelling Jackson's history; they found out he was well travelled around the British Isles, having lived in Southampton, Portsmouth, London and Liverpool, as well as Glasgow. There were rumours, perhaps justified, that he was English and his real name was Johnstone rather than Jackson, and he had been concerned in previous jewellery robberies in London and Manchester. If so, then he had ridden his luck, for a London detective had traced him to Paris and arrested him there, but there had not been enough evidence to convict him. Hugh Carmichael and a determined police officer ensured his luck had run out in Glasgow.

The police made further discoveries as they dug deeper into the mysterious George Jackson. When in his Renfrew Street lodgings, a nosey servant had poked into a box that arrived for him. She saw a selection of saws, the rope ladder and false keys, but was too scared to tell anybody in case she got into trouble.

When he appeared before the Police Court, Jackson gave his name and added, 'I will answer no more questions.' He was tried at the High Court as George Jackson in February and was transported for life. With him departed the answers to various mysteries, not least his real identity and the name of his accomplice. There is one final postscript, however. The jeweller, David Rait, presented Hugh Carmichael with a silver-mounted snuff horn and £100 'in grateful remembrance of his energetic and successful services in discharge of his duty'. That was a nice touch to close a case in which so many mysteries remain open.

7

The Early Police Force

There is a misconception that London's Metropolitan Police were the first modern professional uniformed police force in the world. Although Edinburgh had a system of uniformed city guards as far back as the seventeenth century, these men were normally ex-army veterans who merely quelled riots and placed drunken troublemakers in the Tolbooth. They were not the same as the civil police. Glasgow was the first city in Scotland and in Britain to have a uniformed civil police force. James Buchanan was the inspector in 1779, a full half-century ahead of Sir Robert Peel's Londoners. The force lasted only two years before money troubles defeated the attempt. The city tried again in 1788, with a total of eight uniformed men to keep down crime right across Glasgow. Each man had to swear an oath to be faithful in his duty, and had to part with a startling £50 as security for his 'honest and faithful behaviour'. Only then could he wear the badge inscribed with 'Police' and his personal identification number.

These eight men had a hard task in front of them. As well as patrolling the city day and night to prevent crime and detecting what they could not stop, they were to trawl the low lodging houses for information, check pawnshops for stolen goods and record everything they discovered. In between times, they were to stop begging and obscene or inflammatory songs and quell the occasional riot, plus arrest vagrants and drunkards, as well as ensure cart and carriage drivers were safe to be on the city streets. These policemen had roles vastly different from the brown-coated watchmen, who had a very limited role in crime control. They were preventative policemen whose uniformed and professional presence had an incalculable effect in quietening crime.

It was not the will to police that prevented the initial attempt from being successful, but lack of money. The city council created a committee to manage the new force, and in 1788 this committee appointed James Buchanan as the first inspector and Richard Marshall as Master of Police, while they tried to persuade the Trades Houses to help finance the experiment and Parliament to pass a Police Act for Glasgow.

Despite their best efforts, the police force failed in 1790, and it was not until the passing of the Glasgow Police Act in 1800 that uniformed police again appeared on the streets of the city. The administration came from the merchant elite, who voted for the commissioners who controlled the police, so the ruling classes were very much in control. Nothing else could be expected at a time when the French Revolution terrified the British ruling elite into squashing any hint of so-called radical protest.

A Holistic Community

Although law enforcement was important to Scottish policing, it was only one of a multitude of duties the police performed. The Glasgow Police Act included provisions for cleaning the streets to keep the city healthy, and for lighting, which was in itself a major factor in crime prevention, so the superintendent in charge of the Glasgow Police was a busy man. Policing was one aspect of a holistic Scottish community that sought to provide a decent quality of life for everybody.

In 1800, John Stenhouse, a city merchant, was appointed Master of Police. He had a force of nine men to protect Glasgow from the criminal element; they mustered in November in the Session House of the Laigh Kirk in the Trongate. Stenhouse divided his men into three sections, each of a sergeant and two policemen, who worked twenty-four hour shifts, with one day in three off. When on duty, the men spent one day on constant patrol in the streets and one day in the police office. They were backed and supported by sixty-eight watchmen, who carried long staffs and a hand-held lantern. As their name implied, the primary duty of these men was to watch. They were placed at strategic points throughout the city, acting as sentinels. Glasgow was now the pioneering police city of Britain; where Glasgow led, all the other towns would eventually follow.

The Changing City

There remains a question of why Glasgow decided to form a police force at this time. There is probably no simple answer, but growing concern about an uneducated and restless industrial population, combined with radical politics, may be significant. Demographic change created by rural depopulation and a surge of people unused to town life was also surely a factor. The result was a city of crowded and unhygienic streets teeming with unskilled labourers, where unscrupulous landlords raked in money with over-priced rents. There were footpads waiting in the unlit closes and highwaymen on the roads, prostitutes in the low lodging houses, pick-pockets among the crowded streets, card sharps and con men in the spirit shops and coiners passing false money to unsuspecting shopkeepers. The police had a hard job ahead of them and started with a lack of manpower and a dearth of experience.

They would learn. They had to.

The criminals were not inclined to wait. Petty crime was endemic, with sundry assaults and robberies. For example, on Sunday, 16 September 1804, housebreakers targeted Post Office Court and completely gutted a house of its valuables. However, as well as deliberate acts of theft and violence, the police were summoned to take care of the sordid and sad day-to-day accidents of life. That same September of 1804, a collier named John Park accidentally drowned when he fell into the Forth and Clyde Canal near the aqueduct over the Kelvin. The police helped recover the body. They also gave evidence at the trial of Alexander Colquhoun, a carter who had driven over and killed an elderly pauper named Hugh Taggart near the Gallowgate Toll. Colquhoun was found guilty of culpable homicide.

Already by that year pressure from the police had pushed some of the criminal element out of the city, which unfortunately made the highways outside more hazardous for travellers. This danger was proved on Sunday, 21 December 1804, when two men leaped on a merchant named James Brown as he walked past the Gorbals Toll bar. They grabbed his arms, wrapped a handkerchief round his eyes, tied his wrists together and threatened to kill him unless he handed over his money. Not surprisingly, he did so, and the highwaymen escaped with an astonishing £150. The police scoured the known haunts of Glasgow's bad men and offered a reward for information, but did not catch the robbers.

Early Successes

As well as frustrating failures, there were enough successes for the police to justify their existence and to make the criminals nervous. A year after Brown was robbed, the church at Cheapside in Anderston was hit; at that time Anderston was a suburb to the west of the city. When the morning service finished the congregation went home, and when they were away a thief picked the lock and escaped with the collection, around £10. At that time Glasgow was infested by a gang of cracksmen, but on this occasion the police captured three of them, together with all the tools of their trade.

By 1808 the Glasgow Police had been so successful that criminals were leaving the city for the surrounding villages, and these villages soon decided to follow Glasgow's example. The barony of Gorbals was first, forming its own police force in 1808, and the burgh of Calton in 1819. Five years later, Anderston also formed its own police force, but Glasgow still led the way. By 1813 the Glasgow force alone comprised seventy-eight watchmen as well as sixteen scavengers, the men whose job it was to clean up the accumulated rubbish and filth of the day. Glasgow also had 1,278 lamps, for light was an effective tool in crime prevention, but the vast majority of the closes remained unlit. There was one watch-house in Glasgow as refuge for the policemen, but in 1825 the Central Police Office in South Albion Street was opened.

The innovations were constant. In 1818 the Glasgow Police appointed three lieutenants: Dougal McColl, Alexander Anderson and Peter McKinlay. In 1819 Lieutenant McKinlay became Glasgow's first Criminal Officer, the early name for a detective, although the population were suspicious of these policemen in civilian clothes. Although they were normally employed checking for stolen goods in pawnshops, the criminal officers made an occasional coup. For example, in January 1827 they located a group of forgers in Main Street, Gorbals, with £200 in forged notes.

However, even the Glasgow Police sometimes required military help. There were a number of riots in the first half of the century, as political and social tensions erupted into violence, and during the Dalmarnock riots of 1816, the Radical riots of 1819 and the subsequent Rising of 1820, the military were called in, and again in 1837 when the cotton spinners and miners rioted. That was a bad year altogether, with an economic downturn and high unemployment. There was resistance by combinations, as unions were known, with huge numbers of men protesting in the street and the fewer than 300 police unable to cope. Any *nobs*, as the strike-breakers were called, were liable to be attacked, and in July one nob was shot dead. A £500 reward was offered for information about the murder. Two informants met Sheriff Allison in a vault under the college in a cloak-and-dagger arrangement that included a creep through a back door at night. The informants told of a meeting by the leaders of the combinations in the Black Boy Tavern, and of an alleged plot to murder all the masters and nobs. The Black Boy Tavern was in the Gallowgate, not far from Glasgow Cross, and it had an unenviable reputation for violence.

Superintendent Miller brought twenty police to raid the Black Boy, together with Mr Salmond, the Procurator Fiscal; Nish, the principal

Sheriff Officer; and Sheriff Alison. After stationing his men so nobody could escape from the tavern, Miller moved in. All sixteen of the committee were arrested without any violence and with no resistance. They were all transported for seven years. The Monday after the raid the men were back at work, but although they didn't know it, there was worse ahead, as Europe was on the cusp of the Hungry Forties.

Extending the Boundary

In February 1848 the Glasgow Police boundary was extended to a line from the Kelvin to Tollcross Manse, bringing Drygate Toll, Westmuir, Parkhead and Camlachie into the governance of the police. That month gas lamps were lit in these outlying villages and police constables were out on their streets. The hold of the police was extending.

Some of the early police were real characters. One such was John Lang, who was twenty years in the Clyde Police. Before he joined the police he was a sergeant in the Scots Greys and took part in the famous 'Scotland Forever' charge at Waterloo. His horse was wounded and threw him into the midst of a group of French riflemen. Four Frenchmen attacked him, but he hacked down three and escaped the fourth. He rejoined what remained of the Greys, found another mount and fought through the remainder of the battle. After he was discharged from the Greys Lang joined the police, being commanded by Superintendent Russell, another Greys veteran of Waterloo. Lang died on Monday, 16 December 1850, and was buried in the Southern Necropolis.

The early police had to be tough, as they were always in danger of attack. For example, on Sunday, 4 April 1847, Constable John Colquhoun was on duty at the Bell of the Brae in High Street when a tall man wearing a light moleskin jacket and a dark cap ran up to him and smashed him over the head. Colquhoun's skull was cracked, and he died later in the Royal Infirmary. Despite a reward of £50 being offered to catch the murderer, who was seen running in to a close at 251 High Street, he escaped justice.

But violence was only one danger facing the police. As they dealt with the very lowest strata of society they were also vulnerable to their diseases. For example, on 12 September that same year, Colin Gordon, one of the two night Inspectors of Police and a modest family man, died of typhus, possibly contracted from contact with a sufferer when he inspected the lowest of the lodging houses.

Despite the hazards, the police continued their assault on Glasgow's criminal element. In the autumn of 1847 Glasgow was struck by something like a mini crime wave, as what was thought to be a tight band of professional thieves targeted homes and businesses throughout the city. With Glasgow seemingly under siege, Captain Wilson of the Central District decided to do something drastic. Rather than wait and react to the break-ins, he ordered a number of pre-emptive strikes. On the night of Saturday, 11 September, he gathered his criminal officers into pairs and ordered them to scour the streets for any known criminal and bring them in unless they could prove they were now earning an honest living. Seventeen previously convicted men and women were arrested and charged with being rogues and vagabonds. Wilson's system worked perfectly as the crime figures that night fell dramatically.

As the population of the city rose, so too did the number of police. By August 1853 there were 600 men in the Glasgow Police to control a population of 347,000. The Lord Provost, magistrates and sheriff appointed the superintendent, who appointed the policemen, while a police committee from the town council coped with the administration. By that year the burgh of Partick, as well as the Dundyvan and Gartsherrie iron works had their own police forces, while the Glasgow force helped detect crime in rural Lanarkshire, which still had no police.

Given the size of the Glasgow Police Force and the type of work they had to do, it was inevitable that they should attract some bad characters, and sometimes even the best of them would be accused of ill-doing at one time or another.

Crooked Cops

The early police were certainly not all angels. On Monday, 17 February 1817, three policemen of the night patrol were tried for kidnapping a woman who was innocently walking home. The three constables hustled her along George Street and arrested her, saying she could not leave until she paid them. They were all found guilty, with two sent to the Duke Street Bridewell and the third to prison. Bridewell was a milder punishment, a house of correction where the prisoners were retrained for society.

It was unusual for the police to commit major crimes, but in September 1868 Constable Robert Fraser was accused of culpable homicide.

The situation arose late on 17 July that year when there was trouble in a house in the Gallowgate and Constables Steel and Wyllie were sent to rectify matters. They found that Alexander McDonald, a hefty porter, was happily engaged in thumping his wife. The police tried to mediate, but when McDonald insisted that fists were better than diplomacy, they took him into custody. McDonald was deep in drink and refused to come quietly, but fought every step of the way. As they left the house, McDonald pulled them so they all fell, allegedly with McDonald pitching down the stairs first and Wyllie landing on top, with his knees slamming into McDonald's belly. As so often, people sympathised with any prisoner being taken into custody, and they supported McDonald with the traditional Glasgow greeting of a shower of stones and bricks that had as much chance of hitting the prisoner as the police. A stone cracked against Wyllie's nose but he carried on, bleeding but determined to do his duty.

As a crowd gathered and shouted out for a rescue, the police summoned reinforcements, which included Constable Fraser. They upended McDonald and carried him face down, which they believed helped calm him down. However, when they arrived at the police office in South Albion Street, McDonald remained obdurate. The police dumped him face down on the ground and he refused to stand, but rolled around, kicked out and bit at anybody whose ankles came close to him.

There is some confusion about exactly what happened next. Constables Peter Buchanan and Henry Hill and John McDonald, a clerk in the criminal department of the police force, all saw Constable Fraser restraining McDonald. Buchanan claimed he heard a 'slight struggle' and looked over to see Fraser stamp a foot on the prisoner's neck, then fall on his belly with both knees. Rushing over, Buchanan pushed Fraser away and told him to 'get off for a brute' and stop 'so using the man'. Quite indignant, Fraser demanded how Buchanan would like to be kicked by such a blackguard.

If the scuffle took place, that was the end of it. Constables Steele and Wylie said they had seen nothing of the incident and were adamant that there was no ill usage. However, Buchanan called the police surgeon, Dr McGill, when McDonald complained of a sore belly. McGill made a possible cursory examination, said there was nothing much the matter with him, but recommended he be held in the 'hospital' cell, which was merely a cell that the police inspected more often. When there appeared no deterioration in his condition, McDonald was transferred to an ordinary cell and next morning a magistrate awarded him thirty days. Unfortunately, McDonald did not survive that long; he died the same day of a ruptured bowel.

The question was: did Fraser inflict the injury or had it happened when McDonald dragged them all down the stairs? A jury thought the latter and Fraser was found not guilty.

Johnston's Legacy

Fraser was not the only Glasgow policeman to come before the courts. Robert Johnston was another. Johnston was a Belfast man who, in 1873, moved to Glasgow and became a day constable in the Southern Division. He had only been in the force for a fortnight and was happily perambulating his beat in Gorbals when Superintendent Robb approached him.

'Do you have any money in your pockets, Johnston?' Robb asked.

Johnston looked at him and produced £75 two shillings and eleven pence, and also handed over an empty pocketbook and a purse.

'You had better come with me,' Robb said. 'You are under arrest for theft.'

Johnston went without a complaint. He explained to the superintendent that his father had given him the money and asked him to keep it for safety. That was why he carried it with him on his beat. The superintendent, however, had another theory.

On 24 August, Johnston was in Glasgow with three men, one a fairly prosperous farmer named Kennedy. The farmer asked him if he could find them a cab to Paisley, which Johnston did, and shared part of the journey. Kennedy fell asleep, and Johnston sat at his side.

'Wake up,' one of the others said, but Johnston shook his head.

'He's had a long day,' he said. 'Let him alone.'

Around this time Johnston changed his seat in the cab, moving from one side of the slumbering Kennedy to the other. When they reached the old inn of Halfway House, Johnston left the cab, saying he would wait there for them while they took Kennedy home. As the cab rolled away, Johnston entered the inn and shouted out that his father had sent him money from Ireland; he hauled out a wad of notes and immediately ordered ten glasses of wine and ten drams of whisky. By chance, a local policeman was present, and after a few drinks Johnston presented him with £20, which he kept. By that time Johnston's story had altered, as he said the money had come as a cheque from his siblings. A few moments later, the cab returned and Johnston left the inn.

Next day, Johnston met the policeman again and asked for his money back. When he could not remember the value, the policeman was so suspicious he handed the banknote to the Southern District police. By that time Kennedy had reported the loss of his pocketbook and all his money, and Superintendent Robb put two and two together and came up with Johnston, who had presumably picked Kennedy's pocket in the cab.

Surprisingly, a jury did not believe Johnston's plea of not guilty and he was sentenced to eight years' penal servitude.

As a complete contrast to the miscreant officers, there was James Smart.

Glasgow's First Chief Constable

Glasgow produced some fine policemen in the nineteenth century, but few matched James Smart. He was a local man, born in Cathcart on 22 March 1805, married young and took his wife with him to London, where he worked in the tea trade. That job did not last long, however, and at the end of 1830 Smart became one of the first constables in the Metropolitan Police. He left London and returned to Glasgow in March 1831 to work as a clerk in a factory. When that job abruptly ended in October, he joined the Gorbals Police, left the following April, returned in May and was promoted to Sergeant in August.

Only when Smart rose to Sergeant Major did he realise he was destined to be a career policeman, and he settled down to a serious study of his profession. With his apprenticeship behind him, in June 1835 he became Superintendent of the Calton Burgh Police. At that time Calton had a terrible reputation for crime – theft, prostitution, drunkenness and footpads – and every circuit court had around twenty cases from Calton. Superintendent Smart decided he would clean up his territory. Accordingly, he toured the area, walking up every close and lane, inspecting every street and even every house. With the geography secure in his mind, he investigated the residents, and finally he scrutinised the police themselves.

Smart was not impressed with the quality of his force so he persuaded the Commissioners of Police to increase their wages and attract a higher standard of men. He also altered the perspective of policing, so rather than detect already-committed crimes, the Calton police were instructed to prevent crime by increased vigilance. Smart next ordered each constable to list the brothels; there were thirty-two in Calton. He determined to close them down, as brothels were also thieves' kitchens and the home of pickpockets and every sort of unwelcome rogue known. Accordingly, Superintendent Smart began a campaign of harassment against the keepers of the brothels, arresting them on every excuse, bringing them before the Police Court, where they were fined and imprisoned. But the madams and pimps were tenacious; they had a regular supply of clients whose money not only paid the fines but also created a healthy profit. Smart tried even more drastic measures; he ordered a constable to stand sentinel at the close mouths and stair entrances so the customers could not enter. This economic warfare was effective, and within a year the prostitutes were forced out of Calton to seek safer pastures.

With that part of the district cleared up, the thefts and robberies diminished and Smart concentrated on the cleansing to moderate the amount of disease and improve the lighting so garrotters and pickpockets could not hide in the shadows. He then concentrated on the vagrants and the foul lodging houses from where the lice of itinerant visitors crawled onto the respectable poor and spread typhus. Smart found sickening evidence of filth, with up to forty individuals – men and women, single and married – crowded together in one foul room. From being one of the worst areas of Glasgow, Calton became one of the healthiest, and Smart's reputation was so good that in 1846 when Calton, Gorbals and Anderston merged with Glasgow, Smart was promoted to Superintendent of the Eastern Division of the Glasgow Police. In that position he declared virtual war on the badly run spirit shops, whose customers caused mayhem when they erupted into the city on the Sabbath. He closed many unlicensed shebeens and illegal drinking clubs.

Two years later he was appointed Superintendent of Police of the extended municipality of Glasgow, and in this position he took an active part in suppressing Chartist riots that devastated the city centre. Smart was not responsible only for overseeing the constant battle against crime, he also helped save lives. His duties also included supervising public health. For instance, in January 1848 he created a report on the condition of public wells in the Eastern District of Glasgow. In October 1851 he visited what was known as the 'Carpet Factory Land' in Havannah Close, a building of three flats of thirteen houses, so a total of thirty-nine homes, in which were 167 women, seventy-six men and eighty-six children, but sometimes they held up to 400 people – thieves, prostitutes and beggars and a few desperately poor people engaged in sweated trades. The tenements were 'filthy in the extreme', but when Smart began his inspection, many of the inhabitants swarmed out in case they were arrested. In all thirty-nine rooms there were only six beds, no water, no sinks ('jaw-boxes' as they were known) and all the human excreta was thrown out of the windows. Smart also visited the equally obnoxious Criley's Land in the Old Vennel, where he had to jump to avoid being soaked when a woman in an upper tenement emptied her night soil out the window.

His fight against filth was constant. In January 1849 he advised the people of Springburn how best to fight cholera. The next month he was in charge of relief operations when there was a terrible fire at the Theatre Royal in Dunlop Street; sixty-five people died when a leaking gas pipe caught fire. He also appeared in person when there was a huge fire at John Currie's grain mills at Port Dundas in March 1849. When the burning grain poured down from flat to flat, the whole area became dangerous. There were eight fire engines, and the police had to prevent the crowd from pushing forward into danger. Smart had a similar role in January 1869 when the Prince of Wales Theatre in Stewart Street was ablaze, but this time mercifully without loss of life. He was responsible for organising his area, and in March 1848 he asked that street names and house numbers be put up in his Eastern District.

Despite his awesome responsibilities, he cared for his men. In 1849 he allowed them every third, rather than every fourth, Sunday off to go to church. He also kept a tight watch on the day-to-day business of policing the burgh. For instance, in June that year, he was closely involved when a major fight blew up on Glasgow Green. As Superintendent, Smart also acted as Procurator Fiscal; for example, in April 1850, when he oversaw the granting of licences for 'wee brokers', or small-scale pawnbrokers, of which Glasgow had around 400. He was unhappy at the high levels of interest the pawnbrokers charged and tightened up the system so that only people of decent character were licensed. In a select committee on police in August 1853, Smart claimed that Renfrewshire was one of the worst districts for crime in Scotland, while Paisley was out of date and Glasgow efficient.

Superintendent Smart was known to be hard on drunkenness and prostitution, so when in late summer 1854 some newspapers published a report that he believed teetotallers were unfit to be policemen, there was some disbelief. A number of leading temperance campaigners contacted him to ask if the report was correct, and Smart replied that the report 'is totally without foundation' as he had around 'one hundred men who are teetotallers, and I sincerely wish the other five hundred were teeto-tallers also; they would be better officers and better men'. In March 1857 Smart proved his remarks by reporting favourably on the Forbes Mackenzie Act that restricted the opening times for public houses. By 1857, this act had been in practice for four years, and the effects could be clearly seen.

Despite his high office, Superintendent Smart still worked at the sharp end of policing. In June 1858 he took a dozen officers to escort a doctor who wished to carry out a post-mortem on the body of a workman. The man, John Clyde, had died in the Clyde Iron Works but his family refused to allow the doctor near. Only when Smart and the police arrived did the operation proceed.

In April 1860, Colonel Kinloch inspected the Glasgow Police and found them one of the best disciplined and most efficient forces in the country, under Superintendent Smart's control. Smart also helped stop accidents in the Clyde by posting a constable in Glasgow Green in the winter months to warn people not to stray on the ice, and to stop suicides, mainly by women, in summer.

In 1862 there was another Glasgow Police Act passed, which allowed the title of Chief Constable, and Smart became the first Chief Constable of Glasgow. He had only a few years to enjoy the title, though, for he died on 27 May 1870. His bust remains on watch in the Strathclyde Police Museum, just keeping an eye on things to ensure standards do not slip.

8

That Frightful Locality

It is unlikely there is any city in the world without some less salubrious quarter, an area of high crime where respectable people hesitate to pass after night. The badlands, outlaw territory, no-go areas – there are many names for these neighbourhoods, but the reality is usually the same: squalid, depressing and dangerous.

Tontine Close

In nineteenth-century Glasgow the worst areas were in the centre of the town, the old, dilapidated streets around which the modern city had grown. Here there were ancient streets of tenements punctuated by long narrow closes ten to fifteen metres apart and up to 180 metres in length. Sometimes the tenements that made up the spine of these closes were four storeys, maybe fourteen metres high, with a depth of three metres. Behind the tenements could be a space of around half a metre, and often piled with human waste tossed out of the back windows in the best gardyloo fashion. Of Glasgow's closes, the Black Boy Close, Bush Close and the Tontine Close were amongst the worst, and of these the Tontine Close was arguably the most notorious. It opened up from the Trongate, directly opposite where the statue of King William stood in equestrian splendour and dogmatic challenge.

Tontine Close was a dark chasm between two rows of four-storey-high tenements, unlit for much of its existence and so narrow that sunlight never penetrated the hidden recesses. In this shadowed netherworld, untold hundreds – perhaps as many as 2,000 of the most underprivileged people in Glasgow – seethed in a succession of single-roomed, unventilated, unsanitary homes, planning robbery or worse, and casting predatory eyes on the more fortunate of their fellow citizens.

At one time Tontine Close had been prosperous, but as Glasgow flourished the old centre of the city slumped into decay. Those who could afford it moved away, and the hopeless, hapless and heartless remained. At the beginning of the century there had been a decent tavern here, a virtual palace run by Mrs Pollock, with nine rooms, a kitchen, fine cellars and a busy bar with a loyal clientele, but by 1820 Mrs Pollock was long gone and the quality of the custom had declined alarmingly.

The Tontine Close was already the domain of shoplifters, like the young boy who sidled along the Trongate on the night of 19 February that year, until he looked in a shop window and saw a silk handkerchief he admired. Rather than pay a price he could not afford, he thrust a crooked piece of wire through the hole for the bolt that was intended to secure the shutters, hooked out the handkerchief and scurried into the darkness of the close. His identity was never known; he was just one sneak thief among hundreds.

Fiona McDonald

There was nothing romantic about the thieves in Tontine Close; this was not a fantasyland where there was honour among thieves and the downtrodden poor turned into Glaswegian Robin Hoods. There will have been people driven into crime by poverty, and undoubtedly there were a number of poor but honest people trapped in the horrendous morass of the Tontine, but there were also people who would struggle to ever reach as high as the level of the sewer. One such was a woman who called herself Fiona McDonald, as well as other aliases. McDonald was a tall, rough-voiced woman who lived in the same stair as a blind widow named Mary Blaikie, and on Friday, 14 March 1844, McDonald came into her house offering to sell onions. Blaikie lived in a single room and she was sitting on the only chair, busy with needle and thread as she mended her daughter's gown. She said she did not want any onions, and when McDonald insisted, Blaikie rose from her seat, put her daughter's gown on the bed and ordered McDonald out of the house. McDonald argued but left. Blaikie had heard McDonald moving toward the bed, and when she felt for the gown, it was gone. She called for help and one of the neighbours caught McDonald with the gown. The onion seller spent sixty days in jail.

It is obvious that the inhabitants of Tontine Close could be both victim and culprit, and the day-to-day life there was probably pretty sordid. Drink was an escape from reality so drunkenness was common, with the occasional arrest when somebody was even more obstreperous than usual. Such a case occurred on 26 June 1851, when Mary McFarlane spent the entire night shouting and swearing the length of the close. Eventually the police decided to intervene and McFarlane had thirty days in a cell in which to sober up.

Homicide By Night

Perhaps it is not surprising that the Tontine Close also had a number of killings, some definite murder and others, where death was accidental, termed as culpable homicide. Such a case occurred in early September 1851, when the beat policeman was told that a man named James Jack had murdered his wife. It was midnight, dark enough in the Trongate, but much worse when the policeman entered the foul Tontine Close. His lantern guided him up the stairs to Jack's house, where Mrs Jack lay across her bed, bleeding. She lasted only a few moments before she died. Her husband immediately tried to leave, ostensibly to find her sister, but the policeman hauled him back inside and escorted him to the police office.

With James Jack safely locked away the police began their painstaking enquiries into the death. They soon learned that Jack was a tailor and that night he had come home drunk and had begun to argue with his wife. The neighbours heard loud banging, as if somebody was repeatedly falling down, but whether that was Jack staggering under the weight of drink or his wife being thrown around, nobody could say. One neighbour heard Jack say, 'I'll thraw your neck if you don't hold your tongue,' and then Jack appeared at the neighbour's door, muttering curses and calling his wife every foul name under the sun. Eventually Jack grumbled back home, only to return within a few moments to say his wife was dead. The police charged Jack with murder, but he was found guilty of culpable homicide, as he had beaten his wife up but had not intended to murder her. He was jailed for two years.

Smiling Assassins

Despite the odd killing, Tontine Close was more famous for a much more simple crime. The technique was probably as old as time: a good-looking woman would sweet-talk a lone man into coming with her, and once within the dark recesses of the Tontine, one or more men would arrive, grab the man and beat him up while the woman searched his pockets for whatever she could find.

On Friday, 17 October 1851, a young clerk named William Marshall was inveigled into the close by a girl who gave her name as Helen McGuire. Smiling, she brought him into her den, where they spent some time together, but as he left a group of men knocked him down and McGuire robbed him of a surprisingly respectable £54. Marshall told the police, who knew McGuire well so could guess who her accomplices were. They began to search for a prize fighter named Schofield, and after a hunt through the tangled web of closes and up and down the pestilential common stairs, they found £34 of Marshall's money and arrested Schofield and four other men. It was a minor affair in the life of the Tontine and one that was commonplace.

It will never be known how many such assaults took place, for most were unrecorded; respectable and particularly married men would not want to admit they had allowed an attractive woman to entice them into her house in the Tontine, and may have considered the loss of their money less of a matter than the loss of their dignity and reputation. However, a sufficient number of assaults were reported to the police to highlight the variations on a common theme.

In November 1852 three women – Mary Stewart, Elizabeth Millar and Christine Gordon – flashed encouraging smiles to a young farm servant, guided him into their house in the close and helped themselves to 19/-, all the money he had in the world. They spent the money on drink, and had sixty days to sober up after the Police Court sent them to jail. In November 1855 it was a cattle dealer who was hooked, and the female picked his pocket of £94 and escaped into the dark morass of the close. On other occasions, the thief would wonder if all his labours had been worthwhile.

Joseph Thomson was a long-time bad man. He knew the inside of Glasgow jail but once he had served his time he set himself up with a nice business in the Tontine Close. As a brothel keeper he would be assured of a steady trade, and when that was combined with a little pocket picking on the side, Thomson was quite comfortable, thank you. However, on Thursday, 13 July 1853, he picked a poulterer's pocket when the man was otherwise engaged, and profited by a mere twopence halfpenny. Not only that, but one of the pennies had been bored through and the other was an obvious forgery. However, he kept them both, and when the police searched him later on a completely different charge, they found both coins. As the poulterer had reported his loss, Thomson ended up back in the jail.

The Tale of Lachlan McNeil

Forged coins were not uncommon in the Victorian period and had a nasty habit of biting the hand that stole them. Just after eleven on the night of 12 August 1853, young Lachlan McNeil was walking down the

High Street with his friend John Buchanan, quite happy with life. Both boys were fourteen years old, both were ashore from working on the steam ship *Duke of Argyll*, but only Lachlan carried two bundles of clothes, so that is probably why he was attacked. The boys were passing the close at number 37 when a woman lunged out and grabbed hold of him. Before he had time to protest, a second female joined in. They pulled the struggling boy deep into the recesses of the close and into a house one storey up. Buchanan tried to help, but the women were too experienced in dealing with men to have any trouble with two boys. Within seconds they had robbed Lachlan of his two bundles and picked his pockets into the bargain.

When he realised he could do nothing against these women, Buchanan offered to buy back the two bundles for a shilling, but the women simply snatched that as well. Not surprisingly, the boys ran for a policeman, who forced his way into the house. It was empty of clothes and women. Downcast, they left the house and walked slap into one of the two women. The policeman arrested her immediately. She was Mary Campbell of the Tontine Close. When the police searched her, they found a bent sixpence that Lachlan recognised as being his, and which confirmed she was the thief. The police also found Lachlan's clothes in an outhouse in 37 High Street, but while Campbell got sixty days in jail to ponder the inadvisability of stealing recognisable coins, it is unlikely that Lachlan walked along dark night-time streets with quite the same confidence for some time to come.

Mary Mulloy: Brothel Keeper

The women of Tontine Close were a wild lot. In the early 1850s one of the worst was Mary Mulloy, who kept a brothel and often worked in company with an equally unpleasant woman named Helen McLaughlan. At the beginning of September 1853, Mulloy and McLaughlan attacked William Campbell in Wallace's Court. He staggered under her assault, but recovered and foolishly chased them into the Tontine Close and straight into an ambush. A man named James Gray erupted from Mulloy's house and punched Campbell as both women began throwing bottles at him. Knocked unconscious, Campbell slumped to the ground; two female witnesses tried to intervene on his behalf, but Mulloy and McLaughlan attacked both, and it was not until the arrival of the police that the assault on Campbell ended. Mulloy paid her own £5 fine but did nothing for McLaughlan, who spent the next sixty days in jail.

Mulloy's career continued for another year, when it jarred to an uncompromising close. On the night of 13 April 1854, William Neilson of Townmill Road had enjoyed a night out in the Gallowgate, so was quite happy when an attractive woman smiled to him, called to him by name and suggested they could go together to a drinking establishment. Neilson may have had second thoughts when they turned into Tontine Close, but his companion seemed quite confident and he followed her into a cheerful house, where another woman welcomed them. She said her name was Mary Dawson, and no sooner had she arrived than Dawson told Neilson's friend to leave and a third woman took her place; this was Helen McLaughlan.

Immediately when the women had Neilson alone, McLaughlan grabbed at his gold watch chain. Neilson struggled back, but Dawson held his arms and McLaughlan broke the chain and yanked the watch from his fob pocket, leaving the remnants of the guard chain that secured the watch to his pocket dangling from his neck. They held him against the wall and grabbed his pocketbook, but then Neilson broke free and ran from the house, roaring for the police. He had been in the house less than ten minutes and had been most thoroughly robbed.

Constable Owan Donohue heard the shout and ran up to the house. He found the watch seal lying on the dresser and Mulloy, alias Dawson, lying on a neighbour's bed. Donohue called for a couple of detectives, arrested Mulloy and had the neighbourhood searched. Neilson's gold watch was picked up behind the neighbour's house, and McLaughlan was arrested in a nearby stair. Both women appeared before the autumn court and were transported for fifteen years.

The removal of Mulloy and McLaughlan only clipped the tip of a very sordid iceberg. Month after month women from Tontine Close lured men to their dens to be robbed, assaulted or both. Some cases were recorded, such as the robbery of a man from Canada in November 1856, which saw a gaggle of women in court. The Canadian had been unwise enough to enter the lair of Mrs Adams, a harridan second only to Mulloy in notoriety, and he lost £120 in consequence. Despite the best efforts of the police, the money was never recovered.

That same week an Edinburgh horse dealer fell for the same trick and lost £73 of his employer's money. In November 1855 the police tried a sweep of the close and picked up a number of women who ran what were euphemistically known as 'disreputable houses' but only two were actually arrested; both paid the two-guinea fine rather than go to jail.

'If I Had Been a Cruel Girl I Would Never Have Let Him Out of the House'

Sometimes the victim attempted to get revenge, such as Alexander Niven of Islay, who was robbed in one of the many Tontine brothels. He wrecked the house and smashed all the crockery, but still did not get his money back. On other occasions, the police had success, as in October 1857 when Rachel Broadly got nine months for stealing a silver medal from William Wheeler, a soldier in the 21st Regiment of Foot.

However, while most of the assaults resulted in the loss of small amounts of money and perhaps a few bruises, there were some that had a more tragic ending. On Saturday, 5 December 1857, a sawyer named James Johnstone fell for the usual ploy as a woman named Mary McLachlan lured him into Isabella Campbell's den of iniquity at the head of the Tontine Close. Johnstone gave Campbell a few shillings to buy drink. When Campbell left, Johnstone and McLachlan argued about money. The argument escalated into violence and McLachlan called for her friend Margaret McKay to help. Both women threw themselves at Campbell with fire and venom; he thumped McLachlan with a chair but in turn was kicked, punched and thrown down the steep stone stairs. As he lay there, both women followed him down, turned him on to his back and picked his pockets. When they realised there were only a few pennies, McLachlan voiced her disappointment and McKay kicked the unconscious man viciously in the stomach and ribs. A third woman, Margaret Cook, joined in the fun by jumping full force on top of Johnstone. McLachlan laughed and said, 'If I had been a cruel girl I would never have let him out of the house until I had his throat cut.'

Naturally, the noise brought out the neighbours, but McLachlan and her cohorts chased them away with threats and vile imprecations until at last somebody called the police. With everybody in the stair afraid of McLachlan, nobody told the police what had happened; they believed Johnston had merely fallen down drunk, so it was some time before they learned the truth. By the time they sent for the doctor it was too late; Johnston died shortly afterward. McLachlan and McKay were sent on twenty-one years' penal servitude, while Cook was dismissed for lack of evidence.

Death of a Teacher

The males of Tontine Close could be equally as deadly as the females, and were every bit as prone to violence. In the early hours of Sunday, 31 July 1859, two policemen were called to an unconscious man lying at the Trongate opening to Tontine Close. Supposing that he was yet another drunk, they bundled him onto a barrow and trundled him to the Central Police Office. The police surgeon, Dr McGill, tried to revive him with the stomach pump and by bleeding him, but with no success. The man died that same morning.

Used to the constant trouble in and around Tontine Close, the police made enquiries and found out all was not as it seemed. The dead man was John McPherson, a commercial teacher in his forties, and rather than simply fall down drunk, he had been pushed or tripped down the stairs by two men, Michael Cassidy and Robert Henderson. The full story gradually came out: McPherson and a man named Peter Bennett had gone to Bothwell for the day and returned to Glasgow on the late train. When they left the station they sank a few whisky toddies in Gascoyne's Tavern in King Street, and at about midnight they split up and looked for a cab to take them home. McPherson was not entirely sober, but neither was he roaring drunk as he swayed happily along Trongate.

Cassidy and 'Cockie' Henderson had followed him. As he neared the Tontine Close somebody shouted, 'Bustle him!' Cassidy tripped McPherson from behind, and punched him as he staggered. McPherson fell backward, landing hard and awkward. As he lay stunned on the ground, Henderson jumped on top of him with both feet, then hesitated for a second until a girl gave him a push and called out, 'Run now, Cockie,' and both men fled.

Cassidy ran into Tontine Close, where Constable Matthew Paterson later arrested him, and Henderson sped past Glasgow Cross and toward Nelson Street. Henderson was no stranger to trouble; earlier that night he had pulled a knife on a man named Knox and threatened to rip his guts out, but without coming to actual blows.

McPherson had not been alone for more than ten minutes when Bennett saw a crowd around his prone body. He heard a female call out, 'Murder! A man has been killed!' and saw three men drag McPherson into a sitting position against the wall. The police called for the surgeon, but he could not help. McPherson died of a fractured skull.

At the subsequent trial, the jury considered there was not enough evidence to convict Henderson, but Cassidy was found guilty of culpable homicide and given four years' penal servitude.

Attacking a Seaman

Killings in the close were comparatively rare, but casual violence was commonplace. In March 1855 David Brownlee was fresh off his ship and enjoying being back in Glasgow. He was strolling happily along the Tontine Close, enjoying a pipe of tobacco, when a broad-shouldered man walked toward him, reached out and plucked the pipe from his mouth. When Brownlee protested and demanded his pipe back, the man, a well-known thug, punched him in the face, knocked him to the ground and stuck in the boot. The attacker was James McPherson and when the Police Court added hard labour to his sixty-day sentence, he complained that it was unfair that he was given hard labour every time he was sent to jail.

Just as common was for men and women to act together, as happened just as dawn slipped its revealing light along the Trongate on Sunday, 18 June 1854. Two men, a mason named James Kirkwood and a shoemaker named Robert Currie, were walking down a stair in the Tontine Close. They were separated in the dark, and a woman named Elizabeth Martin called over to Kirkwood. As he stopped to talk to her, John McLauchlan, a muscular man, rushed up and punched him to the ground, and then both he and Martin jumped on his body and kicked him about the head. Fortunately, Currie was still close by and he shouted out, which attracted the attention of other passers-by. Having kicked Kirkwood unconscious, Martin and McLauchlan fled, but the police recognised their descriptions and arrested both later that morning.

Jane Faucet and Her Ilk

More petty assaults were ten a penny. Most would never be recorded, and only if the police were called and the case came to court would the world be aware of the violence that simmered beneath the surface in the close. To list them all would be both pointless and tedious, but there are many examples to choose from. For instance, on 2 July 1858, two women named Jane Faucet and Janet McFarlane were fined for assault in the close. On 31 August 1859, a man named Peter Newton was given sixty days' hard labour for attacking his mother when she did not feed him to his satisfaction, and in January 1856 a shoemaker called James McGrory was given sixty days for biting his wife on the shoulder, knocking her down and kicking her. On 31 January 1860, a man named George Boyce was sent to prison for forty days for assaulting his wife. John McDonald was another wife beater; in June 1860 he thumped his wife across the head with a poker and paid a two-guinea fine for her pains.

Jane Faucet was in trouble again in May 1860 when she was fined £5 for assaulting a man named Dennis Murray. She was indirectly involved in another case in April that year when a man and two women were found guilty of stealing over £300 in notes and cheques from a man who was in her house. The thieves got a substantial four years' penal servitude each. That type of theft normally took place within low lodging houses or brothels, so perhaps Faucet ran one of these. The list of men supposedly decoyed into brothels to be attacked and of drunken men assaulted in the close is long and sordid.

There was a typical and fairly simple case of assault in August 1859 when four women – Ann Lyons, Mary Ann Lee, Jane Kennedy and Catherine Sinclair – attacked a Govan weaver named John Blakeney and stole £1 10/- from him, but that same week the Glasgow Police Commission appointed a three-man committee to look into affairs in the 'disorderly state' of the close, with Superintendent Smart of the police giving the benefit of his vast experience.

There was more to the Tontine than just assaults and robbery. There were also terrible accidents, such as when Mary Roder got herself so drunk she did not notice when her wide skirt drifted into the fire and ignited in June 1859. A neighbour heard her screaming, rushed in and doused the flames but the badly burned woman had to be taken to hospital. There was also the odd suicide when things got too much for the desperate people who had to live surrounded by filth and squalor and saw no way out.

Drink was a two-edged sword; on one hand it provided a relief from a life devoid of hope, but on the other it seeped away at health and ate the few pennies that was all most of the inhabitants of the close could earn. As well as a substantial tavern, Tontine Close had a number of shebeens, illicit drinking dens where men and women could get blind drunk on whisky that was not always of the best quality. In July 1855 Catherine Young was fined £7 for running one of these dens in the close. The following April, Rachel Broadly, already mentioned as a medal thief, was found with five people drinking spirits in her house and was hit with the same fine. Others were to follow.

As well as violence and drink, simple theft was common in the Tontine. There was the theft of lead from the Tontine Hotel in December 1855, when the thieves climbed onto the roof of the tenements of the close and stepped over to the hotel roof. They got eighty feet of sheet lead, which would fetch a pretty price at a scrap metal merchant.

Sometimes the thefts were more personal, as when Agnes McDougall stole a bedcover and two blankets, and ended up with four years' penal servitude as a reward. The police knew the identities of most of Glasgow's habitual thieves, so when Mrs Bullock's spirit shop in Wilson Street was robbed on the first of July 1860, Detective Officer McBryan knew who the most likely suspects were. He was on duty at Glasgow Cross in the early hours of next morning and saw two thieves, Donald and Archibald Sinclair, slinking through the shadows and he followed them into the Hell's Kitchen of the Tontine Close. Rather than chance walking alone into an ambush, McBryan whistled up some uniformed assistance and crashed into the Sinclairs' house.

It was fortunate that he had reinforcements for there were six men in the house, none of whom appreciated being raided in the small hours of the morning. The police made a thorough search and found a great quantity of money and a fine selection of housebreaker's tools. The house was the headquarters of a gang of thieves who used a pair of young apprentices, boys who were small enough to slide in between the bars of a window and then open the front door to let in the professionals. The police collected the lot.

There were many other thefts and incidents, month in, month out. In July 1860 Mary Henderson lured a man into a house to be attacked; in February 1862 Sarah Jackson leaned out of her window and threw burning coals onto the heads of passers-by; in August 1864 a Motherwell man named James Kennedy followed the well trodden route of allowing the rustle of petticoats and the flash of a female eye to lure him into a house in Tontine Close, where a pair of she-devils leaped on him in hopes of his pocketbook. Not inclined to allow that, Kennedy ran to the window and jumped the fifteen feet to the ground. He sustained severe spinal injuries. However, Margaret Holmes, the lady of the establishment, gave a slightly different story. She claimed Kennedy had entered the house, gone mad and immediately tried to jump out of the window. The women, of course, had been trying to hold him back.

These are just examples from a long, long list of thieves and returned robbers, suspicious deaths and mass brawls, prostitutes and pickpockets and the desperate unfortunates.

It was not surprising that the general perception of Tontine Close was not good. In September 1860 the *Glasgow Herald* called it 'that frightful locality', and when the authorities decided to clean up the city and improve communications, Tontine Close was high on the list to be cleared away. In 1862 the new Glasgow Police Act allowed the corporation to put lamps in private closes and stairs but send the bill to the property owners. The idea was sound; thieves and robbers work best in the dark and there was nowhere darker than the Tontine Close. Even before the Glasgow Improvement Act of 1866, which was intended to open up Glasgow traffic and remove the worst of the city centre slums, the corporation had begun to buy up some of the worst areas of the city; however, there were ugly rumours of corruption when people found out that some men, such as

Bailie Watson, had bought property in the area and then pushed for the Improvement Act. For a while it was believed that councillors and bailies, such as Watson, had bought cheap with the intention of selling the property to the city to make a profit, but it appeared that the accusations were false. Those gentlemen who had bought into the Tontine Close were more interested in improving the area than increasing their bank balance.

The facts were simple. In 1861 a consortium of benevolent and prominent citizens of Glasgow had started a fund to buy some of the worst slum property to try and improve the look and function of the city. The group included James Watson and Sir James Lumsden, both of whom became Lord Provost, and Archibald Orr Ewing, an MP. Each man contributed £1,300 and after the Improvement Act was passed in 1866 the group sold ten of the properties to the Improvement Trust, making a 25 per cent profit, which averaged at about £750 per man, so hardly a huge return after five years. The Council appeared pleased with the deal they got, but the *Daily Mail* stirred the murmurings of corruption until 1872 when the Lord Provost took the paper to court over its accusations. The Lord Provost won his case, with damages of £575.

There is a postscript to the story of the Tontine Close: in June 1865 when the houses in Buchanan Court, just beside the Tontine Close, were being demolished, the workmen found a pile of human bones, including skulls. At the time it was presumed that the bones had been dumped there by medical students, but given the history of the area, there may have been a more sinister reason.

9
Official Retribution

Once the police caught the criminals, there were a number of levels of justice available. The first step was the Police Court, where justice was swift but limited to small fines and up to sixty days in jail for simple assaults, drunkenness and petty theft. For the next level of crime, or after a number of offences, the culprit was sent to the Sheriff Court. Until 1856 the Sheriff Court could order the convict to be transported to Australia, but after that it could only impose jail sentences of up to eighteen months. After somebody had appeared twice at the Sheriff Court, or for major offences, he or she would be sent to the Circuit Court, then finally the High Court, both of which could impose a death sentence.

The Circuit Courts had a history that extended back to the Middle Ages. With travel difficult, it was easier for a judge to journey to local courts than for a host of criminals to congregate in Edinburgh, so the judges left the capital for a tour, or 'circuit'. They travelled in style to principal burghs, including Glasgow, and stayed at the best inns. The Circuit Courts always opened with impressive ceremony. For instance, in September 1848 judges the Honourable Lord Moncrieff and Lord Cockburn stayed overnight at Carrick's Royal Hotel and travelled to the Court Hall with the band of the 27th Regiment of Foot marching before them and a cavalry escort of the 2nd Dragoons backed by the police in their best uniforms.

Except for those that included a sexual element, trials were open to the public and there was often a large audience appreciating this free entertainment. However, in his *Circuit Journeys*, the judge Lord Cockburn said that 'of all the judicial spectators in Scotland, those of Glasgow are the worst. They are the least attentive and by far the most vulgar.'

Execution of an Innocent Man

One of the most telling arguments against capital punishment is that there can be no reprieve once the sentence has been carried out. Once a man is hanged, he is hanged, and that is the end of it. In Glasgow in 1864 there was a case where a man proclaimed his innocence right to the final moment and there is still doubt about the validity of his execution.

Reilly's alleged crime was about as typical a case of murder as it was possible to find. On 8 December 1863, a man named Laffy was due before the Police Court on a minor charge, so his wife gathered together as much money as she could and left her home in Newarthill to come in and pay the expected fine. However, the judge was less than kind and Laffy was jailed instead, so Mrs Laffy was left with nineteen shillings in her pocket and no husband to keep her company.

It was the most natural thing in the world for her to enter a public house and fortify herself for the walk home. It was equally natural for her to talk to a man she met there, and after an hour or so she said her good-byes and began the walk home. Next morning her dead body was found at the roadside, bereft of money. The police believed that a thirty-one-year-old labourer named John Reilly had murdered her, mainly on circumstantial evidence. They believed he confirmed his guilt when he vanished the same day the murder occurred, and they put a full-scale manhunt in place. They followed his trail southward, right across the Borders to Redesdale in Northumberland, where he was arrested, imprisoned and brought to trial for murder.

There was nothing spectacular about Reilly; he was an Irishman from County Monaghan, had spent six years in the 60th Foot, mostly in India, but had been discharged through ill health in 1856. Since then he had married but had no children.

Despite the gravity of his situation, Reilly remained composed throughout his trial and even when sentence of death was pronounced, he did not break down or become agitated. He claimed innocence throughout the trial and when he was held in jail, he was respectful to the jailers despite his imminent death. His lawyers sent off an appeal for mercy, and when that was turned now Reilly knew there was no possibility of life.

On Friday, 13 May 1864, William Calcraft, the bearded, aging London executioner who officiated at such occasions, arrived in Glasgow. He stayed in the South Prison, an impressive neo-classical building at the foot of the Saltmarket opposite Glasgow Green. Much to Calcraft's disgust, an Edinburgh man with experience of executions in India was appointed as his assistant. Calcraft considered that appointment a slight on his professional abilities.

As the day of the execution neared, Catholic chapels across the city prayed for their co-religionist, who they called 'Reilly the Martyr', although what he was a martyr to they never made clear. Reilly was brought from Duke Street Prison to a cell on the ground floor of the South Prison on Sunday, the day before his execution. From there he would probably be able to hear the sounds of the scaffold being erected outside, and know that he would shortly be standing there. There was a tried and tested method for executions, with a wide space cleared from the bottom of the Saltmarket to Hutcheson Bridge, a barricade to keep the crowds back and a three-and-a-half-foot-high screen erected so the crowd could not witness the final agony of the condemned. A large proportion of the Glasgow Police were also to be in attendance.

In the early morning of Monday, 16 May, the crowd began to gather in front of Jail Square and in the Green as far as the incongruous gaiety of Barlow's Circus. By seven o'clock there were around 25,000 people there, waiting for Reilly to be hanged. Most of the crowd came from the working classes, with as many women and girls as men. They were excited but not too boisterous, although here and there the police cracked their batons across an unruly head.

When Reilly appeared shortly after half past seven, the crowd gave an excited buzz then lapsed into relative silence. Not surprisingly, he was pale, but he made no statement and climbed the stairs of the scaffold with dignity and said a short prayer and shook hands with the minister and bishop. Calcraft put the noose over his head and at eight minutes past eight he was hanged, with his guilt as much in doubt as it had ever been. It took three hard minutes for him to die.

The Execution Spots

John Reilly was only one of a host of people to be hanged in Glasgow during the course of the century. Most were probably guilty, although there will probably always be debate whether death is the most suitable punishment or not. One thing is for certain: a good hanging provided free public entertainment.

At the beginning of the century all executions were carried out at the Cross, usually on a Wednesday between two and three in the afternoon. The day and time were not arbitrary; Wednesday was market day so there would be a gathering from the surrounding countryside as well as townspeople, with the crowds peaking in early afternoon, people walking in from as far as Paisley to watch the fun, men and women carrying stools to stand on so they had a better vantage point and the conversation centred around who was getting hanged and why and how long they would dangle before they eventually choked to death.

The last execution at the Cross was on 19 November 1813, when William Muir and William Mudie were hanged for highway robbery. Both were relatively young men, with Muir from Dalry in Ayrshire being around thirty-four and Mudie five years younger. Both were colliers and both had been soldiers, but both had deserted the Royal Scots and eventually fell foul of the law. The Irishman Mudie had been married since he was thirteen and had three children, with one more on the way. Muir had a wife and five children. Their state of mind is impossible to gauge as they contemplated leaving their widows to struggle and bring up a family in a very unforgiving world.

The procedure for hangings followed a set pattern of judicial formal killing laced with Christian compassion for the soul of the condemned. Mudie and Muir were held in their cells until two o'clock, when the guards led them out into the hall of the prison. They had an hour before execution, and the Reverend Balfour helped them prepare for their next life beyond death. At three o'clock both men were escorted to the scaffold and their last few moments on earth. As the crowd watched, the condemned men sang a soft hymn and listened to a prayer intoned by a Reverend Campbell. By that time they were feeling the strain; Mudie nearly collapsed and had to be helped to the platform. Once there the executioner placed the nooses around their necks and was about to place the hoods over their faces but Mudie fainted. Calder, the Town Officer, ran up the steps from the street below and supported him before he fell off the platform and injured himself. The hoods, called caps, were put over their heads and as the *Caledonian Mercury* put it: 'at quarter past three they paid the penalty of their crimes'. These two were fortunate as they died quickly with no protracted struggles, and after hanging for forty minutes they were brought back down.

The death of any human lessens the whole of humanity, but an unnecessary and untimely death is always more tragic. Yet by the standards of the time both these men deserved to hang. Muir had a bad past. He had been jailed in Glasgow in 1808 for highway robbery but had escaped to commit more crimes; together with Mudie he had robbed John Fraser, an Edinburgh builder, on the high road to Bathgate. They had also broken a washing line full of clothes belonging to Sir James Stewart of Coldness. Today these would not be considered too terrible crimes, but in 1813 the combination meant a capital offence.

Not people known for waste, the city fathers had sold the gallows immediately after their executions. According to legend, an eating house bought the platform and used it as a table.

Executed at Jail Square

All subsequent public executions took place outside the New or South Jail that had been erected in 1812 at the Saltmarket, overlooking the Green. The Glasgow 'town wright' built a new gallows, modelling his design on that used in London, and came up with a simple, ugly but effective structure. It was basically a black painted box on small wheels, with two nine-foot-tall vertical beams surmounted by a crosspiece at the top, like a large goalmouth in a football pitch. The hanging rope was suspended from the middle of crossbar. Underneath the rope was a small raised section, with two hinged leaves forming a trap door. The condemned man stood on this section and at the appropriate time the trap door opened and he fell to be hanged, either by a quick jerk that broke his neck or by slower and more painful strangulation. This gallows was positioned in front of the jail, in Jail Square, now termed 'Jocelyn Square', and lasted until the era of public executions ended in 1868. There was a special building just for the gallows, behind the jail and perhaps aptly beside the slaughterhouse.

The first guests of the new improved gallows were William Higgins and Thomas Harold in October 1814. They were both Irishmen convicted of highway robbery. Between October 1814 and the end of July 1865, seventy people were executed here, including James Wilson in 1820. He was the last man in Scotland to be publicly beheaded for High Treason after the 1820 Republican Rising.

Beheaded for His Patriotism

James Wilson was a popular man, with much public sympathy. He was a sixty-three-year-old weaver, who had been heavily involved in the 1820

Scottish Republican Rising, the Radical War, in which the weavers had hoped to gain a fairer society, marching under the motto 'Scotland Free or a Desert'. Wilson was so popular the authorities tried to blacken his name by spreading false propaganda. They said Wilson had blasphemed Christianity and burned a Bible, both heinous crimes in those religious times, and smacking of the Jacobinism of the atheistic French Revolution. An establishment minister, Dr Greville Ewing, also told Wilson he was not a political martyr for liberty but a criminal condemned in the sight of God. Even worse, the authorities sent their pet minister, the Reverend James Lapsie, to Wilson as he languished in his condemned cell. Lapsie was a turncoat; he had been a Radical himself but had accepted his thirty pieces of silver to inform on his fellow strugglers.

Wilson was executed on Wednesday, 30 August 1820, weather-wise a bright day, but morally dark as a brave man was martyred for a cause that tens of thousands believed to be just. The crowds gathered from an early hour, but rather than jocular and cheery they were quiet, resentful. They did not approve of this execution. There were around 20,000 people gathered by mid-morning, and Major General Reynell, in charge of the military guard, was worried there might be a rescue attempt at the least. He ordered the 1st Battalion of the Rifle Brigade to patrol the streets of Glasgow and the 33rd Regiment of Foot to guard the gallows and support the 3rd Dragoon Guards.

Wilson was dressed in a white suit for his execution. He was quiet but determined as he joined in Psalm 51 and drank his last glass of wine. Dr Ewing, speaking with the voice of authority, told the crowd that Wilson's death was a lesson to the evil-designing people in Scotland; he meant those who sought suffrage and a more equal society. The executioner waited. He wore a grey coat, with a fur hat on his head, and his face was masked by black crepe. On this occasion he was Thomas Moore, a volunteer, a twenty-year-old medical student from Glasgow's Bridgegate.

Wilson and Moore had left the jail by the south gate. Wilson was tied, arms behind his back, and sat in the rear of a black hurdle. Moore sat opposite, with the blade of his axe pointing at the condemned man. A detachment of the 3rd Dragoon Guards acted as escort, their equipment jingling and their sabres unsheathed, balanced on their shoulders and gleaming dully in the sunshine. At the rear was all the pomp and majesty of Glasgow authority with the Lord Provost presiding over all.

The crowd hissed. They booed. They shouted 'Murder', but with the Dragoons and hundreds of riflemen in the vicinity, they could do little more than utter vocal protest. The hangman placed the noose around Wilson's neck; Wilson dropped his handkerchief to signify he was ready to die. As Wilson fell, there was an outpouring of disgust from the crowd and one of the cavalry officers ordered his men to charge the crowd. The memory of the battle of Bonnybridge and the massacre of Peterloo was still vivid and the shout came out, 'The cavalry are coming,' but this time there were no deaths except for Wilson's. The executioner let the corpse hang for half an hour and at half past three Wilson was taken down and placed across an open coffin with the head on a wooden block. As was the tradition, Moore removed the death cap and calmly chopped off Wilson's head, to the screams of disgust from the crowd. He lifted Wilson's head and shouted, 'This is the head of a traitor!' The crowd disagreed, shouting that Wilson was a martyr who bled for his country.

There were many more hangings to come.

'I Bid You a Long Farewell'

On the morning of Wednesday, 1 November 1826, Edward Kelly and Andrew Stewart were hanged for street robbery. They had not acted together, the crimes were on separate occasions and they only had two things in common: both were robbers and both were executed in front of the same gawping crowd.

Andrew Stewart was a handsome, single twenty-five-year-old man from Belfast, but his good looks hid a bad past. A weaver and one-time publican, his life was punctuated by drunkenness and wild women. He had been one of a group of blackguards who had followed a man in the

Gallowgate in the dark hours of early morning, thumped him on the head and stolen his watch and chain and a couple of pounds. They had run to Glasgow Green to divide the spoils.

On the other hand, Kelly had acted alone when he stole £108 from an elderly man in Bridgegate Street, but that had not been his first offence. Although he was only twenty-one years old, strongly built, and well able to hold down a good job, he had lived beyond the law all his life. He had been in and out of jail since early childhood, so it was unlikely he would ever have reformed.

The magistrates and prisoners gathered in the hall of the jail shortly after eight in the morning, where they drank a fortifying glass of wine before the main event. There is no way of knowing how the condemned men felt as they left the building for the short climb up to the scaffold and a look over the masses that had come to see them die. Stewart would see his mother in the front of the crowd. She stood there, a respectable, soberly dressed woman who now lived in Calton. Her eyes would be terribly sad as she watched her son.

Stewart faced them and gave the customary speech, possibly the only thing he had ever said in his life that would be remembered. It was a short speech, but to the point: 'I have a few words to say to you all, friends. Beware of drunkenness, obey your parents and do not profane the Sabbath day, for these are the crimes that brought me here. I bid you a long farewell.'

Kelly, a Glasgow born man, did not speak. The two condemned prayed together and shook hands, then Stewart gave the signal and the executioner pulled the lever. Until then Stewart's mother had been silently praying but when the trap opened and the rope tightened around his neck she gave a loud shriek that was heard over the sudden hush of the crowd. Although Mrs Stewart had the agony of witnessing her son's execution, at least she did not see him suffer. He died quickly, unlike Kelly, who kicked and struggled for long, terrible moments as he slowly strangled to death.

Yet not all the hanged were men; women also made their final farewell from the fatal Glasgow gallows.

'Do It With As Little Pain As You Can, Sir'

A number of women were executed in Glasgow during the nineteenth century, but few deaths were as cold-blooded as that of twenty-five-year-old Margaret Hamilton. She was hanged on Thursday, 31 January 1850, for murder and forgery. Her story was brief and sordid. Her sister-in-law, Jean Hamilton, had £20 in the Strathhaven Bank, but Margaret Hamilton found the deposit receipt, forged her sister-in-law's name and took the lot. To cover her crime, Hamilton poisoned Jean Hamilton with arsenic; Jean became ill on 21 June 1849 and died on 6 July. Margaret Hamilton was arrested and tried, with Lord Cockburn sentencing her to death, despite the jury's plea for mercy. Cockburn mentions the case very briefly in his *Circuit Journeys*: 'One, a female prisoner, was doomed to die . . . [she] had first stolen a bank deposit receipt, and then finding that she could not get the money without the owner's signature, she forged it and then . . . murdered the victim in order to hide them.' There was also an appeal, but the Home Secretary refused to alter the sentence.

Hamilton did not give up her life lightly. She constantly refused to admit her guilt and went to the length of writing a letter asking others to confess. Two ministers and her husband, Andrew Hamilton, visited her in jail, with Andrew nearly hysterical with grief when she gave him a lock of her hair as a keepsake. Superintendent Smart led 500 police to guard the scaffold when she was brought out to a crowd that grew to around 20,000. Many of the crowd were middle-aged or older women, with lesser numbers of the respectable on the fringes, but they were all curious, for it had been seven years since the last execution in Glasgow, so people had forgotten the vivacious thrill of watching others suffer while they were safe.

The day before the execution Hamilton's composure cracked as she realised there was no reprieve and her time was running out. She requested a psalm from the minister, wrote a letter to her husband and that night she fainted. When she was revived, she repeated her claim of innocence. At four in the morning the prison matron helped her get dressed in the clothes she would wear to her death. There was the usual religious service before the hanging and the usual glass of wine, but while most condemned put on a brave front, Margaret Hamilton was perhaps more honest. When the hangman tied her arms, she pleaded with him, 'Don't make it tight to hurt me.' By that time there was only one executioner for the whole of Scotland, an eighty-two-year-old man named Murdoch, who walked with a stick.

Two prison guards had to support Hamilton as she staggered, whimpering, through the underground passage between the prison and the courthouse, where she had to slump into a chair with her long black hair trailing from under her white night cap and onto her black dress. Two men helped her to the scaffold and up the ladders. She was white-faced and trembling as the hangman arranged the rope around her neck and pulled down the cap that covered her face. She put her head close to him. 'Do it with as little pain as you can, sir,' she asked.

She refused the handkerchief that she had to drop to signal she was ready to be executed. Then she fainted again and swung sideways with the rope the only thing preventing her from falling to the platform. The crowd gasped, the chaplain stopped in mid-prayer and the hangman pulled the bolt so Hamilton was hanged in her unconscious state. She died very quickly and was buried inside the prison. By ten o'clock the scaffold was removed and the crowd dissipated; Hamilton had been executed and the city returned to normal.

The Hangman's Rest

Many cities have their stories of hangmen and the hanged, and in Glasgow the hangman was said to go to a pub for a quick dram after he had performed his duty. Tradition claims he used to slink away to Wilson Street in the old Merchant City, where the establishment was later named The Hangman's Rest and, long after the hanging days had ended, a noose dangled from the ceiling with typical black Glaswegian humour. Although there were many – perhaps far too many – people hanged in Glasgow, most criminals faced other sentences, including transportation to Australia.

Lesser Sentences

Transportation could be a cruel punishment that separated an offender from his or her family forever, or it could give an unlucky man or woman the chance of redemption and the opportunity to carve out a new life in a different environment. However, transportation did not always work. For instance, there was a man named McColgan, whom Lord Cockburn sentenced to be transported for ten years, but who returned within a year to Glasgow to garrotte somebody, was sentenced to fifteen years, but was released and committed a third robbery before finally being sent to Australia.

In the early years of the century, punishment could be more brutal. On Wednesday, 8 May 1822, Richard Campbell had the dubious honour of being the last man to be whipped through the streets of Glasgow. He had been prominently involved in the attack on a paint factory in Clyde Street, was arrested, charged and sentenced to be flogged. To ensure there was no crowd trouble, Mr Hardie, Superintendent of Police, had called up a powerful body of police and sheriff officers, backed by the jingling harness, tall horses and long sabres of the 4th Dragoon Guards.

At noon the police escorted Campbell out of the north door of the jail and tied his wrists to the back of a waiting cart. With a party of Dragoons riding in front and behind, the cart rumbled to the south side of the jail. The public hangman, an old man named Thomas Young, stripped off his shirt, hefted a cat of nine tails and gave him twenty powerful lashes. A large crowd watched but did not try to interfere; they seemed to approve the punishment. Then the cart moved on to the bottom of the Stockwell for another twenty; the head of the Stockwell for the next batch and the final twenty at the Cross. After eighty, Campbell was in a bad way. He had yelled at the bite of the cat and now warned the crowd not to become involved in any riot.

With the whipping complete, Campbell was returned to jail and his wounds were treated. When he was recovered, he was transported to Australia to ponder his sins.

On the Way to Australia

Once they were sentenced to transportation, a long journey awaited the convicts even before their time abroad could begin. From confinement in Glasgow jail they were carried to Edinburgh, then shipped south to the hellish hulks of the Thames until the next convict transport for Australia was ready for them. However, the Glasgow convicts were not always ready to bow the knee to an authority that had just sent them into what could be a living hell.

On Monday, 4 September 1815, a mixed bag of convicts was thrust out of Glasgow Jail on the first stage of their trip south. There were thirteen of them, ten from Glasgow and three from Ayrshire, and a huge number of Glaswegians came to see them off. The crowd included wives and husbands saying tearful goodbyes to spouses they would probably never see again, mothers saying goodbye to their children, children having a last glimpse of their parents, friends, well-wishers and no doubt a sprinkling of pickpockets and the idle curious.

Some of the sentences seem disproportionate by the standards of the twenty-first century. There was Alexander Sutherland, sentenced to fourteen years for shoplifting; Hana Peebles, who got the same length for reset of stolen goods; the quiet Robert Rankine and Matthew Gardner, fourteen years for shop breaking and theft; John Campbell and Andrew Howie, both sent south for seven years for theft; Felix McLaughlin, who got seven years for a number of acts of violent conduct; and the undoubtedly unpleasant John McNeill, known as 'Teapot', who was little more than a violent footpad, who was off for seven years.

Chained two by two, the prisoners were escorted to a carriage that was to trundle the first forty-odd miles to Leith, where the ship for the Thames awaited. As always, there would be a number stuffed inside the carriage and the rest would perch precariously on the roof to brave the autumn weather. As soon as the coach began its jolting journey the convicts began to show their contempt for authority, or perhaps just their natural truculence. Within a few moments the men shattered the coach windows and Teapot McNeill, who was on the roof, passed the time by kicking at the streetlamps of Glasgow. The coach stopped at Airdrie when Teapot made a dash for freedom, pulling the quiet Rankine with him. The force of their fall dragged the other outside convicts down as well, so there was a tangle of five men struggling to escape, with wrist chains hampering them and the guards dragging them apart. The guards changed at Linlithgow, and when they arrived in Edinburgh at four in the afternoon, the prisoners' shackles were finally removed.

As soon as the prisoners were freed they began to riot, fighting and swearing and attempting to escape, and it was only the intervention of a party of Edinburgh's much maligned city guard that restored order. Once more chained together, the prisoners spent the night in jail, and on Tuesday were bundled into carriages and sent off to Leith and from there to the hulks of the Thames.

They could be equally unpredictable inside the jail.

Breakout

Jails of the nineteenth century have left a formidable reputation. The image is of great stone walls, tiny cells, grim guards and the treadmill. They were designed to break the spirit and the mind as much as to contain the body, but the men they were constructed to hold were not easily subdued. On Tuesday, 2 January 1827, there was a multi-breakout of Glasgow jail. Of the four men involved, two were very well known to the police: Peter Lappin, a notorious forger, and Angus McLean, a locksmith. When Lappin was arrested, a hoard of nearly 600 forged banknotes had been found in his house; he was no small-scale operator.

It took patience and skill to escape but these men had that, as well as plenty of time. They were confined on the upper storey of the jail and knew that the watchman left his post for the night at half past six. The governor and a pair of turnkeys lived in the premises, but their last inspection of the day was at half past five. McLean's expertise came in handy when they picked the locks of their cells. They emerged into the lobby of the jail, dug their way through the outer wall, tied a rope of blankets to the lightning rod and clambered down. Once out they vanished into the spider's web of Glasgow's ancient streets.

There were other breakouts and attempted breakouts from Glasgow's jails. On 6 December 1848, it was the turn of the North Prison at Duke Street to be breached. The prison was overcrowded, with an ominous figure of 666 inmates that December, twenty-eight of whom were waiting to be transported to Australia and probably not relishing the prospect. Cells intended for single occupancy were crammed with three men, with the inevitable result of plots and plans.

High on the third storey of a newly constructed wing of the jail, three men crammed into one of these cells, but rather than wait for transportation, they planned to escape. They were locked in at seven in the evening and remained so until early next morning, so there was plenty of time for determined and resourceful men to work. There was a watchman who patrolled outside the cells all night, so they piled their bedding against the door to deaden any noise and set to work. Not long before, workmen had been busy inside the jail, and one of the prisoners had stolen an unguarded file. Now in the classic manner he filed through one of the iron bars of the window and tore the top two-thirds free. Three prison hammocks provided enough material to form a rope. They had been trained as tailors while in prison, so stitching the hammocks together was nearly as easy as tying the makeshift rope to the stump of a bar and swarming to the ground below.

It was four on a winter's morning, black as a politician's promise and they knew the routine of the yard watchman well enough to avoid them.

Yet although they were outside the prison building, they were still within the prison grounds. The outside wall remained as a final barrier between them and freedom. Two of the men hoisted the third, John White, onto their shoulders and gave him a boost so he scrambled up the wall, and then they waited for him to reach down and help them up.

But he did not. Instead, White slipped over the wall and ran, leaving his companions to be caught. Abandoned, they searched frantically for an alternative way out, but Governor Mullen's dog heard them moving and started to bark, which alerted the yard watchman and he soon had the two men back in a cell. White was more fortunate and escaped.

Juvenile Punishments

In the nineteenth century, as today and possibly as in every period of history, there was concern at the behaviour of youths and juveniles. In April 1850 the Glasgow Police magistrates debated the increasing amount of juvenile crime in the city. They believed that imprisonment was not the answer, and suggested corporal punishment, which apparently was effective in Edinburgh.

On Monday, 29 March 1852, an eleven-year-old boy named O'Hara faced the Central Police Court after he had been convicted of stealing a handkerchief from a shop doorway in the Gallowgate. The magistrate awarded him fifteen stripes, but the officer wielding the tawse must have had a very light hand, for within the hour O'Hara was back at the police office, cheekily demanding the return of twopence that the duty lieutenant held for him. That same court ordered Donald Fraser, a young pickpocket, to have twenty stripes, but the police were already doubtful if whipping young boys was a remedy for their crimes. The youngsters were said to 'squeal frightfully' when they were being whipped, but as soon as they were released they 'put their fingers to their nose' to show their contempt for the punishment or perhaps authority in general.

Even as youngsters, Glasgow criminals showed a defiant spirit.

10

The Poisoners

Although the murders of Burke and Hare and Jack the Ripper are perhaps remembered as the epitome of nineteenth-century crime, such barbarity was unusual. More typical of the period were drunken assaults or the secret murder by poison. Glasgow seemed to be particularly prone to this latter type of crime, and women were more likely to be the perpetrators, or at least to be caught for the offence. Three women suffered the ultimate penalty but have been forgotten by history: Mary Steel, who together with her husband was hanged in October 1831 for poisoning a man with laudanum in a spirit cellar, then robbing the corpse; Mrs Jeffrey in 1838, who used arsenic to murder a man and woman in Carluke; and the previously mentioned Margaret Hamilton in 1850. In September 1854 there was an even sadder affair in Inverkip Street in Greenock when a spirit dealer named Mrs Dick bought some vitriol to clean her scales. She poured the vitriol into a cup and left it on the kitchen table. When a customer came in, she walked into the front shop, but her eighteen-month-old child drank the vitriol. She died the next day.

Others have been better remembered.

The Dowanhill Poisoning

Nineteenth-century Glasgow, architects and poison seemed to be linked. Take the case of John Burnet, for instance. He was an influential Glasgow architect, associated with the Greek temple of Elgin Place Church, the Clapperton/Middleton warehouse in Miller Street, ship owners' baronial houses of Auchendennan and Kilmahew, as well as the Clydesdale and Union Bank. He also designed his own house, named St Kilda, in Victoria Circus in Glasgow's fashionable Dowanhill area, and it was within his own walls that a scandal of poisoning occurred in 1893. Burnet was not directly involved, however, and no hint of blame seemed to have attached to him, but as the victim was one of his servants, there may have been whispers of mismanagement in his household at St Kilda House. The servant was Margaret McAllan, a young girl from Caithness.

Margaret had been recommended to the Burnets as a willing worker and a quiet girl. She started work at St Kilda House in May 1893, and as she was young, clever and attractive, it was not unexpected that young men should soon be taking notice of her. One of her most persistent admirers was an equally young man named John Smith. The friendship progressed very well and within a few weeks Smith and Margaret were sweethearting, and then were engaged to be married. It was only then that Margaret found out that her fiancé was overly fond of the bottle. He turned up the worse for wear a few times, not drunk but definitely not sober, and Margaret raised her voice to him, pointing out the error of his ways.

At the end of July the drinking led Smith into more serious trouble than Margaret's tongue, when he tried to gain access to St Kilda House while undoubtedly drunk. He was thumping the door and ringing the bell without success when the beat policeman asked what he was doing. Rather than give a civil reply, Smith swore at the constable and was promptly arrested and taken to the police cells.

Smith was fined fifteen shillings, but as he had no money, he sent a message to Margaret, asking her to pay for him. Margaret refused. She would not pay his fine and moreover, she was very annoyed that he had involved her. In turn, Smith was angry that she had refused to help him. The couple fell out, with Margaret again lecturing Smith about his drinking habits, but he still continued to visit St Kilda House and the engagement was still live. Sometimes Smith would bring a bottle with him, which Margaret appeared to allow. At that time the Burnets were away for the summer, as was quite common among the upper middle-class in Glasgow, so their son and daughter, Mr Lindsay Burnet and Miss Burnet, had been left to run the house and look after the servants.

On Saturday, 19 August, the younger Burnets joined their parents, leaving Margaret alone in the house. At three in the afternoon, Smith called again. He was not quite sober and still had not forgiven Margaret for refusing to pay his fine. He told her he thought she had 'not treated him well' and the subsequent argument ended with Margaret storming upstairs to Mrs Burnet's bedroom.

For a few moments Margaret remained there, possibly just keeping out of Smith's way and allowing things to cool down. As the maidservant she had full run of the house and opened a press in the corner where Mrs Burnet kept medicine bottles. One full bottle was marked 'Poison' and she opened it, but replaced the cork very quickly because of the pungent smell. For some reason she kept the bottle in her hand when she went back downstairs and she still held it when she rejoined Smith in the kitchen. Their anger seemed to have cooled by then, but Smith had been drinking and was asleep on the chair. When Margaret woke him he snatched the bottle of poison from her hand.

'Smell that,' she said, and he did, but when she asked for it back Smith slipped it into his pocket. He still had it when he left the house sometime after eight in the evening. He returned next day. Margaret tried to refuse him access as he was drunk again, but he pushed past and staggered in. Margaret asked him to hand back the bottle of poison, but he kept hold of it and still had possession when he left in the middle of the afternoon. He came back again the next evening, singing drunk and carrying a bottle of port wine. He was obviously in high spirits for he offered a drink to Margaret and then tried to be amorous, but she was having none of it. When he persisted, she fled into the drawing room and stayed there, relatively safe, while Smith blundered drunkenly about the house.

Margaret waited until seven and returned to the kitchen, hoping Smith had left, but he was still there, wide awake and annoyed with her. He called her over to him and again tried to get romantic, but she repelled him once more and locked herself in the study. She spent the night there, ignored Smith's lustful banging at the door and felt great relief when he withdrew into one of the bedrooms and fell asleep.

Early next morning Margaret crept downstairs. Smith was not in the bedroom or in the kitchen, and for a while Margaret thought he had left. She returned to her own room, but the door was locked and Smith was inside. She knocked for entry and Smith let her in; she said she was scared, lifted a knife from the table and asked Smith to leave. He refused. She looked closer, noticed he had a tattoo of a crucifix on his arm and asked if he was a Catholic.

That was apparently not a good thing to ask, as Smith lost his temper and shouted at her. They must have calmed down, though, for Smith followed Margaret to the butcher's shop later that morning, bought some more port, and slipped back into St Kilda. They argued again; Margaret ordered him to leave and said she would call for the police, but he countered her threat by saying he would happily do eighteen months in prison to get his revenge. Margaret changed tack and once again asked for the return of poison, and this time Smith promised to return it before he left the house. He followed that by taking hold of her, but she shook him off and ran to the drawing room. When he came in behind her, Margaret told him that Mr Lindsay Burnet would be home soon and he had better leave. He refused, but the reminder seemed to curtail his romantic pursuit.

Margaret was playing the Burnets' piano later that day when Smith interrupted her. 'You still say I am a Catholic?' he asked. Not having learned from her previous argument, Margaret said she did. Smith stormed out of the room, but returned with a peace offering. He offered Margaret a tumbler full of something she thought was port.

'This is for you,' he said, and she drank it at once.

Immediately as Margaret swallowed the contents of the tumbler, she wished she had not. The liquid seemed to burn her throat and choke her at the same time. With the flair for the melodramatic that seemed common at the period, she leaped up from her seat, dashed her tumbler into the fireplace and screamed, 'You've poisoned me!'

Holding her throat, she tried to run outside, but Smith grabbed her sleeve and hauled her back into the room. She next ran toward the pantry to find something that might make her sick, but again Smith stopped her, saying he would also take the poison.

'If you knew what I am suffering,' Margaret told him, 'you wouldn't take it.'

Maybe her words convinced him, or perhaps he was just making idle boasts, but Smith did not drink out of the bottle. Instead, he grabbed Margaret when she tried to get outside. She asked him to run for a doctor, but he refused, so she asked him to at least leave and let her die in peace. Smith told her, quite callously, 'I will wait and see the last of you.'

Margaret ran up to her bedroom, opened her mouth and screamed for help. The local beat constable came into the house and found her lying on her bed, still screaming.

'Oh, he's poisoned me!' Margaret said. 'Oh, he's poisoned me!' When the officer asked who, she only said, 'Oh, he is cruel.'

The constable sent for Dr Snodgrass, who gave Margaret chalk and water, followed by olive oil, while Smith admitted, 'It was me who gave her it.' He handed the poison bottle to Dr Snodgrass and said, 'I gave her what was in that bottle,' and, 'I gave it her for a lark.' Smith helped Snodgrass support Margaret into a cab that took her to the Western Infirmary, where she was confined for three weeks.

Inspector James Cairns investigated the case. He found the bottle contained concentrated hydrochloric acid and it must have been mixed with port or Margaret would have noticed the very pungent smell. The acid was used as an additive in flour when baking, as well as for removing iron moulds from clothes. Smith was arrested and charged with attempted murder. He was suspected of having poured hydrochloric acid from the poison bottle into the tumbler of port he gave to Margaret. He pleaded not guilty, and at his trial in October 1893 the defence produced a letter wherein Margaret said, 'This is the last you will hear from me on earth.' The defence argued that this phrase showed Margaret had suicidal tendencies, while she said she had only intended to end her engagement. The jury sided with the prosecution and found Smith guilty. He was sentenced to ten months with hard labour.

Margaret survived her brush with poison, but others were not so lucky.

Glasgow's Own Doctor Death

Edward Pritchard was an Englishman who came to Glasgow and set himself up as a general practitioner. He was born in 1825 and at fifteen became an apprentice naval surgeon, eventually serving at sea for four years. Although his doctoring skills may have left much to be desired, he was most definitely popular with a certain type of lady: those with low morals and a nature that was easily swayed by charm. He worked in Hunmanby in Yorkshire, but according to rumour, he had to leave when the number of angry husbands became too many for him to avoid. Even uglier rumours followed him as he came to Glasgow in 1860.

Pritchard was a tall man, with the beard that was so fashionable at the time, although he was balding on top, and seems to have been immensely vain. Indeed he paraded around the centre of Glasgow, sniffing out likely ladies and handing out postcards of himself in the full fig of a Masonic Master.

Despite his amorous pursuits, Pritchard was a married man. In 1850 he married Mary Jane Taylor of Edinburgh, with whom he had five children. It had been Mary's parents who bought Pritchard out of the navy and financed his doctor's practice in Yorkshire. Perhaps their money enabled him to buy the certificates of Doctor of Medicine from the University of Erlangen and Licentiate of the Society of Apothecaries of London, for his qualifications were certainly more impressive than his skill. The Taylors' money may have enabled Pritchard to better cheat on their daughter too, but possibly he used his silver tongue for that. The same tongue talked him into the Freemasons, so he became master of Lodge St Mark, and into the Glasgow Royal Arch and the Grand Lodge of the Royal Order in Edinburgh. In fact, Pritchard eased himself into any society that could help him. His fellow doctors in Glasgow, however, were less awestruck.

In 1863 Elizabeth McGirn, Pritchard's maidservant, died at a fire at his Berkeley Street home. Despite Pritchard's increasingly dubious reputation, a police investigation found nothing untoward. The Pritchard family moved home, first to Royal Crescent, then Sauchiehall Street, with the Taylors again footing the bill. Then, in the autumn of 1864, Mary became quite seriously sick. She left her husband to live with her parents in Edinburgh. Once in the capital she recovered quickly and returned to Glasgow, only to fall sick again. The received wisdom of the period attributed illness to unhealthy air, and the Taylors thought the industrial pollution of Glasgow was somehow to blame. But when Mary was languishing in her west coast sickbed, Dr Cowan came from Edinburgh to check on her. Despite Pritchard's occupation, Cowan, a relation, recommended that Mrs Taylor come through to help look after her daughter.

At the same time as Mary was ill and her mother was taking on the nursing duties, Pritchard was having yet another affair, this time with Mary McLeod, a child of seventeen who was one of his maidservants. 'If my wife dies,' Pritchard told her cheerfully, 'I will marry you.' When young Mary McLeod fell pregnant, Pritchard kindly carried out an abortion of his own child. Mary Pritchard was well aware of her husband's cavorting and doubtless fumed in the background.

As Mary's health deteriorated the Taylors sent a succession of medical men to check on her. When Dr Gairdner from Glasgow University visited, Pritchard informed him that Cowan had advised treating Mary with chloroform and champagne. Gairdner recommended bread and milk. Only while Mrs Taylor nursed her did Mary show some improvement, but then the Pritchard household was struck with a double death. First Mrs Taylor died, and then, three agonising weeks later, Mary herself. Pritchard himself completed the death certificates, with Mrs Taylor apparently dying of apoplexy while gastric fever had killed her daughter. It was significant that others in the house, including the unfortunate Mary McLeod, also became ill if they tasted Mary's food. However, Pritchard continued to go his merry way, seemingly invulnerable to illness or blame. Before Mary was lowered into her grave, he insisted that the coffin lid be unscrewed, and he gave her a parting kiss.

But despite his over-elaborate grief, others were suspicious of the suave but slippery doctor. One of the many medical men who had attended Mary, Dr Paterson, suggested that she had been poisoned, and a chemist mentioned that Pritchard had bought quite substantial quantities of tincture of aconite and potassium tartrate. Both substances were poisonous.

When a post-mortem found traces of both aconite poison and antimony in Mary's body, her mother was exhumed and also examined with the same results. The police pursued their investigations and discovered that Pritchard had not disposed of his wife purely to pursue fresh sexual conquests, for he had also opened up quite substantial insurance policies on Mary and her mother. Strangely, he had made insurance claims for jewellery in the aftermath of the Berkeley Street fire as well. A jury found no difficulty in finding him guilty and the judge ordered that he be hanged.

As he waited in Duke Street Prison, more stories emerged about the life and career of Dr Pritchard. The rumours suggested that he had poisoned some of his patients while working in Yorkshire, including an elderly lady named Betty Chandler. Whether he intended to kill them or was simply a very incompetent doctor is uncertain, but Pritchard was said to have quickly disposed of all the medicines he had used to unsuccessfully treat his patients. There was also some evidence that he had indeed started the Berkeley Street fire. Although the fire had started in the middle of the night, when the police came to the door Pritchard was fully dressed. Even uglier rumours claimed that Pritchard had first got McGirn pregnant, then murdered her. She had been burned on her bed, but everybody else in the house had survived, while the fire had not even wakened her. Mary's character did not escape unscathed either; there were people who thought she had been blackmailing him about the deaths and affairs, which was why he disposed of her.

On the day before his execution, Pritchard pretended piety and gave audience to a whole host of ministers. The crowd that watched was estimated at anything from 30,000 to 100,000, and Pritchard gave them something to remember him by. He dressed up for the occasion, with a brand new suit, shiny patent leather boots and his beard all washed and combed. Only then, when it was obvious there was no reprieve, did Pritchard confess to the murders of his wife and mother-in-law, and he died facing the crowds on Glasgow Green. Although they did not know it, those who saw him 'turned off' were witnessing history, for Pritchard was the last man to be publicly hanged in Glasgow. It was 28 July 1865, and three years later the government ordered that all future executions would take place behind prison walls.

Martyr or Murderess?

Although every crime is a tragedy and every criminal is unique in his or her own way, there was something very special about Madeleine Smith. She was young, intelligent, eminently respectable, attractive, charming and involved in one of the most celebrated cases of poisoning Scotland has ever seen.

Smith was the eldest daughter of the architect James Smith and the granddaughter of the neo-classical architect David Hamilton. As such she was firmly in the upper level of Glasgow society. The family lived at fashionable Blythswood Square and owned a house near Helensburgh. As young people tend to do, Smith fell in lust, or perhaps even love, with the wrong man, in her case Pierre Emile L'Angelier, an apprentice nurseryman from Jersey who worked in Glasgow. She met him in 1855 and they had a series of romantic liaisons, despite coming from vastly different social backgrounds. L'Angelier was around thirty, a handsome, vain man who dressed well and boasted of important connections in France, where his father had been born. L'Angelier either hoped for social advancement or genuinely liked the sight of Smith, for he manipulated a meeting with her as they promenaded along Sauchiehall Street. One meeting escalated into many and the two became attached.

They sent each other a great number of love letters and occasionally managed to meet unchaperoned, which was pretty scandalous for Smith's class at the time. They exchanged small talk, letters and kisses at the basement window of the house in Blythswood Square and in a number of other locations. Even more scandalous was the fact that L'Angelier eventually managed to seduce Smith, who was presumably not terribly difficult to persuade, into bed. Unfortunately for both, Smith's parents had more conventional ideas for their daughter and when her father found out about the affair he ordered her to call a halt. At first Smith seemed to accept her father's authority and bid L'Angelier a fond adieu, but once her father's back was turned she continued to meet her chosen man. Indeed the affair became more serious. L'Angelier attempted to control Smith's life, but Smith was a social butterfly and graced balls and events which were suitable to her position, and to which L'Angelier would never be invited. Smith's life changed completely when her father found her a much more suitable partner in William Minnoch, a wealthy cotton manufacturer.

Now Smith lived a double life with her open friendship with Minnoch and her secret, scandalous liaison with L'Angelier. The Jersey man sought acceptance in Smith's social circle, but Smith knew that was impossible. She spent more time with Minnoch, less with L'Angelier, and eventually Minnoch proposed. Either realising her position, being dragooned out of her affair or genuinely falling out of love with the Jersey man, Smith attempted to break free of the relationship. She asked for the return of her love letters, telling him, 'I shall feel obliged by your bringing me my letters and likeness on Thursday evening.'

Instead L'Angelier again revealed his nasty side and refused. He threatened to use the letters to expose the relationship to her father unless she agreed to marry him. If that had happened, Smith's reputation would have been shredded and the possibility of any respectable man marrying her would be very slim.

The blackmail centred on the letters. L'Angelier had retained around 200 of them, as well as the drafts of some of his replies. Now he threatened to have them published, which would certainly have damaged Smith's reputation and future marriage prospects. The early letters appear innocent to the modern eye, with phrases such as: 'I do not feel as if I were writing you for the first time . . . we have become as familiar friends. I often wish you were near us. We could take such charming walks.' However, after a time the phrases became more personal and the wording more intense. As Smith's trust for L'Angelier grew, she opened her heart to him and the letters contained her dreams and hopes. She wrote of a clandestine trip to Edinburgh for marriage, and the Jersey man became her 'own darling husband'. Rather than L'Angelier leading Smith astray, it seemed that she was looking for more physicality, and was not afraid to write of 'being fondled by you, deal Emile' while he attempted to return to a morality more acceptable to the day and age.

As with many upper middle-class Glasgow families, the Smiths owned property at a Clyde resort and they spent the summer of 1856 at Rowaleyn, their house at Rhu. It was there the affair reached its inevitable climax. Smith's subsequent letter to L'Angelier reveals not only what happened, but also her feelings. After they made love, Smith wrote: 'if we did wrong last night it was in the excitement of our love' and revealed her previous physical innocence: 'I did not bleed in the least last night.' However, her Victorian sensibilities also shone through as she accepted the guilt: 'were you angry at me for allowing you to do what you did – was it very bad of me? We should . . . have waited till we were married'.

Having seduced the younger woman, L'Angelier immediately heaped the blame of his actions on to her. Rather than reassurance, his letters spoke of his being 'wretchedly sad' and asked, 'why . . . did you give way after your promises?' He told her, 'you had no resolution' and, 'it was very bad indeed'. He asked her to 'think of the consequences if I were never to marry you'. But rather than consider her good name, L'Angelier said, 'What reproaches I should have.' In that letter surely L'Angelier revealed a selfish, ugly character. By asking Smith to consider him, he was adding emotional blackmail to the guilt her class and respectability would have already burdened her with.

After L'Angelier's threats of exposure, the story gets a bit murky. L'Angelier asked to see Smith again and she agreed, possibly with the hope of persuading him to hand the letters over. The relationship continued, albeit haltingly. The couple met, Smith made cups of hot chocolate and they talked. On 19 February, L'Angelier's diary recorded: 'saw Mimi [Smith] a few moments. Was very ill during the night.' The next day they met again, and again L'Angelier was sick. On 22 February, the same thing happened. Every time he met Smith he was sick, vomiting green bile. He told a number of people he believed Smith had poisoned him. Smith was also acting differently, visiting Murdoch Brothers, the Sauchiehall Street chemists, to buy arsenic for the house at Rhu.

Until that time Smith had not told L'Angelier she was to marry Minnoch, but the engagement was due to be made public. She tried to send L'Angelier away, but once again she visited a chemist and bought arsenic mixed with indigo. On 21 March, L'Angelier left his flat; he came back in the early hours of 22 March, very ill. On 23 March 1857, he was found dead. When the police searched his flat, they found Smith's love letters.

Smith had vanished. Minnoch guessed she would be at Rhu and brought her back. L'Angelier had already been buried, but he was exhumed and a post-mortem found traces of arsenic. Smith was arrested for murder and tried in the High Court in Edinburgh. She never denied her affair, and claimed she had used the arsenic as a beauty aid. On the other hand, L'Angelier was known to have a melancholic temperament and to have spoken of suicide. He was also familiar with the use of arsenic.

It was not an easy case to decide, but the jury thought the evidence circumstantial and found the case not proven. It remains not proven. Did Smith poison her lover, or did he commit suicide as a twisted act of revenge against the woman he had seduced? Smith's case was one of Glasgow's most celebrated and the correct outcome has never been satisfactorily decided.

Murder By Wife?

Poisoning appears to have been a difficult crime to prove. On Sunday, 17 October 1847, an Irish labourer named James Keenan spent the night drinking in some of the Glasgow shebeens. He returned to his home in Hunter Street and continued to drink, but next morning he was found dead. At first there was no real suspicion, but when various people whispered 'foul play' to the police, Criminal Officer Clark began his enquiries. Keenan was in his early forties, a married man with three children, but he had been on bad terms with his wife Mary Ann for some time. Mary Ann had been seen to buy two pennies' worth of laudanum, and witnesses claimed to have seen her mix the laudanum with his whisky.

When the police surgeon carried out a post-mortem he found that Keenan had indeed died of laudanum poisoning, and so his wife was arrested and charged with murder. The case came up before the Glasgow Spring Circuit, but had to be abandoned as most of the defence witnesses had returned to Ireland and could not be called. A new warrant was issued and Mary Ann Keenan appeared before the High Court in Edinburgh in July, but the jury could not agree and she was found not proven of murder so walked free.

Where the Madeleine Smith case made headlines and created nationwide interest, the Keenans' case barely got a mention. In suspected murder, as in so many things in the nineteenth century, class was very important.

11
Nautical Crime

Glasgow's position as a major maritime city gave an international angle to many of the crimes. It also gave the resident thieves even more opportunities for illegal gain. As well as stealing from vessels moored at the Broomielaw or in the ever expanding docks, the constant coming and goings of ferries on the Clyde provided a whole new world of victims. By their very nature ferries were the temporary abode of strangers crowded together for a short space of time and then parted by arrival. This environment was perfect for a pickpocket, who could slide among the unwary, snatch what he wanted and vanish again, to commit the same crime day after day with different people. In the 1840s Glasgow was infested by a number of thieves up from London, and some targeted the Clyde coast steamers. Their method of operation was to wait until the passengers crowded on the wooden gangplank prior to departing, and then dip as many pockets as possible before vanishing with the loot.

In late June 1845 the police began to combat the thieves by sending a number of plainclothes detectives to travel on the boats and watch for anything suspicious. There could not have been many men spared for this hit-and-miss operation, but the threat of being detected must have worked, as the spate of thefts on the Clyde diminished after that date.

Sometimes, however, even the Glasgow Police could make a mistake.

The Arrest of Miss Mary Brown

On Tuesday, 16 April 1850, the Partick-built Inman Line steamer *City of Glasgow* left the Broomielaw on her maiden voyage. An estimated 60,000 people gathered to watch her leave, standing on both banks of the Clyde and perched on every elevated position so they could watch the first steam ship to make the voyage direct from Glasgow to New York. She eased away from the Broomielaw shortly after two in the afternoon, grounded briefly in the river, but with a fussy tug in attendance and her screw churning the water white, and as bands played and guns roared farewell, she steamed down the Clyde until, two hours later, she sat in splendour off the Tail of the Bank.

For the vast majority of the crowd, the memories were of a majestic Clyde-built ship and the pageantry of a new passage, but one young woman had a vastly different experience that day. Mary Brown was a lady. She came from a very respectable Glasgow family and had bought her ticket for the passage, intending to travel from New York to Toronto, where her relatives were expecting her. However, just as *City of Glasgow* was about to leave the Broomielaw, two sheriff officers clambered up the gangplank and arrested Mary Brown. Her protests attracted a crowd, but the officers had official papers that claimed she owed her brother money. Brown denied the charge and claimed she was a victim of 'gross persecution and oppression' and refused to leave the ship. The officers contacted the Clyde Police and they bundled Brown ashore, much to the disgust of the passengers and crew of the ship, as well as many of the crowd on shore.

As *City of Glasgow* sailed away, Mary Brown was hustled into a cab, which clattered through the streets to the sheriff's chambers. There the document was examined and found to be in error. Brown's brother had no claim against her at all and she did not owe him anything. The sheriff officers released her, but the ship had long sailed. Miss Brown was not a lady to give up, and she ran for the late afternoon train for Greenock, caught the connection to Gourock and arrived there to see *City of Glasgow* still sitting offshore. There was only a short stretch of water to cross now, so Brown hired an open boat, got herself rowed across and as the passengers cheered, she held her hat with one hand and clambered up a rope ladder onto the deck of the ship. She was obviously a determined lady.

Racing By Steam

The Victorian period was one of intense competition. Firms struggled for supremacy, churches competed to fill pews, stagecoaches raced each other to their destinations and sports, from curling to football, attracted huge interest. This competition extended to the sea, where clipper ships competed to bring the first tea and packet ships fought to be first at the pier. However, reckless competition sometimes led to disaster.

In the middle of the century there were a number of steamship companies operating in the Clyde, each one eager for the maximum number of passengers, who often chose the fastest ships. In July 1850 two of these vessels were *Victoria*, commanded by John Campbell, and *Eclipse*. The ships were racing from Greenock to the Broomielaw, both desperate to arrive first with their passengers.

Both vessels had arrived at Greenock at quarter past seven on Monday, 29 July. *Eclipse* was first to pile in her 500 passengers and leave, with her side paddles churning the water to a creamy froth, but *Victoria* was only a few moments behind her. Captain Campbell got steam up and followed in *Eclipse*'s choppy wake. What happened next was the crux of the matter. The prosecution said that Captain Campbell had recklessly steered *Victoria* into the stern of *Eclipse*, while the defence claimed that *Eclipse* had steered a zigzag course so that *Victoria* could not overtake her. What was not in doubt was the result.

Victoria's bow ran straight into the stern of *Eclipse*, smashing her boat from its davits. Not surprisingly, the passengers panicked as the sharp prow crashed a few feet from them. Although nobody was killed or even seriously injured, there were a number of minor injuries and one woman on the quarterdeck fainted.

The River Bailie Court considered the case for a full seven hours and thought Campbell was to blame. He was fined £5, plus the costs of the court. Other cases were on a much larger scale.

The Curious Case of the Vanishing Ferret

Constable James Davidson liked to read. That was no secret. In particular, he liked to read the Scottish newspapers for sometimes he felt homesick, away out in Melbourne in Australia. In June 1881 he read the 12 February edition of *The Scotsman* and found an article that interested him very much. Apparently a ship named *Ferret* had been chartered in Glasgow the previous year and had vanished completely. There were rumours that it had foundered with all hands at the entrance to the Mediterranean, but some people were putting forward darker theories of theft and fraud. Mr Chamberlain, President of the Board of Trade, had said the government was taking steps to find the missing vessel.

When Davidson read the account of the vanished ship he realised he had seen a similar vessel lying in Hobsons Bay, just off Melbourne. He remembered her well because her master had been most reluctant to come close to shore, but the pilot had insisted. Now she sat there with her crew banned from stepping ashore and steam rising, as if she was waiting to run, even though her owner had put her up for sale. Her name was *India*, not *Ferret*, but the description was so close that Davidson was virtually certain she was the same ship.

Davidson informed his superiors of his suspicions, and the Commissioner of Customs, Andrew Clark, checked *India* on Lloyd's Register of Shipping. When it was obvious she was not listed, and therefore was not officially registered, Clark led a party of marine police, backed by armed Royal Marines, to raid the mysterious steamer. The crew on board surrendered without a fight, despite there being a quantity of arms and ammunition on board. As Captain Clark and the authorities investigated further, they unravelled part of one of the most amazing stories of nautical theft and fraud of the nineteenth century.

How to Steal a Ship

It all began in Glasgow in the summer of 1880 when two very well set up gentlemen approached a yacht chandlers and wished to charter the 460-ton, ninety horsepower steam ship, *Ferret*. The men called themselves George Smith and Joseph Walker and appeared to be gentlemen with plenty of money to splash around. *Ferret* had been on the Glasgow to Belfast crossing, but the Highland Railway Company had bought her for service in the north-west. Now Smith and Walker were proposing to take *Ferret* on a six-month pleasure cruise through the Mediterranean with a party of friends. Mr Smith made an instant hit in Glasgow; he said he was related to Mr William Henry Smith, bookseller and then First Lord of the Admiralty, who was possibly to become the model for Sir Joseph Porter in Gilbert and Sullivan's *HMS Pinafore*. The Highland Railway Company investigated Smith and Walker, but both appeared genuine. They banked with the Standard Bank in London and had a pile of documentation to authenticate their positions.

With the paperwork in order, *Ferret* steamed south to the Clyde to be refitted for her new role. The contract was given to Steele and Company of Greenock, who were top quality shipbuilders. They had built *United Kingdom*, for a while the largest paddle steamer in the world, and had been a prime builder for Cunard, but were arguably best remembered for their supreme tea-clippers.

It was obvious that Smith and Walker wanted only the best workmanship for *Ferret*, so firms clamoured to get their attention. Russell and Company, ship-store dealers of Glasgow, must have rubbed their hands in glee when they were selected to supply the ship's stores, including an eye-poppingly extensive wine list. Russell sent Smith and Walker a bill for a staggering £1,400 for stores alone. McMillan, a Greenock butcher, got the order for the beef supplies and a host of small Glasgow companies were involved with the minor supplies, such as candles and stationery. Some people thought *Ferret* had taken on board enough stores to last a year, although the owners had said the Mediterranean voyage was to last only six months, but that was quietly smiled away.

When Captain Watkins appeared with a riot of gold decorating both his cap and the sleeves of his tailored uniform, some people commented that it was unusual for a 'man of colour' to command a British ship, but most were unconcerned about such a minor detail and concentrated on fitting out *Ferret*. No expense was spared in making her a beautiful vessel inside and out. When the work was completed and *Ferret* ready for sea, Smith and Walker came up to the Clyde and took over the ship. There were no complications; all seemed in order, and *Ferret* sailed to Cardiff where her party of gentlemen passengers was waiting. She coaled there, and in October 1880 set off for her pleasure trip to the Mediterranean.

Ferret's first port of call after Cardiff was intended to be Marseilles, but that was the last heard of her until the spring of 1881. The creditors waited for their bills to be paid, but nothing transpired. There were rumours and reports of sightings: she had been seen passing through the Straits; she was seen in the Bay of Naples; she was sighed at Malta; she had sunk in a gale and there was wreckage found in the Bay of Biscay. But these were just rumours. The solitary truth was shocking. Mr Walker and Mr Smith had been fraudsters; they had not only obtained the stores and fittings for *Ferret* for nothing, but they had also stolen the entire ship.

But that was just the tip of a massive iceberg. The theft of *Ferret* was the beginning of a fraudulent scheme, the full scope of which has never been discovered. As soon as they suspected the theft, the Board of Trade telegraphed around the ports of the world to watch for *Ferret*, but they did not find her. In the meantime, *Ferret* roamed the world on her own terms. Captain Watkins had taken on temporary crew at Greenock.

Known as 'runners', these men sailed her to Cardiff, where they were replaced by a brand new bunch of hands. The voyage was gradually worked out. After Cardiff, *Ferret* sailed to Milford, where they shipped a cargo of coal, and then passed through the Strait of Gibraltar at the entrance to the Mediterranean. So far everything was as it should be, but once she had passed the Rock, *Ferret* waited for night, turned off her lights and made a spectacular U-turn back into the Atlantic.

Here Watkins ordered that lifebuoys with the name *Ferret* on them should be thrown over the side, together with one of the ship's lifeboats. When some of the crew objected, they were told that the running of the ship was not their concern. With the supposed wreckage laid, Watkins ordered the name *Ferret* to be removed from the stern and bows, from the bell and the register, and the name *Benton* added instead. Her chart-room and wheelhouse were moved so her profile was altered, she was repainted, her official registration number was erased and a new number added and, even stranger, each member of the crew was given a new name. Henry Coffin, the chief steward, became Henry Martin. When Walker told Walter Rudd, the boatswain, he was now William Jones, Rudd merely looked at Walker and shrugged. He did not care; he just obeyed orders. He had already helped throw the lifeboat overboard. The seaman, Matthew Robinson, became Matthew Rug; John Wilson, seaman, who had been at the wheel when the buoys were put over the side, became Samuel Boyd. Mr Walker was now James Stewart Henderson, or Mr B.

There were mysteries within mysteries as well. Take Joseph Brown, the second steward, for example. He joined *Ferret* at Cardiff and was obviously educated above his apparent station. Henderson recruited him as a clerk, so he witnessed a great deal more than most. Brown was rumoured to be the son of an English clergyman who chose a career at sea and fell into evil company. If so, it was a classic Victorian melodrama. Brown created lists of stores and forged a host of documents, destroyed genuine bills of lading and made false ones, altered the names in the crew lists and made new ship's papers. He became James Henry, a false name to alter an already fake identity, and sometime during the voyage he saw Smith using a variety of writing styles. The man may have been a master forger.

Somewhere in the Atlantic Walker must have heard murmurings of discontent among the ranks, for he called all hands to his cabin. He told them he was a colonel in the US Army on a secret mission and if everybody was loyal and did their duty, they would be well taken care of, but if they tried to betray him, he would blow their brains out. At this point he displayed a revolver and a bottle of grog – death or loyalty. Not surprisingly, all the crew chose the grog and swore their loyalty.

The newly named *Benton* picked up ballast and water at Santo Antão in the Cape Verde Islands then steamed to Santos in Brazil, where she re-coaled and bought a cargo of coffee, again paying with worthless banker's drafts. *Ferret* had loaded too much coffee and not enough coal, so the crew had to burn part of her cargo to keep steam up as they re-crossed the Atlantic to Cape Town. Here Captain Watkins left and the first mate Robert Wright took command, under the watchful eye of the owner, Mr Walker, alias Henderson.

Mr Smith also had a new name: William Wallace. He became the ship's purser. About halfway to Cape Town *Ferret* had another name change, and it was as SS *India* that she sailed into South African waters. Walker sold the cargo for around £8,000. He kept around £2,000 of the cash, with the remainder being in bills for the London partners, who could draw the cash from their bank there. From Cape Town, *India* claimed to be sailing for Bombay, but instead made for Mauritius. The idea may have been to load a cargo of sugar, but she left empty and sailed to Albany, West Australia, for coal and from there to Melbourne. On 20 April 1881, *Ferret*, now *India*, sailed through the Heads and into Hobsons Bay.

While Walker and Smith scrambled ashore and pretended to try and sell the ship for £10,500, the crew were busy painting her with a red star on her black funnel for her next reincarnation. It was then that Constable Davidson gave the alarm and the authorities had the crew arrested. As the police searched the ship, they found an array of incriminating evidence to show that *Ferret* was part of an amazing plot that had its headquarters in London.

They found rifles and ammunition, a bag of 626 gold sovereigns, a roll of Brazilian banknotes, discovered that the supposedly official number 77942 carved into the combings of the main hatch was false, and a close investigation revealed four digits of *Ferret*'s number 63864 inscribed beneath. They discovered that the original name had been filed off the ship's bell, the logbook had been tampered with and the name cut out, and a single advance note between the pages had the name *Ferret* across the head. They found rubber stamps of various company names, blank documents, bills of lading, crew sheets and a printing press. Possibly most damning of all was the discovery of a codebook for sending telegraphs. Some of the coded messages hinted at a wholesale plan to buy cargoes with non-existent funds and claim insurance for lost cargoes. The codebook held such phrases as: 'Vessel seized. Everything U.P. Could destroy nothing'; 'game is up; all discovered; destroy or hide everything and make yourself scarce. Communicate with me and through the arranged channel.'

The authorities towed *Ferret* to the lee of the ironclad HMS *Cerberus* and she remained under the guns of the Royal Navy, in case someone should attempt an escape. However, there were still mysteries in the *Ferret* story. The real owners were not known, and nor were the people in London with whom Walker corresponded. The ultimate end of the fraud was also not known, but there was wild speculation that Walker intended scuttling the ship and murdering the crew. Given the new paintwork and the documents found on board *Ferret* with the name *Raven*, it seemed unlikely Walker genuinely intended to sell her. It was more likely he would take the money, hand over false ownership and registration papers and steam away into the night.

With the ship in custody, the Melbourne authorities searched for Walker, Smith and Wright. Smith seems to have been arrested fairly easily, but Walker vanished and had to be tracked down in the outback.

Wright was also hard to find, but he was arrested on a quite different charge, recognised as the master of *Ferret* and held for sailing under false papers and forging the ship's register. He was also known as Edward Rashleigh Carlyon. Walker tried to make bail, saying that the government already held £10,000 worth of his property so he would not run away. The Melbourne authorities listened but refused, and Walker remained locked up.

When questioned, the crew denied nothing. Only a few men had been with the ship during the entire voyage, but there was enough evidence given to convict three of the four chief players. Watkins, who had disembarked at Cape Town, was never seen or heard of again. There was some dispute as to who would try the prisoners, and on what charges, but although there was a desire to bring them to Greenock for the theft of a ship, they eventually appeared in a Melbourne court on the lesser charge of sailing under false papers. The defence was simple: the ship was on a secret mission to carry arms to Peru, currently engaged in a war with Chile. The frequent name changes were to enable the ship to run the Chilean blockade. However, the jury was not convinced. Walker/ Henderson and Smith/Wallace – whatever their real names – were sentenced to seven years' penal servitude; Robert Wright, or Carlyon, an older man, was given half that.

There was a hint of romance when Walker's wife, known as Mrs Henderson, appeared in court. Young, slim and attractive, she sat patiently and quietly through the proceedings, and a benevolent judge granted her the 600-plus sovereigns found on *Ferret*. However, Russell and Co. of Glasgow put in a counter claim for their unpaid bill, and Mrs Henderson had to go without.

Ferret was sold to South Australian owners and the case faded from the public mind. There was a slight reminder the following year when six of *Ferret's* seamen searched out the owners and demanded wages and compensation for the voyage, but by that time there were events grabbing the headlines other than the voyage of an obscure Glasgow ship. Yet the case left a major mystery unsolved: who were the men behind the fraud, the mysterious men in London with whom Walker corresponded? That truth will never be known.

Death of a Ship

The death of a ship is always a tragedy, and especially so when it could have been avoided. Ships could be driven ashore in foul weather, lost without a trace, struck by icebergs or tropical storms or catch fire. There were also occasions when the master or mate deliberately sank them in an attempt to claim insurance money. In the nineteenth century there was a rash of such attempts at scuttling, and one case came before the Glasgow Court in December 1888.

The vessel involved was the 984-ton, three-masted barque *Gryfe*. Like many quality vessels, she had been built in Massachusetts, but was now past her best, being over forty years old. Originally named *Independence*, she had undergone two changes of identity, also being known as *St John* before she became *Gryfe* in 1874.

In 1888 *Gryfe* was English owned but registered in Quebec. She operated as a timber carrier between Canada and the Clyde, and that year her master and mate were charged with trying to scuttle. As usual the story was confused and contradictory, but the second mate, Charles Robinson, gave what may be a reasonably accurate picture, so the gist of the story is based around his account.

Robinson signed articles on *Gryfe* at Quebec a few weeks before she sailed, when Captain Robert Tait was in command, and there were ongoing repairs. In early July they sailed for the Clyde, but after only a few days the barque began to take in water. *Gryfe* was a wind-powered vessel with no engine; they were under a full press of sail, beating off a lee shore, and when Robinson found ten feet of water in the hold he thought it safest to put into port. Captain Tait agreed and they headed for St John's, Newfoundland, where *Gryfe* was beached, the deck cargo unloaded and the hands discharged. Captain Tait ordered that the hull should be caulked – that is, the seams patched – to three feet of her keel.

A Mr Sanson was in charge of the repairs and he was meticulous, checking the work every day. However, Sanson also mentioned that *Gryfe* was 'fully insured to her total loss', which was perhaps an unusual statement to make. When the repairs were complete, *Gryfe* was surveyed. She seemed seaworthy, so another crew was signed on, including some of the original men, and a new master and mate appointed, with Robinson back as second mate. The new master was Louis le Bourdois, with his brother, Joseph le Bourdois, as chief mate. However, Captain le Bourdois ordered Robinson to keep the log, as his brother was unable to write English.

Robinson tried his best to keep an accurate log, but Captain le Bourdois interfered, ordering him to alter some entries and rip out sundry pages. In a ship at sea, the master's word is law and to disobey is mutiny so Robinson did as he was told. He tore out the page that detailed the repairs carried out at St John's, and inserted false entries stating that there was a greater depth of water in the hold than had actually been the case, on 17, 19, 20 and 21 August. For example, whereas Robinson remembered there being three feet of water in the hold on 17 August, the amended log entry claimed there was six feet five inches. The amended log also stated that all hands were pumping, rather than just one watch, and it also claimed the weather was worse.

It took the hands two days to pump *Gryfe* dry, but on the third day Captain le Bourdois told Robinson that he did not want to remain in the ship. He planned to abandon her once they were clear of the Newfoundland Banks, for they would then be on the main shipping lanes. According to Robinson, Captain le Bourdois did not explain why he wanted to leave the ship. Following the captain's orders, Robinson told the crew they were going to abandon the ship, and had them prepare the lifeboats. That same day the captain approached Robinson privately and ordered him to bore a hole in her bows so she took in water, adding that they were now directly on the steamer routes.

Despite knowing the risks of refusing a direct order, Robinson declined. He said he lacked the skill for such a job, but as the chief mate Joseph le Bourdois was a carpenter, he would be the best man. Accordingly, the chief mate sharpened an auger and in the deep dark of midnight he asked Robinson to accompany him. They worked by lantern light inside the hold, boring a hole an inch and a quarter in diameter through the wooden hull. 'That's all right,' the captain said as *Gryfe* began to take in water faster than the pumps could cope.

'Don't kill yourself with the pumps,' Captain le Bourdois said to the hands, and ordered the steward to make sure they had plenty to eat as they were going to leave the ship soon. The men pumped for two days, and then they saw the smudge of smoke that signified a steamer. When she drew close Robinson ordered that they hoist a distress signal. The steamer was *Persian Monarch*, Clyde-built and en route from New York to London. When she came to investigate, Captain le Bourdois launched a lifeboat with six men to ask her master if he could lend some hands for the pump and some provisions. Simultaneously, he ordered Robinson and the chief mate to take the remainder of the crew to knock out the bow ports. That would allow the sea to flood in and hasten the demise of *Gryfe*.

However, Robinson had helped put in the bow ports and knew they were watertight. He had no intention of sinking the ship and deliberately bungled the job. He returned on deck to report that he had failed to knock out the ports, and was informed that Captain Irvine of *Persian Monarch* asked to see Captain le Bourdois. When the captain returned from the steamer he ordered the crew to throw their deck cargo of timber overboard to try and keep *Gryfe* afloat, and if that failed they would abandon her when the next steamer happened along. By now the crew was fully aware what was happening and refused to stay aboard a ship the captain was obviously determined to sink.

Le Bourdois again ordered the bow ports to be knocked out, but again Robinson refrained. The captain then ordered his brother to bore another hole in her hull but that attempt also failed. The captain's next plan was to cover the cabin and living quarters with oil and set fire to the ship; as a timber carrier she would have burned like a torch. While some of the men obeyed, Captain le Bourdois took eight men across to *Persian Monarch*, leaving Robinson, the chief mate and the boatswain on board to transfer when the boat returned.

Some of *Persian Monarch*'s crew came aboard, where they commented on the oil and found over eleven feet of water in the hold. When the boatswain of *Persian Monarch* said *Gryfe* 'could be trusted a little further', Robinson dropped his bombshell. He refused to leave *Gryfe*. Believing that the men from the steamer wished to clam the barque as salvage, he said he would remain on board. As seemed normal practice, the boatswain had disabled the pumps so *Gryfe* would sink faster, possibly to ensure she would not be a hazard to shipping. When some of the crew tried to persuade Robinson to come to *Persian Monarch* with them, he produced the captain's revolver and said he would 'shoot the first man who tried to force him away'.

In the face of that threat it is not surprising the seamen retreated, and Robinson squared the mainsail and headed eastward, a lone man attempting to sail a 900-ton vessel the full width of the Atlantic. The master and crew of *Persian Monarch* left him to his fate. However, he was not alone for long. In a surprising twist of events, Captain and Joseph le Bourdois approached *Gryfe* in a small boat and after initially trying to persuade Robinson to leave the vessel, they eventually joined him as *Persian Monarch* steamed away.

The voyage was not easy. The first night *Gryfe* was sluggish with seventeen feet of water in the hold, but they left her to sail herself as they struggled to block the hole in the bow. After that it was constant toil until they were off Queenstown, Ireland, where they found a tug that towed them to Greenock. Once safe on land, negotiations began. Captain le Bourdois sent Robinson to the agent and offered him a third of the men's wages as reward for staying with the vessel, but when they were both in the office of Mr Orkney, the shipping agent, Robinson was also expected to sign documents that would perhaps remove any claim Robinson had to salvage money. At first he refused to sign or accept anything until after the inevitable Board of Trade enquiry. Nevertheless, Robinson was persuaded to accept a cash payment of £10 if he signed the paper, so, fearing he may lose everything, he signed. Captain le Bourdois handed him a further £5 on condition he disappeared to France.

Naturally the story spread and the case eventually came to the court in Glasgow, where Robinson's version of events came under challenge. When a succession of seamen from *Gryfe* gave their evidence, some said that it was Robinson who ordered the lashings of the lower bow ports to be cut, and it was Robinson, not the captain, who gave an order to unship the pumps and break open the cask of oil. Thomas Brown, the steward, claimed that Robinson said he would make a thousand dollars from this trip as he would 'stick by the ship' and use the money for his forthcoming marriage. He also claimed it was Robinson who told him to give the men 'plenty to eat', as the food would all be going to the bottom anyway, and they said Robinson gave the order to take the spears out of the pumps so they could not be used to save the ship. However, Brown also said that when they left *Gryfe*, the captain ordered them all to sign a paper claiming the barque had been unseaworthy.

A seaman named William Johnstone claimed Robinson had said he would be 'quite safe in the ship alone' and another steamer would pick him up. Robinson admitted that he took the captain's revolver, but claimed that le Bourdois had intended to shoot one of the men. Then a seaman named William Roberts gave further damning evidence against Robinson. He had joined the ship in St John's and was suspicious when he saw the boats prepared a day or so after the hands had been pumping the hold dry. He saw Robinson with the fore hatches open, which itself was unusual when they were at sea, and working with two men to bore a hole through the hull so every time *Gryfe* dipped, water gushed in. He said Robinson also ordered him to knock out the bow ports and to cut away the rigging, spread paraffin around and set fire to the ship. Roberts believed that Robinson had great influence over the master and mate.

The hands seemed to agree that while Captain and Joseph le Bourdois were quiet men, Robinson was a forceful, even a bullying character that it was best to avoid. He had been jailed in St John's for theft, and reinstated as an ordinary seaman before being appointed to the position of second mate. The evidence of the crew made it appear as if Robinson was more involved in the initial scuppering than he admitted. It is possible he was quite happy to have the ship appear partly waterlogged, but remain on board himself and claim at last part of the salvage.

A judge and jury, however, decided that Louis and Joseph le Bourdois were guilty of attempting to sink *Gryfe* to defraud the insurers of a total of £9,490, and the brothers were sentenced to ten years' penal servitude.

That was not the last of the misadventures of *Gryfe*, however. That was to come in November 1891, when, en route from Quebec to Liverpool with a cargo of oak and deal, she hit foul weather and was wrecked off the Irish coast near Kinsale. Eight men died as the unlucky ship met her end.

12

Orange and Green

Religious troubles have often arisen in the history of Glasgow. The best known is the clash between Catholic and Protestant, which has surfaced in various guises. In the sixteenth century armies of the two factions under their figureheads of Mary, Queen of Scots and King James came to a full-scale battle at Langside, near present-day Hampden Park. After that the differences withdrew to a quiet simmer rather than out and out war, although rival factions of Protestantism clashed in the seventeenth century. As Scotland became firmly Presbyterian, save for a scattering of Episcopalians and even fewer Roman Catholic enclaves, so the religious divide lessened in importance, but in the nineteenth century the troubles began again.

First came the Highland Clearances and an influx of Catholic Highlanders into Glasgow, and then came immigrants from Ireland. The religious divide had became more bitter in 1798, when Scottish soldiers helped put down what was seen as an Irish rebellion. The Scots served side by side with Protestant Irish Yeomanry, who only a few years previously had formed the Orange Order for mutual protection against what they perceived to be a threat from the Roman Catholic majority. When the uprising was subdued, many of the returning Scottish soldiers opened up their own Orange Lodges. The number of these military Orange Lodges in

Scotland grew, and by early 1820s there were around forty, mainly concentrated in the centre and west of the country. As the number of Catholics in the Glasgow area increased, the Orange Lodges were not allowed free rein. The Roman Catholic rivals were known as Ribbonmen because of the green ribbons they wore. As with the Orange Lodges, their origin and spiritual home was in Ireland.

By 1822 the Orange Lodges around Glasgow were keen to show their strength and their support for their religion and beliefs. They planned a Grand Orange Procession through Glasgow on Friday, 12 July, the anniversary of the Protestant victory at the Battle of the Boyne in 1690. However, the Glasgow magistrates refused permission for the march.

The situation remained at stalemate for a while, with the Lodges adamant they would parade and the magistrates saying no, but at nine o'clock on the morning of 12 July the Orangemen gathered for the march. With sashes, swords and banners, they formed up opposite the Duke Street Barracks in the East End of the city, and all 127 of them paraded to Fraser Hall in King Street. The outward march was a success, with no opposition, and the Orangemen reached Fraser Hall in triumph. However, news of the procession had spread and crowds clustered outside. Many of the crowd were Catholics seeking confrontation.

Around ten in the morning a lone Orangeman left the hall and a number of Catholics shoved him around and knocked him down. Naturally, other Orangemen emerged to support their colleague and face down the Catholics. For a while it seemed as if serious bloodshed would erupt as the Orangemen clustered outside the hall and the more numerous Catholics formed a semi-circle around them. There were shouts and threats and the brandishing of fists. While some of the Orangemen drew swords, the Catholics had a variety of weapons; one bold lad had sharpened a pitchfork on the pavement and jabbed it in the direction of the Orangemen. The situation remained tense until a magistrate brought along a strong body of police officers to diffuse the situation. There were a number of arrests, but with so many angry men still squaring up to each other, Sheriff Robertson called the army and marched a strong body of red-coated infantry to King Street.

Rather than separate the sides, the soldiers formed around the Orangemen and paraded them back to the Court. Not surprisingly, crowds gathered to watch the colourful spectacle of the Orange Lodges, complete with sashes and regalia, being escorted by what appeared a guard of honour, with the magistrates marching in front. When they reached the Court, the magistrates said they were not under arrest but had been escorted there to save them from attack. The situation had been resolved, but there were far more dangerous confrontations to come.

Billy and Dan

Daniel O'Connell, known as 'The Liberator', was one of the main figures opposing British rule in Ireland during the grim middle years of the nineteenth century. He had a chequered career, but was consistent in his support for the cause of the indigenous Catholic majority against the landlords, and was staunch in calling for the repeal of the Union between Great Britain and Ireland. With opponents as formidable as Wellington and Peel, his star still shone bright even after his imprisonment for sedition and his name is still remembered. In 1875, twenty-eight years after his death and with agitation for Irish Home Rule still alive, the centenary of his birth was marked with processions. Inevitably there were clashes as Orangemen opposed what they called Ribbonmen. Partick, then just outside the Glasgow boundary, saw some of the worst violence.

The demonstrations to mark the centenary of O'Connell's birth took place on Saturday, 7 August 1875. There were bands playing, people marching in a fairly orderly fashion and colours on display but on the whole Glasgow was peaceable. It was not until the marchers returned to the neighbouring burghs that celebration degenerated into chaos and red blood polluted the emerald green of the marchers. Given the passions for and against Home Rule, it was nearly inevitable that a brief flicker of trouble would lead to whole-scale rioting that involved police from three forces: special constables, Volunteers and had the army on standby.

Trouble

The trouble began around eight on the Saturday night when around two hundred men – a fragment of the main procession – returned to their homes in Partick. They were in high spirits, singing and displaying their banners, and it is possible that some carried sticks, either to help them on the march or in case they were opposed by the more aggressive members of the Orange party.

Although the parade had been ostensibly to honour the life of O'Connell, there was an underlying and more contemporary motive, for Ireland was in the throes of a Home Rule movement and the supporters of O'Connell, called the 'Dans' after his first name, were often supporters of that Irish cause. To the Orangemen, and perhaps also to a number of themselves, the Home Rulers were sometimes known as Ribbonmen after the Catholic Irish association of that name.

Quite a crowd had gathered to watch the return of the marchers to Partick, including a number of people who were more inclined to the Orange or Unionist side and were openly hostile to Home Rule. For some unknown reason, one of the marchers thumped one of the crowd, who retaliated by punching the man in the mouth. Others joined in the fun and in minutes what had been an orderly, if raucous march became pandemonium. The few Partick police moved in and snatched some of the main participants, which helped calm the situation. However, the spark had flown and the tinderbox that was Partick exploded into violence. The police were kept busy dashing from place to place, trying to keep the peace as the two parties clashed with sticks and stones and the night-time peace was shattered with the faction war cries of 'Billy!' and 'Dan!' There were bloody casualties among the police as well as the public, with one officer smashed on the head with a brick. The noise subsided around midnight, by which time the police had arrested forty of the rioters.

The daylight hours of Sunday passed without incident, but there was a feeling of growing tension as the evening drew to a close. The police were in readiness. They patrolled the streets and watched at Partick Cross, the natural centre of the town where two roads intersected. Those five constables at the Cross must have felt like the loneliest men in Scotland when a force of pro-Home Rulers – estimated at between 200 and 300 – targeted them.

The mob came from Glasgow, shouting as they surged toward the Cross, 'Come on, boys. We'll take the town!' However, the constables were not as isolated as they thought. A number of the inhabitants of Partick came to their aid and the combined force pushed the attackers back over the old Kelvin Bridge to Glasgow. The local Orangemen, including the Star of Erin Band, later claimed the credit for providing this reinforcement and this may well be true. The invaders were not yet defeated and tried more than once to gain a foothold in Partick but were repulsed each time. No sooner had the police scattered one mob than another – about 200 strong – charged over the second, new bridge to the burgh and assaulted the police at their stronghold at the Cross.

By that time more police had arrived and Captain Edwards had thirty men under his command, but rather than wait for the Home Rulers to come to him, Edwards ordered a baton charge just as the attackers launched a preliminary barrage of stones and bricks. Although the police were vastly outnumbered, they were also disciplined and had a single purpose. The Home Rulers were pushed back again, losing twenty of their number to the police. Some of the rioters resisted strongly and there were many tough struggles before the ringleaders were in custody. There was rough work in Bridge Street when the inhabitants of an attic flat bombarded everybody below with a barrage of stones. One man even stood on the roof, throwing slates. The police charged into the stair and up the dark steps, booted open the barricaded door and arrested all six people inside. The Orange Hall was targeted with the windows and the lamp outside smashed by stones.

Naturally, Provost Thomson was unhappy to see his town turned into a battlefield. He contacted his southern neighbour, the Sheriff of Lanarkshire, and asked for whatever help was available. He also called out the Volunteers, the Victorian equivalent of the Territorial Army, and enrolled thirty of them, plus other respectable people, as special constables. One of these specials was a woman, Mrs Rachel Hamilton. Over six feet tall and about seventeen stone, she was better known as 'Big Rachel', and it would be a brave rioter who tackled her. Provost Thomson also willingly accepted police help from Glasgow and Hillhead. The Glasgow Police did not come into Partick, but Superintendent Brown of the Central District ensured his men guarded the bridges that led from Glasgow to Partick and kept strong patrols on the main streets.

Crowds congregated at the Cross and the atmosphere in Partick remained tense, with the occasional sudden burst of noise an indication of unseen trouble in the dim backstreets. People leaned from the upper windows of tenements to hurl stones and other missiles at the groups of youths and young men who roamed the darkening streets, with a scattering of casualties. Passers-by and the unwary were challenged with the threatening, 'Are you a Billy or a Dan?' with the wrong choice meaning a possible trip to the nearest hospital.

Newton Street was the scene of a fairly major confrontation, with every ground-floor window smashed and the Roman Catholic chapel and the windows of the house of Father Gallagher, the local priest, especially targeted. Father Gallagher had been in the area for twenty years and was a man who spread peace among his flock. As a mark of their respect, some of his male parishioners had offered to protect him, but Father Gallagher turned the offer down in order to minimise trouble; it was a decision he may have regretted when the bricks came in a constant hail and the chants sang out from the night, 'Billy! Billy! Billy!' Further west, past the gasworks, the night was relatively peaceful.

The Specials were stood down and sent home at one in the morning. The day division of police were retained for another two hours, then dismissed with orders to return at seven after a hard-earned four hours' sleep. The deep dark passed, but in the grim early hours of Monday morning men returned to work in the town, or sidled to the Cross to meet their companions and wonder what excitement the day would bring. They saw the streets littered with bricks, roofing tiles and rocks, and pointed to the broken windows and ominous pools of drying blood. The shopkeepers opened up for business but kept the protective shutters in place.

At ten in the morning there was a surge of movement to the court-house, where the prisoners, complete with swollen lips, cut faces and black eyes, were to be tried. They were not at all subdued. They joked, sang, rattled their metal drinking cups from the cell bars and waved to their friends as they were remanded in custody for another day. Groups of both factions roamed the streets, ignoring the faces that stared at them from tenement windows. There was some confusion in the town when a rumour spread that a mob was coming down the Dumbarton Road from Glasgow, and scores of men moved to the Kelvin Bridge to confront the supposed invasion, then returned to the Cross when the bridge remained disappointingly empty. Only three men crossed the Kelvin, and despite the fact they were probably innocently looking for work, they were accused of being 'spies for the Ribbonmen' and set upon. Two, Samuel Gallagher and Patrick Harvey, were badly cut and bruised.

The tension did not abate. The authorities sent telegrams to the military barracks at Hamilton and Gallowgate: cavalry and infantry were readied to march to Partick. Chief Constable McCall whistled up more Glasgow police to patrol the western streets of the city. In the early afternoon thirty of them arrived in Partick Court Hall and waited for the trouble to begin as Provost Thomson ordered the Partick pubs to close and asked Superintendent Cornelly of the County Police to supply men from the Hillhead District. Cornelly obliged by sending fifteen constables. In the meantime, crowds gathered at the Cross, seething, simmering, waiting. There was an occasional shout for Billy and at five o'clock, as more workmen appeared and women began to drift from their windows to the streets, Provost Thomson appeared and read the Riot Act, which gave him the authority to dispel crowds with as much force as necessary. He allowed one hour's grace. Many in the crowd cheered. Some drifted back to their homes. There was desultory street violence; the police helped the victims. In Glasgow the police on the Dumbarton Road broke up groups of potential troublemakers and cracked a few heads, not all of them innocent. An omnibus rattled over the bridge from Glasgow with twenty more police. They waited at the gasworks, ready to defend the western boundary. Menace lurked in the gathering darkness.

Around half past eight there was a scare that hundreds of Ribbonmen were cutting staves from the woods around the Three Tree or Pear Tree Well, an old holy well beside the River Kelvin. The police sent a small force to check on the story but a priest, possibly Father Gallagher, got there first and shooed away the dozen or so young boys whose presence had started the panic. Once more the Volunteers proved their worth as they patrolled the town and helped the police, while bands of Orangemen picked on anybody they suspected of Home Rule sympathies.

Once again trouble arrived with oncoming darkness. The crowd at the Cross began their nightly barrage of stones, combined with the usual pointless dashes to places where the Ribbonmen were rumoured to be gathering. There was a more serious incident when a man named Patrick Smith appeared with a loaded Colt revolver at the west end of Dumbarton Road. Sticks and stones were one thing, but firearms added a different complexion, so the police and Volunteers combined to capture him. Smith ran into Crawford Street and ducked into a tenement stair. The specials followed and caught him in the top flat, but after Smith was arrested the crowd surged forward to rescue him and there was a smart stramash before he was hustled to the police office.

A rising roar from the Overnewton Toll signalled more trouble as the police wrestled with a large body of men armed with pointed staves; a mob tried to cross the bridge over the Kelvin and the police grabbed the ringleaders. The police and Volunteers also responded to other alarms and disturbances, stamped on the worst of the problems and arrested who they thought were the most dangerous. In the course of the night they also collected a fine variety of weapons. As well as the revolver, they raked in a sword bayonet, pokers, a hatchet, a mallet, a pair of tongs, a long length of iron fashioned like a sword and a dagger, lovingly inscribed with the word 'faith'.

By Tuesday, 10 August, Patrick had returned to near normality. The shopkeepers removed the protective shutters, and although there were still police patrols in the streets and a crowd at the Cross, the tension had eased. There was a flurry of excitement at eight in the morning when the crowds cheered a short convoy of omnibuses that carried the prisoners from the police office in Anderson Street to Duke Street Prison. An hour later, the specials were sent home. Normal life resumed.

The prisoners were charged mostly with minor public order offences and were given brief sentences of a few weeks in jail. With a few exceptions, they treated the procedure as a joke, laughing with the audience. Among the prisoners was John Drummond, who had knocked down a policeman and run to the middle of the River Kelvin, where he was arrested – he got sixty days; and William Lafferty, who led a squad of men that attacked the original procession on Saturday and got forty days to think about it. William Crawford and John McDade were charged with throwing stones and carrying offensive weapons in the shape of pokers. Crawford said he had taken the poker from a man who attacked him, while McDade denied having a poker at all, despite the police having found it in his possession. Both got sixty days, but when McDade heard that he replied, 'I can do that on my head.'

Even when the riots faded away there was desultory party violence throughout Glasgow with people questioned as to their allegiance to Home

Rule or King Billy. A mob attacked Archibald McLaren and James Woods in Partick, knocking Woods down and stabbing McLaren, while in Anderston, Isabella White stabbed the Home Rule supporter Ann McDade. Rumours abounded. Catholics were going to attack Orange houses in Partick; Orangemen were planning to attack the Bridgeton Home Rule Instrumental Band as it marched through Rutherglen, Orangemen planned an assault on the Catholics in Partick. All proved false. Gradually peace returned, but the incipient violence simmered beneath the surface, waiting for an excuse to burst out again.

The Muldoon Mob

In many ways the nineteenth century was a precursor of the twentieth, and crime was no exception. The major gang troubles of the twentieth century were prefaced by skirmishes in the nineteenth, when groups of young men ran riot. Religion was cited as the excuse if not the reason for one bunch of young lads from deprived backgrounds attacking another bunch of lads who shared exactly the same problems. One of the most notorious gangs of the early 1880s was the Muldoon Mob.

Hurray for Billy

This group of angry young men professed to be Catholic, and targeted anybody they believed to be openly Protestant as they continued the disputes of the seventeenth century many of their forefathers had carried with them from Ireland. They finished 1879 in style, when on 8 November a howling group of them attacked a young apprentice fitter named Samuel Woods. It was around seven in a dark evening when Woods was marching through King Street as a member of the Apprentice Boys' Band. The band was playing 'Boyne Water', which one observer thought was likely to cause trouble. Cries of 'to hell with Dan' and 'hurrah for Billy' created some tension among the mixed crowd. One young boy, John Dewar, thought the tune was called 'To Hell with the Pope', which may help explain what happened next.

For some reason, Woods had fallen about forty yards behind the others and was quietly walking past the assembled crowd when four youths burst from the mouth of a close. The youths shouted, 'Are these the sons of William?' and suddenly they leaped on Woods. One punched him in the face and he staggered, but he quickly recovered and ran for the shelter of a nearby shop. It did little good, though, for they were right behind him. Woods tried to struggle through the shop door but they hauled him back, and the boots and fists were flying. They gave him 'a smash apiece', which knocked him to the ground, and then the boots hammered on his face and head until he was kicked unconscious.

As the Muldoons retreated in triumph, a woman came from the crowd to help. She took Woods to her house and washed the blood from him, but he was in a lot of pain. After he reported to the police office he was admitted into the Infirmary, where it was found his skull was badly fractured. The surgeons had to operate to remove a section of splintered bone that was pushed into his brain, so Woods was fortunate to survive. Three of the four attackers, David John Warden, John Muldoon and Michael McDermid, were sentenced to fifteen months with hard labour.

Trouble simmered throughout 1880 with minor disputes, and slogans of the rival parties were frequently heard in the streets. Whether the cry was for 'Billy' or 'Dan', the background of the people involved was so similar it makes the whole dispute appear utterly sad. In June 1881 there were a number of skirmishes in the East End, and although the reports are contradictory and confused, it seems that a man named Flynn from the Muldoon Mob was attacked by Matthew Brown of a rival Orange gang. Brown, who the magistrate called an 'insignificant wretch', had taken off his belt and smashed the buckle on Flynn's head. However, despite the best efforts of a witness with the suggestive name of 'Green Orator McIntyre', the case was not proven and both mobs were set free to continue their venomous careers.

The magistrate was not impressed with the part the police played, either. He accused them of being quick to arrest women traders with barrows but of running away 'out of sight whenever rows of these kind occur'.

'I'll Put a New Head on You'

There was a spate of such incidents that June, each one minor in itself but symptomatic of the larger problems of sectarianism and youth crime within the city. For example, there was fifteen-year-old Patrick Docherty, who was fined a guinea for shouting out, 'Hurray for Billy' in Bell Street, Calton, at midnight on Saturday, 4 June 1881. His ten-year-old brother Thomas was also in court for throwing bricks at the police, but instead of punishing him the magistrate sent him home and gave the boy's mother a stern warning about the conduct of her children, as well as the late hours they were keeping. On the other side there was Thomas Baker, who fastened his belt around a broken tumbler and ran riot at the head of a gang in Abercrombie Street, roaring, 'Hurray for Dan!' His mob crowded around two innocent men and demanded, 'Are you for Billy or Dan?' When the men hesitated, Baker helped them decide by adding, 'If you're not for Dan I'll put a new head on you and make a football out of the old one.' The magistrate did not appreciate his wit and gave him ten days in jail.

That same Saturday night there was a party scuffle in High Street and the police arrested two men, David McCallum and David Symington. As the two constables were taking their prisoner to the police office, a crowd gathered and demanded the release of the prisoner. The police refused and moved on, with Sergeant Guy coming up in support. Two brothers, Henry and John Miller, rushed up and attacked Guy, punched him to the ground and used the boot. The Millers were fined 63/- each.

Again that same night there was trouble in Bellgrave Street when Thomas Flannigan headed some of the Muldoon Mob. He took off his belt and swung it around his head so the heavy brass buckle whirred past people's heads. 'Fight me!' he challenged, but instead the police arrested him and threw him in jail.

That month saw more trouble in the Gallowgate when the rivals proved their allegiance to their respective faiths by bombarding each other with stones across the width of the street. In October the Muldoons were at it again, as one of their members, Mark Devlin, attacked a younger boy in Castle Street. This time the police were quick to react and Devlin, who already had a record for assault, spent the next sixty days in jail.

In the twentieth century, Glasgow would see gangs hundreds strong battling it out with bayonets and cut-throat razors, but in the nineteenth the gangs were small-scale, if still dangerous to lone passers-by.

The Barrack Street Penny Mob

As well as the gangs who fought for the sake of religion, there were those who were purely out for profit. In nineteenth-century Glasgow a peculiar type of gang emerged in the case of the 'penny mobs' of the 1880s and 1890s. The name said it all really, as the gangs roamed a certain area looking for some vulnerable victim, who they would approach mob-handed and demand a penny. Drunk men were favourite targets as they were seldom in a condition to defend themselves, and the ubiquitous penny could often expand to every penny the man possessed. Usually these petty thugs escaped scot-free, but occasionally they were caught and brought to court.

On the very early morning of 2 January 1889, one of the penny mobs was patrolling its territory in Barrack Street. They were about a dozen strong, aged from around fifteen to eighteen, and they pounced on three drunk men in quick succession. The first victim was John Forrest, from whom they stole £1 fourteen shillings, an ounce of tobacco, a knife and a box of matches. The second was Thomas Shannon, who they robbed of a massive 5d, and last was John Burns, who lost seven shillings to the gang. This particular penny mob was well known in the area, but constant success had made them over confident. A local resident, Ann Boyle, had watched their endeavours from her kitchen window.

Boyle also watched the aftermath as the youths fell out over their loot, argued and nearly fought. The police arrested five of them, who appeared in the Glasgow Sheriff Criminal Court on 15 January. They were James McGuire, Joseph Kean, Robert Barbour and Alexander Mulholland. Of the boys, Mulholland, believed to be the leader, was also the oldest and was jailed for a year. McGuire got nine months, Kean and Barbour five months and Montgomery, the youngest, two months.

As soon as the sentences were announced, the boys waved their hats to their friends in the public gallery and shouted 'Cheer up' across the courtroom. The gangs of the nineteenth century may not have been as numerous as those of the twentieth, but they were every bit as brash.

13

The Fraudsters

There were a number of ways of taking money from people apart from straightforward robbery, and the Glasgow crooks knew them all. One of the simplest but most effective was to look for trusting people.

Cold-Hearted Tricksters

On Wednesday, 11 October 1826, the smuggler James Cairnie stalked the streets, along with a tall, elegant man in a fine blue coat and fancy boots who claimed to be McIlvain, a merchant from Belfast. They hunted together, and when they saw the open face of a sawyer named David Keir as he walked along Jamaica Street, they knew they had their man. McIlvain made the first move. He emerged from the shelter of a close just behind Keir, pointed to the ground and pretended to find a silver sixpence.

'Did you drop this, sir?' Honest McIlvain asked.

'Indeed, no, sir, I did not,' Keir replied, after checking his pockets.

'Well then, sir, it is a shared good fortune,' McIlvain said. 'I propose we repose to the nearest tavern and spend it between us.'

The offer of a free drink was too good to refuse, so Keir accompanied McIlvain to the pub, where McIlvain lost no time in spreading news of their fortune to two other gentlemen, one of whom happened to be Cairnie. The two men joined them at a table; the drams of whisky encouraged the flow of conversation from luck to fate and then to friendly games of chance. Cairnie suggested that he and his companion toss coins for guinea stakes – heads against tails – and the table became a scene of friendly competition and laughter. McIlvain joined in, but his luck was obviously out that evening, as he lost far more games than he won.

Keir watched but did not participate until Cairnie leaned closer and whispered that McIlvain was a 'young gentleman who had nothing else to do but sport his money; he had been left £6,000 by a rich relation, don't you know'.

Keir fell for the trap. His purse was quite slim so a few of McIlvain's guineas would be most welcome. He agreed to gamble.

'Good man,' his companions chorused. They used Keir's hat as a depository for the stakes; each man put in what they had, with the winner to take all. Keir dropped his £1 17/- on top of the soft sheen of the golden guineas and watched as Cairnie moved to the door, where there was better light to count the coins. And then Cairnie ran, with McIlvain and the other man joining him. Keir was not quite the dupe he seemed to be and hollered for help; half the men in the pub joined in the chase, and Cairnie and McIlvain were captured, together with Keir's cash, but the final man escaped.

Bailie Graham had no sympathy for the sportsmen and awarded a prize of sixty days in jail, while Keir retained his money.

The Devious Captain Lang

Captain Lang was a charming man who claimed to have been an officer of the 64th Regiment of Foot. He descended upon a succession of lodging houses across Scotland and left without paying the bill and usually with a number of household possessions tucked into his travelling bag. He moved quickly from place to place, always keeping ahead of the police, who knew his game but could never quite catch him. They had an excellent description of him: he was around twenty-four, dapper in appearance, held himself as erect as a guardsman and was around five foot six in height. He had a dark complexion, and his eyebrows met above his nose. The police even knew what he wore: either a brown coat or a blue one, but still he evaded them time after time.

At the end of November 1818 the police traced the elusive captain to Edinburgh, where he was suspected of having graced a New Town lodging house before leaving it short of a few towels, six silver teaspoons and a pair of silver tongs. From Edinburgh he slipped across the country to Glasgow, where he formed a partnership with a like-minded but unfortunately anonymous man. Their original plan was to pretend to be agents for Prince Gregor MacGregor, who was then searching for finance and emigrants for the country of Poyais in Central America. Ironically, and unknown to Captain Lang, MacGregor was probably the greatest confidence trickster of the century, and surely one of the greatest of all time. The country he claimed to represent was a complete fantasy, yet he fooled the authorities in both Britain and in France; he had false money and documents printed, and sent boatloads of paying emigrants over to what in effect was a malarial swamp. Many died.

Captain Lang was not at that level, but he did his deceitful best. Together with his new partner he slipped across country to Perth and acted the dandy, with fancy coats, hired horses and footmen, to give the impression of a rich man. He pretended to be raising recruits for MacGregor, and accepted money from eager volunteers who wanted to become officers in MacGregor's army and were willing to pay both for the privilege and for their passage. However, whenever Lang and his companion were discovered as frauds, they ran to find fresh victims elsewhere.

MacGregor had genuinely been a soldier fighting for the independence of Venezuela from Spain. Arriving in South America as a private, he had shown real military genius and had risen through the ranks of Simón

Bolívar's army to become a general; one of the many Scots who fought for the independence of other nations. Although Lang claimed the rank of an army captain, he had no such distinguished background. The police suspected he was nearly illiterate, and his military career extended to a spell as a private in various militia regiments that had never experienced the foul fog of war.

With Perth drained dry, Captain Lang moved back to Glasgow. His new trick was to pretend to be a commercial traveller, dupe a gull into taking a journey with him in a hired gig and rob his victim while out in the country. However, when he tried this less-that-subtle approach with a Paisley man, it backfired, and Captain Lang was tossed into jail and banished from Glasgow under the threat of a lot more time behind bars. But Captain Lang was nothing if not confident, and he returned yet again to the city and recommenced his old game of charming landladies into allowing him free reign of their homes so he could walk off with whatever took his fancy.

His career lasted a few more months, during which he ripped off a number of trusting dupes. First he rented a parlour and bedroom from the widow Mrs King in Hutcheson Street and decamped with her much prized silver toddy ladles. Then he graced the home of John Ewing Wright in Dempster Street, where he stole a pair of silver sugar tongs and six silver teaspoons, as well as a number of other articles. His next stop was the inn of John Homes in Finnieston, which kindly provided a silk shawl, £8 in banknotes and a handful of silver coins.

Perhaps the people of Glasgow were growing wise to the silver-tongued pseudo-captain, but he began to resort to more direct action to gain his prizes. On 17 December 1818, he used a picklock to break into the property of Thomas Arnot, a publican in McAlpin Street, and found a lovely new shirt for himself, and on the same day, in the same street and by the same method, he added a silk handkerchief to his collection. The previous owner, Daniel Murray, surely did not need it any longer. However, that was Lang's last haul. On Sunday, 20 December, the police picked him up in Anderston and held him secure. When they searched him, they found a silver watch and other items, but they could not trace the owner.

In late April 1819 Captain Lang made his appearance in court. He came ready for his big day, dressed in a blue surtout and with a black silk handkerchief to show his gentlemanly status. However, the jury was not fooled, and the judge sent him to Australia for seven years to see if his charms would work in a warmer climate.

The Gudgeon Strikes Back

No area of life was safe from swindlers, cheats, confidence tricks or forgers. When they were buying in the markets, Victorian Glaswegians had to be aware of false weights and diluted foodstuffs; when they were serving in the shops, they had to look for forged coins and attempts to swindle them. There were beggars with false credentials and servants with false references, as well as bogus workmen and baby-minders who used laudanum as a means of keeping their charges quiet. Even when they were travelling, Victorians had to have their wits about them, as pickpockets and card sharps infested ships and railway carriages.

It is hard to imagine that gamblers could haunt railway trains in Scotland, with there being such short distances between stations, but card sharps were seemingly as common on Scottish routes as they were on the much longer distances in the United States. The gamblers tended to ride on trains to the big cities and look for dupes or 'gudgeons' to fleece.

On 19 February 1856, a commercial traveller named Charles Robertson was travelling on a Glasgow-bound train when he fell in with a gang of three card sharps. He had only a few sovereigns and, as was usually the case, what started as a friendly game with him winning more than he lost soon became serious, with him losing all that he had. By that time Robertson was hooked, however, and he put forward his much treasured gold watch as a stake. He lost that as well. Robertson was not pleased at that outcome, and arranged to meet the gamblers at the Royal Hotel where he stayed so he could buy it back at its full valuation of £15. By then Robertson had realised he had been conned, and he decided to work a little revenge.

Rather than greet the card sharps himself, Robertson recruited the largest and most muscular of the hotel porters to act on his behalf. The porter agreed, so when the sharp appeared with the watch and a hopeful leer, he was shown into a small room where the porter waited. The interview was very short and very sweet, at least for Robertson. Nearly as soon as the door closed, the porter recovered the stolen watch, grabbed the sharp around the throat, dragged him out of the hotel, turned him around and booted him hard up the backside so he virtually flew into the street. That was the last Robertson saw of the gambling gang, but others were not so fortunate.

Despite their humiliation at the hands of the porter, the sharps returned to their operations on the Glasgow train, with an unknown number of victims over the next few days. One unfortunate was a church minister, who should have known better than to gamble, but he lost £10 for his sins; and then the gang found a German on the Caledonian Line from Liverpool. The sharps saw he was a foreigner and sidled up to him with the same technique. They started with a friendly game, gambled for small stakes at first and then, when the money in the pool increased, stripped him of every penny he possessed and a fine German gold watch worth £60. Not surprisingly, the German was most unhappy and reported his experiences to the station master at Buchanan Street Railway Station. The station master immediately locked the sharps' carriage and called the police. One fraudster escaped, but the police took the remaining two to Cowcaddens Police Office. They admitted they had the money and the watch, but claimed they had won them fair and square, and without proof the police could only warn them and let them go. The German never saw his watch again.

Other frauds were more elaborate.

A Dead Man Giving Evidence

A death in the family is always a sad time. The feeling of immediate loss is followed by numbness as the realisation of finality slowly sinks in. Sometimes there is an overwhelming expression of grief, particularly if the relationship has been close.

That seemed to be the case when Hugh Jamieson visited Dr Connor's consulting room on 17 August 1881. He claimed his first name was William, but he was so upset he could barely articulate his sorrow. His wife Margaret had to explain what the matter was, and Dr Connor calmed him down in case his howls alarmed the shopkeeper next door. Jamieson's father had been fit and well two days before, but had been struck by sudden pains in his side, aggravated by a cough. He had died the previous day, before Jamieson even had time to send for a doctor.

Dr Connor listened with sympathy. He had known Mrs Jamieson for upwards of six years, so he had no qualms about issuing a death certificate when they asked for one. He knew the Jamiesons were not well off, and if he had gone to inspect the dead man he would have had to charge them for his time, so he trusted them and filled in the form. He claimed to have been the medical attendant at the scene and stated that heart disease had caused the death.

It was a small, routine matter in a century when death struck without warning, so Dr Connor bid the Jamiesons farewell and got on with his day. It was November before he saw the Jamiesons again, and this time they were accompanied by a woman named Bridget McDonald. This time it was McDonald who was grieving, crying with such violence that Dr Connor had to intervene to soothe her. McDonald told the doctor that her father, Allan McDonald, had died the previous night after suffering a terrible cough and severe pains in his left side. His death had been too sudden for anybody to call a doctor, but the Jamiesons had been in the house and would certify to the truth of his statement. Hugh Jamieson claimed he was the son of the dead man.

Kindly Dr Connor again saved the family the expense of a home visit by issuing a medical certificate without inspecting the body. He put the death down as bronchitis and wrote:'I hereby certify that I attended Allan McDonald. He died on 21 November 1881 at 205 Duke Street. I last saw the deceased on that day, and the cause of death was as understated.'

The doctor did not admit that, although he had known Mr and Mrs McDonald, he had never met Allan McDonald, Senior, in his life. He was the second doctor the Jamiesons had approached for a death certificate. The first, Dr James Mullan of Crown Street, was disappointingly conscientious and actually tried to see the body. Mrs Jamieson brought him to Duke Street, but when she refused him access to the supposedly deceased man, he said, 'This is all humbug,' claimed she was swindling him and stormed away. Only then did the Jamiesons and McDonald approach Dr Connor again.

Gradually the scheme was revealed. The Jamiesons were trying out an insurance scam. The supposedly dead men had been insured through the Prudential Insurance Company, the Scottish Legal Life Assurance Company and the City of Glasgow Friendly Society. Overall, Hugh Jamieson, Senior was insured for a total of £28 2/-, and Allan McDonald for £49 15/-. When the case came to the Circuit Court, the supposedly deceased Allan McDonald was called to appear and, as well as being obviously alive and well, denied all knowledge of the fraud. Hugh and Margaret Jamieson were both found guilty of six charges, while Bridget McDonald, Hugh's sister-in-law, was found guilty of two. The judge, Lord Young, sent Jamieson to jail for eighteen months, his wife for six months and McDonald for four months.

The Drowned Missionary

Women were every bit as good at fooling the public as men were. In spring and summer 1844 there was an attractive woman knocking at the doors of respectable gentlemen in Glasgow. She claimed to be Miss Smith, the daughter of Mr Smith, the missionary who was drowned when his ship was sunk. The supposed Miss Smith only approached men of means, but after a while she came to the house of a man more sceptical than usual. This man asked the name of the ship in which Mr Smith drowned, and when he could not trace her in Lloyd's List, he notified the police. Neither her looks nor her charm affected the constable who picked her up, and she proved to be a well-known fraudster named Mrs Neil.

False Money

Throughout the century, the people of Glasgow had to be careful of the money they used. Forgeries were so commonplace that in April 1804 the Glasgow magistrates issued a warning about the different types of counterfeit coins in circulation. There were two types of false shillings. One was made of copper and finished with a silver colour, but it did not look quite right and if rapped against a solid surface it did not ring true. The second type was from Ireland and was made of silver, but was about half the thickness of real shillings. There were also seven-shilling pieces that were supposedly made of gold, but were instead made of copper gilt. The magistrates advised that anybody accustomed to handling gold would recognise these coins instantly by their lighter weight. During that period foreign currency was quite common in Scotland, and the Spanish silver dollar was also easily forged. However, the coin was too shiny and the copper base shone through the thin plating in places, while the king's head was very shallowly struck into the coin.

The Irish Connection

Much of the base coinage used in Glasgow originated in Ireland and was imported by ship, sometimes in surprisingly large quantities. One such case was discovered in July 1848 when two criminal officers, McColl and

Patrick, were engaged in a crackdown on pawnbrokers suspected of resetting stolen property. They pushed into the Bridgegate shop of Mr and
Mrs Smith. As the detectives spoke to Mr Smith they realised his wife
was trying to hide a portmanteau behind her back. Naturally suspicious,
they took hold of her and grabbed the case. It felt heavy, so they opened
it and found it crammed with forged pennies and halfpennies of Queen
Victoria and King George IV. There were 900 coins, all made of lead,
thinly sheeted with copper and packed together in tubes of 120. Mrs
Smith had brought them over on the packet boat from Ireland.

In another, similar case, on 21 April 1847, Chief Criminal Officer
Brown of the Gorbals Police was doing a routine search of a Bridgegate
pawn dealer when he came across a few obviously false copper coins. He
continued the search and found more. He ordered the people in the house
to turn out their pockets and then to strip. One of them, a lodger named
John Hanley, was found with a large number of pennies all dated 1843.
Brown was suspicious of the coincidence of date and checked the coins
thoroughly. They were all identical, as if they had come from the same
mould, with the same flaws; they were too light and the copper was not
pure. After some questioning, Hanley admitted he had brought the coins
from Ireland.

However, all these frauds pale in insignificance compared to a disaster
that rocked the city to its foundations in the late 1870s.

The Great City of Glasgow Bank Crash

Some crimes were sordid, personal and very violent. Others were imper-
sonal in nature but created ripples that affected the lives of thousands.
The great City of Glasgow Bank crash of 1878 was one of the latter. It
was a white-collar crime in an institution that was considered rock solid,
but whose directors had led the investors and shareholders into massive
debt. In an age when shareholders held unlimited liability, they paid a
heavy price that resulted in bankruptcies and suicides.

The City of Glasgow Bank had specialised in small investors ever since its foundation in 1839. It was a friendly business that opened late in the evening so that men could deposit the takings from their businesses, and it had a solidly Glaswegian headquarters, first in Virginia Street and then Glassford Street. The bank expanded steadily and paid annual dividends of between 9 and 12 per cent, and by June 1878 there were 133 branches, and it was licensed to print its own notes, backed by deposits of eight million pounds. That month the directors announced the welcome news that the bank would pay the shareholders a dividend of 12 per cent. However, the joy turned to unbelieving despondency on 1 October that same year when the news came that the bank, a cornerstone of finance in the Second City of the Empire, had collapsed.

The directors had known of the looming disaster for some time and had tried to sidestep the crash. They had caused their own problems by poor judgement and investing in risky speculation. The initial investments were in United States Railway stocks and in mining companies, but when these failed to bring in a return the directors attempted to recoup their losses. In place of American investments they looked to the colonies, granting massive loans of some £6 million to four firms in India and into New Zealand and Australian sheep farms and land, without properly checking the viability of the outlay. When they realised the bank's money was vanishing, the directors panicked.

Until that point the directors' acts had been foolish rather than criminal, but now they began the great cover-up. They created false reports concerning the amount of gold reserves the bank held to back their paper notes, secretly bought their own shares to push up the price to over £230 for a £100 share and published ludicrously optimistic reports of the bank's financial position. With no reason to doubt such an ostensibly stable organisation, small businessmen continued to invest their life savings and shareholders continued to trust their directors. Only when the directors realised they were deep in trouble did they ask their neighbouring banks for help.

The general managers of nine of the most important Scottish banks met in the Bank of Scotland headquarters in Edinburgh on Monday, 30 September 1878. When the directors of the City of Glasgow Bank confessed they had falsified their figures, the collective general managers appointed an accountant named George Jamieson to check the books and have a report ready within twenty-four hours. Astonishingly, Jamieson managed to meet this deadline and reported a loss of around £3 million. He also said the figures had been wrongly entered for years. The last published balance sheet of 5 June 1878 had stated that the bank had a capital balance in excess of one and a half million pounds. In reality, by the end of September there was nothing in the kitty, and creditors were demanding over five million pounds. Rather than offer assistance, the other banks bade a soldier's farewell and refused any help, on the basis that to do so would damage the integrity of the entire system.

There was only one thing left to do. The directors of the City of Glasgow Bank slammed shut their doors, 'until further notice', to prevent any withdrawals and declare their business at an end.

Nevertheless, the other banks were not totally heartless. They continued to accept the notes of the Glasgow Bank to help prevent a general panic; pure self-preservation rather than compassion for a drowning bank. Naturally, crowds gathered outside the Virginia Street headquarters of the bank, hoping to withdraw their savings. The police were on alert for trouble but rather than a riot there was an aura of deep gloom as the investors contemplated a future of unemployment and poverty. The crowds may have been slightly cheered at the astounding spectacle of the directors, three of Glasgow's most respectable citizens, being arrested by the police. But however gratifying it may have been to see white-collar criminals being treated the same as those with dirty fingernails, the ripple effect proved unpleasant for the city.

The worst affected were the 1,200 shareholders, who had to bear the entire burden of the loss. For example, if a businessman held £100 in shares, he was liable for £2,750 of the bank's debt, an almost unthinkable sum for an ordinary man. The next affected were the several hundred small businesses that used the bank. Many collapsed, ruining the owners and putting their families on the bread line. The Inverness-based Caledonian Banking Company was a major shareholder and nearly went to the wall, damaging business across the Highlands. People lost confidence in banks and demanded gold in exchange for banknotes, which was good news for the pickpockets who waited outside the banks to target the unwary. There is a story, perhaps apocryphal but which highlights the mood of the period, that one elderly man stalked Virginia Street with a loaded rifle, hoping to catch sight of one of the bank directors. Other investors took a more passive approach and committed quiet suicide.

So while a garrotter or burglar could ruin the life of one victim, the white-collar bankers had destroyed hundreds at a stroke. The collapse of the City of Glasgow Bank caused a great scandal, and the press covered the High Court trial of eight of its officials. The accused men were Lewis Potter, who was also a city merchant; William Morrison the accountant; the bank manager Robert Stronach; and a mason, a magistrate and three businessmen, including a man named James Morton. As the trial continued, details of the fraud emerged. Morton had drawn out several thousand pounds every week with only two men, Stronach and Morrison, aware of the transactions. Morton used the money for the bank's wild colonial speculations.

After twelve days of intense interest, the trial came to its conclusion. Lewis Potter, a director for twenty years, was given eighteen months for fraud. Robert Stronach, the manager, got handed the same. Four other directors and the secretary were locked up for eight months.

The sentences seem very light for a crime that affected so many people and which created Glasgow's worst financial crisis of the century. The Scottish public demanded heavier sentences, but the court seemed to consider white-collar crime less worrying than casual assaults or petty theft that could end with the perpetrator given a ten-year sentence. There was an upside, although it came too late to help those involved in the crash. The 1879 Companies Act allowed Joint Stock Banks to become limited liability, so shareholders would not be responsible for the entire debts of the company. Companies also began to publish detailed and hopefully accurate balance sheets, with regular audits. Nevertheless, even in the second decade of the twenty-first century, banks still collapse and distrust remains.

14

Offences of a Sexual Nature

In common with every other city in the world, Glasgow was afflicted with sexual crimes. There was the usual variety: rape, sex with a minor and criminal assault. This chapter will look at two cases where sex was a major factor, but both are widely different from each other and both raised public interest at the time.

'In the Name of God and the Queen, Help'

The first case took place on Saturday, 14 July 1864, at Sandyknowes Common, on the Govan Road, which was then about two miles outside the City of Glasgow. An elderly farmer named Thomas Learmonth and a young man from Edinburgh were chatting quietly as they strolled along East Loan Road. They both looked up as two people hurried toward them. One was a woman, the other a young boy: mother and son. The woman was agitated, pointed behind her and pleaded for them to go and help as a 'man there was murdering a woman'.

Learmonth and the youth hurried on until they heard a long, low groan and found a half-dressed man lying beside an unconscious woman. The man was about thirty, tall and strong, and looked like a labouring man, with his moleskin trousers and canvas jacket. Learmonth noticed blood on his jacket and on the exposed underclothes beneath.

Without hesitation, Learmonth grabbed the man, who wilted immediately. When the man asked if he could get dressed, Learmonth agreed. The man seemed passive, but as soon as Learmonth began to take him back down the road toward Glasgow, he leaped on top of the old farmer. Although outmatched by a much younger and more aggressive opponent, Learmonth sent his companion for help and struggled on. The fight attracted a crowd, mostly of rough-looking labourers, and although Learmonth begged, 'In the name of God and the Queen, help', they only watched as the younger man gradually wore him down. As a farmer, Learmonth was strong but if help had not arrived he would have been overpowered.

The man who came to help was a fireman named Andrew MacPherson. Between him and Learmonth they dragged the supposed rapist to the nearest police officer. He proved to be Michael McGlinchey, an Irish labourer in his early twenties, and a private in the Londonderry Militia. As the police escorted him to the office, they asked why he had raped the woman. McGlinchey's reply was unusual: 'I did nothing to her, and although I should get twenty years, I will get my meat anyhow, and that is all I can get by working.'

Gradually the story came out. The young woman was Margaret Addie, a very respectable young lady who lived at Weymouth Terrace, off the Paisley Road. She had been visiting a friend in Murrow Place in Govan, but had left late at night to get home. The night was cool and clear, ideal for walking, but when she came to the lonely Common near the Cessford Nursery outside Govan, Addie walked a lot faster. When McGlinchey shouted out to her, Addie put her head down and tried to ignore him, but McGlinchey was persistent.

When McGlinchey then reached out to take hold of her, Addie screamed and tried to run, but he grabbed her. She tried to break free. McGlinchey was stronger and held her tight. She opened her mouth in a terrified scream, pulling this way and that as she struggled, but McGlinchey slapped her brutally on the face and knocked her to the ground.

When Addie tried to scream again, McGlinchey hit her another time. 'Hold your tongue,' he ordered. Grabbing her by the hair, he dragged her further from the path and into a field on the nearby farm of Heathery-hall, knocked her helpless and raped her.

After Learmonth rescued her two men from Ibroxholm helped Addie to a doctor, who found she had a broken nose, a burst lip, a gashed fore-head and a number of other abrasions. Her clothing was ripped and sodden with blood, and she was so weak with shock and loss of blood that there were fears she would not survive.

As Addie lay in bed in her own house, the police inspected the scene of the rape. They found the ground trampled and speckled with Addie's blood, her hat yards away from her hair cushion, her belt and her brooch all scattered across the ground and smeared with blood. They also located two girls who had seen McGlinchey hanging around shortly before his attack on Addie. They said he had looked so menacing that they had altered their route to avoid hm.

A more significant pair of witnesses was the mother and son who had initially told Learmonth about the rape. The mother was Catherine Boyle and her son was thirteen-year-old Robert. Catherine Boyle had seen McGlinchey savagely kicking Addie as she pleaded, 'Let me alone. Let me alone.' McGlinchey told her to keep quiet. Catherine Boyle had grabbed her son's hand and run away. She met Learmonth and gabbled out her story to him.

The police also heard McGlinchey's side of the story. He had spent the day drinking in Glasgow and claimed to have little memory of what had happened. However, the arresting officers said he had been sober.

The case caused quite a stir in Glasgow, possibly because it was the rape of a gentlewoman by a labouring man. There was extensive news-paper coverage and a number of letters in the local press suggesting the use of the cat of nine tails for rapists, and a fund was started to raise a reward for MacPherson, the fireman who helped Learmonth. When the case came to court in December 1864, a number of character witnesses spoke highly of McGlinchey, saying he was a quiet and inoffensive man, but the judge was not impressed and gave him penal servitude for life.

A Beastly Affair

The second case here also had a strong sexual nature, but this time the victim was a man of equal social standing to Margaret Addie, and nearly equal innocence. The story is a tangle of money, debt, revenge and deceit, with a Union Street solicitor and Writer to the Signet (WS) named Francis Paterson as the fly in the spider's web. There were a number of spiders, with the two principals being John Boyle and his wife Margaret Boyle.

John Boyle was the tenant of a small broker and cloth merchant's shop in McAlpin Street, a short walk from upmarket Argyle Street, and only a spit from the firm of Barclay and Curles on the Clyde, but either business was not good, or Boyle was unwilling to pay his dues, for in 1858 he fell behind with his rent. The owner of the shop, George Hunter of Renfrew, and his factor, Francis Paterson, took Boyle to the Small Debt Court for £11 6/8d due for unpaid rent, with a threat to 'poind' if the money was not paid within ten days. Poinding was a peculiarly vicious legal action in Scotland where a debtor's goods could be dragged out and sold to pay the debts. It was an act of public humiliation that caused great resentment and shame.

The Boyles certainly resented being dragged before the court with the threat of poinding hanging over their heads, and they planned their revenge. On 25 February, the day after Paterson created the decree against the Boyles, Mrs Boyle met him in the street, apparently by chance. She seemed slightly agitated and said she did not have any money with her, but she would pay him £5 of the rent money if he came with her to the McAlpin Street shop, but not to tell her husband, as he did not know she had any money. Paterson suggested that if she paid that £5 and her husband dropped in to the office and paid £5, he would call the bill settled, but she must tell her husband.

Paterson got no money that day, and he believed the Boyles intended to 'do' him for the money, but they were in touch with him later. They asked him to call in to their shop for part of the debt. Paterson agreed, and on Wednesday, 2 March, he pulled on two overcoats against the chill, set his hat square on his head and, accompanied by a clerk named John Stewart, walked to the shop. There was quite a crowd of people gathered inside. Mr and Mrs Boyle were both there, together with a group of friends and customers. As they approached the shop, one of the men, James Boyle – no relation at all, but coincidently a man with the same surname – took Stewart aside while Paterson entered the shop alone. The shop consisted of two apartments, a front shop where the business was done, and a back shop that the Boyles had sub-let to a Mrs McDougall, although there was also a small private room used for storage.

No sooner had Paterson entered the shop than Mrs Boyle told him there was some trouble with the water pipe in the storeroom, and as the factor he should do something about it. Paterson agreed, and Mrs Boyle accompanied him to point out the fault. When Paterson walked into the back shop he noticed the lower part of shutters were closed and the room was in darkness, but as soon as he bent to examine the water pipe, Mrs Boyle grabbed hold of his collar. Caught by surprise, Paterson had no time to resist as Mrs Boyle hauled him into a dark corner of the room, where she dragged them both to the floor. 'Murder!' Paterson screamed, and, 'Please let me out! They're robbing me.'

There was no help. Paterson continued to yell for help, promising, 'If you let me out I'll reward you', and perhaps also, 'Please let me out, mistress'. The cries continued for about eight minutes; all that time, Mrs Boyle held him there in the dim room.

The neighbours heard the screams, shook their heads and looked the other way. They had no idea what was happening, but one neighbour,

Mary McCaig, thought that Mrs Margaret Boyle was 'licking her husband'. Such happenings were not uncommon in the backstreets of any Victorian city. So Paterson's calls for help were completely unheeded until the door opened and a press of bodies rushed in.

If Paterson thought he would be rescued, he was soon made aware of his mistake. The newcomers were anything but friendly. It was only then that Paterson realised that Mrs Boyle's skirt was up around her waist and her personal parts were exposed. As he looked, shocked, two men and two women crashed toward him. When James Boyle grabbed hold of his collar, Paterson screamed in fear. He yelled again as Mrs Boyle reached up and ripped her nails down his face, drawing blood in two different places. Paterson backed away, and within seconds Margaret Boyle and James Boyle chased him around the room.

Charles Kerr, a companion of the Boyles, came close and put a hand in Paterson's pocket; at the time Paterson thought Kerr was going to rob him, but on reflection he thought Kerr's hand was very close to the button that fastened his trousers.

There were a few moments of pandemonium as somebody called out, 'Police!' Margaret Boyle again draped herself artistically on the ground with her skirt lifted high, and somebody threw a bottle at Paterson's head. The bottle smashed against the wall as Paterson fled, ducking a second bottle. He retreated to Mrs McDougall's shop, where quite a crowd was gathered, including Sarah Vass, who lived in the flat above John Boyle's back shop. Vass knew Paterson as a modest man and was curious why his face was bleeding. He told her, 'Oh, that woman, that woman.' She thought he was very excited and upset. When Vass asked Paterson if he had hit Mrs Boyle, he replied, 'God forbid, Mrs Vass, that I should ever strike a woman.'

Paterson was still there when the police came, and he accompanied them to the police office.

The police took four people to the office: Paterson; Charles Kerr; young Margaret Boyle, who was the daughter of John and Margaret

Boyle; and James Boyle. Mrs Boyle remained behind, having apparently fainted.

Paterson was not quite the dapper figure he had appeared when he had set out. His face was bleeding from Mrs Boyle's raking nails, his right hand was cut, his shirt was ripped asunder and his hat had been battered and trampled in the back shop stramash. He told the police what had happened, but rather than sympathise, Lieutenant McLay said he would not consider Paterson's claim against Mrs Boyle; instead, he believed the Boyles' version of events.

The Boyles claimed that Paterson had both physically and sexually – then called 'criminally' – assaulted Mrs Boyle. The daughter, Margaret Boyle, claimed that Paterson had thrown Mrs Boyle to the floor and then kicked her. After an hour and a half, the police let Paterson free, but took a pledge of five guineas from him to assure his return to answer charges. Next day Superintendent McKenna told him he was accused of criminal assault, and would certainly be convicted.

At this distance of time it is impossible to judge Paterson's feelings, but he probably felt extremely uncomfortable when he appeared before Bailie Playfair at Anderston Police Court. Paterson was an eminently respectable man. He had been a WS since 1845 and was a Procurator in Hamilton; however, the evidence of six witnesses weighed heavily against him. They claimed he had taken Mrs Boyle into the back room and had closed and locked the door, then put his hands around her throat, knocked her to the ground and raped her. They also claimed he offered a reward if they did not report him to the police, hinted he was the proprietor of a brothel and said he had offered a bribe to a near neighbour, Helen McCall, if she backed him up.

Paterson denied all these charges, said he had never been in a brothel in his life and said that he had offered a reward to anybody who released him from the room. More intriguingly from a man who had been married for two years, Paterson also said that no woman had ever taken hold of him in that manner before. Both sides then waited for the verdict. Despite the best efforts of the witnesses, the judge found their evidence contradictory and implausible. Consequently, he found Paterson not guilty and threw the case out.

But Paterson was not happy. In response to the accusations thrown at him, he scouted around for witnesses who could speak in his favour, but in so doing he further angered the Boyles and their supporters. For the next few months he lived in terror as the Boyles stalked his footsteps, but in October 1859 the Crown prosecuted them for conspiracy and perjury. The case came to the Glasgow Circuit Court. The Boyles pleaded not guilty.

The prosecution had gathered a large number of witnesses, and they all told a similar story. They mentioned hearing Paterson's screams; the crowd gathered outside the shop; that Mrs Boyle had closed the shutters so that Paterson, known as 'the Laird', would be fumbling in the dark when he entered; and that the Boyles' daughter Margaret said that Paterson had kicked her mother.

The police on duty, William Carmichael and Duncan MacTavish, William Humphreys and Campbell Craig, said that John Stewart claimed Paterson had attacked Mrs Boyle and 'exposed her person'. He described Paterson with his face bleeding and his coat dusty, while James Boyle said it was 'a beastly affair', and indicated where Mrs Boyle was. When he entered the back shop he found Mrs Boyle lying in the place she had carefully positioned herself. Naturally, Mrs Boyle had accused Paterson of assault right away and asked the police not to let him away, while James Boyle claimed he had dragged Paterson away from her.

However, it was the evidence of Helen McCall that possibly proved Paterson's case and condemned the Boyles. She told the whole story of the conspiracy against Paterson. She mentioned Paterson's small debt case and said the Boyles had offered her a new dress if she assisted them in incriminating him. McCall refused to help hold Paterson down, but agreed to act as a witness. She told of the whole plot: bringing Paterson into the shop and having young Margaret Boyle scream for a policeman and then a number of witnesses swearing they saw him criminally assault Mrs Boyle. She also told that all the conspirators shared a half mutchkin of whisky in a pub later, and John Boyle joked they had 'the old chap safe enough now'. Only after being held for five weeks in prison did McCall agree to tell of her part in the affair. Lord Ardmillan, the Circuit Court judge, found them guilty of a conspiracy to extort money, and sentenced Margaret Boyle and John Boyle seven years' penal servitude each and James Boyle and Charles Kerr five years' penal servitude.

Although sexual crimes were as common in the nineteenth century as they are now, this type of entrapment was unusual. The extensive press coverage of this case revealed the interest of the public, who were obviously disgusted with the actions of the perpetrators.

15

Crimes Involving Children

Crime is sordid and unpleasant, but crime that involves children is worse. This chapter looks at a few of the thousands of cases in Glasgow where children were either the victims or the perpetrators.

The False Doctor

Jean Lapsley was not a woman blessed by luck, life or anything else. Poverty stalked her footsteps, so she shared a one-roomed flat in Renfrew with four other adults and her son John. In September 1811 John was two years old, a fine boy but one who grew up without knowing his father, who had never been married to Jean. Sharing a room with one child and four adults was not easy for Jean, particularly when John was a poor sleeper. There was one particular man who disliked the child's constant night-time crying, and he let his feelings be known quite loudly. This man was an ex-soldier, who had been invalided out of the army after the disastrous Walcheren expedition of 1809. Like so many veterans, he had caught a form of malaria known as Walcheren Fever.

With his sickness making him irritable, the soldier said if Jean did not keep John quiet he would make her put him outside in the night. Jean had nowhere else to go and did not want to live with discord in her home.

She walked to the nearest doctor and asked him for something to make John sleep. However, although Mr Carswell called himself a doctor, he had never been to university and had no medical qualifications. What he did have was decades of experience, a high opinion of himself and a supply of laudanum. He sold Jean a penny's worth and asked if she meant to poison somebody, but gave no advice on how little or large a quantity to administer, even when Jean told him about her sleepless son. Jean gave the boy a large dose and he fell into a deep sleep. At first Jean was pleased with the result of the laudanum, but when John did not wake up she became alarmed and hurried back to Carswell. Unfortunately the doctor was not interested and said that the boy would wake up soon. After a few hours John was still unconscious, and a distraught Jean again ran to Carswell and pleaded for his help. Once again Carswell refused to come, and not long later young John died.

Jean Lapsley was charged with murdering her son by giving him an overdose of laudanum. The case came to court but the defence and the judge both turned the evidence round and put the blame firmly on so-called Dr Carswell. Rather than find Jean guilty of murder and the inevitable sentence of death, the jury found her not guilty and the judge did his best to prevent Carswell from practising medicine again.

Poisoning Her Own Daughter

Sometimes crimes seem so hideous that people can only feel repulsion for the perpetrator until they learn the facts behind the incident, when sympathy and understanding take over. Such a case occurred in July 1868 when Lydia Dodds of King Street tried to poison her six-month-old baby daughter. Mrs Dodds was thirty years old, married to George Dodds, who earned good money in his position as a hammerman, and she was as respectable as any other woman in the street. There seemed no reason for Mrs Dodds to take her daughter into a close off the Saltmarket and give her sixty drops of laudanum, and then drink the remainder of the bottle herself.

When the police came, they revived both the mother and her child, but charged Dodds with poisoning her daughter. Dodds denied nothing. After weeks in prison she was taken before the Autumn Circuit Court in September, and there she told her story.

For the past year, things had not been well in the household. Perhaps it was because Mrs Dodds had been with child, but her husband had taken to slapping her around, as well as spending time and money with another woman. With a young baby in tow and her life falling to pieces around her, it was not surprising that Mrs Dodds should get depressed. Matters came to a head on Monday, 6 July, when she challenged her husband as he sat with his other woman in a pub. The result was perhaps predictable, as George Dodds punched and kicked her as the other woman watched.

Mrs Dodds ran away after that, but the next day she again tried to pull her husband away from his girlfriend, with exactly the same result. In Mrs Dodds' own words 'he struck me again and again' until she was 'mad with grief and shame and . . . thought to end it all'. It was then she gave her daughter the laudanum. Rather than hiding what she had done, Mrs Dodds remained at the head of the close, crying, and when one of her neighbours came to ask what the matter was, she admitted everything at once.

When the case came to court, the judge, Lord Ardmillan, said he hoped Mrs Dodds was no longer living with her husband, but as the memory of what she had done would be a dreadful enough punishment, and as the child had recovered, he sent her to jail for only six months.

Mrs Dodds was driven to attempted infanticide by her husband's behaviour, but in a period when millions of people lived on the edge of poverty and having an illegitimate child could carry a social stigma, disposing of an unwanted child was terribly common.

Buried Alive

On the evening of Friday, 15 March 1844, two boys saw a respectable-looking woman walking into a quarry at Hillhead, near the Kelvin viaduct.

They thought it strange that a decent woman should visit such a place at such an hour, and being children and therefore inquisitive, they watched, saw all but did not tell an adult.

A week later, one of the masons made a disturbing discovery. He was working in a secluded part of the quarry when he saw something protruding from the soft mud. When he stooped closer he saw it was a tiny human foot, so he investigated further and uncovered the fully dressed body of a baby boy. About a month old, the baby was well dressed in flannels, with a shift, bellyband and an embroidered double cap. The quarry owners called Dr Easton, and he gave the shocking news that the baby had been buried alive and had been suffocated by the mud.

The two boys who had witnessed the event came forward and gave a full description of the blonde woman in a green tartan they had seen, but the murder was never solved.

Other children were slightly luckier.

Thrown on the Fire

Janet Hay was probably not the best example of a mother. In December 1853 she gave birth to an illegitimate son, but having long since split from the father, she found it hard to support both herself and her baby. On the night of 11 February 1854, she carried the baby into her mother's house in Calton. For some reason, Hay and her mother argued and, in a fit of temper, Hay threw her son onto the fire. Her mother snatched him out, saw he was unhurt and carefully tucked him in Hay's apron, but Hay immediately threw him to the ground. When her mother handed her to the police, Hay spent the next sixty days in jail.

Sometimes the child was the centre of an adventure.

Moses on the Railway

The Biblical account of Moses is too well known to recount in detail. The majority of people know that the Israelites were held as slaves in

Egypt and the Pharaoh ordered that all male babies were to be killed. One mother tried to save her son by placing him in a basket and floating him down the Nile. The basket was found by an Egyptian lady, and Moses was brought up safely, to eventually lead the Israelis to safety out of Egypt and into the Promised Land of Israel.

But early Victorian Glasgow had its own variant of the Moses story, with the railway being the nineteenth-century version of the Nile. In late August 1844 a porter at Ayr railway station was sorting through the goods unloaded from the half past six train from Glasgow. Among the various packets and bundles was a white willow basket. He did not notice it particularly, but treated it with as much care as was normal. All the packets in the goods office were for delivery in Ayr, so the next morning the porter grabbed the basket and was about to put it on his trolley when he realised there was something moving inside. At first he thought it might be a dog or a cat that was being sent as a pet, but when he heard faint crying sounds, he knew it was not an animal. He opened the unsecured lid, saw a little baby girl staring up at him, and he smiled. The girl was only a couple of weeks old and seemed quite healthy, considering the ordeal she had just survived. All she needed was changed, washed and fed; the first two the porter did himself, and he called for a wet nurse for the third.

The Glasgow Police made their usual enquiries and discovered that a boy had delivered the basket to the railway booking office in Glasgow. The addressee of the basket helped all she could. The police asked around the city for any information about mothers who no longer had children with them or mothers with any connection to Ayrshire, followed a number of leads, lost the trail a few times, and in the middle of November they had the full picture. Unsurprisingly, the mother was not married to the father. Her name was Rachel Gibson; the father was a small farmer in Ayrshire, and Gibson had sent his daughter to his mother in Ayr, hoping she could either look after the child or pass it on to the father. When the nurse and the little one were required in Glasgow for a hearing, the railway company provided a first-class compartment for free, which is an example both of public relations and humanity that showed the Victorians at their best.

In the Circuit Court of January 1845 Rachel Gibson was charged that on 28 August she enclosed a female child in a basket and addressed it to Mrs Murdoch, Cassels Place, in Ayr. At first Gibson was accused of drugging the baby with laudanum, which was quite a common practice at the time, but that was disproved, and Gibson was shown only to be a desperate woman who did not know what to do with her child. She was jailed for three months. Unlike Moses, the Glasgow child in a basket did not rise to lead a nation, but she was termed a healthy and interesting baby, so that was good progress for an infant who started her life with such a traumatic adventure.

Other children had equally lucky escapes.

'Inhuman Wretch'

Drink played a huge part in the lives of the Victorians, so much so that it could lead to violence, theft and family grief. However, there was one occasion when events moved in an ever worse manner than normal. It was in November 1826, a time when Scotland lived in fear of the Resurrectionists, the men who dug up dead bodies and sold them for medical research. One Glasgow woman had become addicted to alcohol, so she had sold all her clothes for drink money, except for those she stood up in; then she sold her husband's clothes as well. Her house was stripped of furniture, but her thirst was still raging, so she took her baby boy and approached one of the surgeons in the University. She offered to sell him the baby for dissection, but instead he informed the police. When she appeared before the Police Court, the woman seemed very sorry and claimed she would not have tried to sell her baby if she had been sober. The magistrate was a bit nonplussed, perhaps not surprisingly, but as no crime had been committed he merely called her an 'inhuman wretch' and released her with a reprimand.

Sometimes children could be stolen.

Plagium

Plagium was an unusual crime in Scotland, but it did happen. It meant child stealing. On Friday, 7 July 1848, Mary Morrison was stolen. Her father, John Morrison, was a pattern drawer who lived in Love Loan. Mary had gone out of her house about two in the afternoon, and at quarter past her mother stepped outside to call her in, but the child had vanished. Mrs Morrison searched frantically but in vain, and ultimately told the police. Criminal Officer William Fotheringham was soon on the case and making enquiries, which led him to Bell Street in Calton. John Morrison came with him, anxious to find his daughter, while the mother remained behind in case Mary should come home.

They knocked at the door of Margaret Park, who had been seen with a young girl who was not her own. A woman answered the door, but when Fotheringham asked if Park was at home she replied, 'No. Margaret is not in just now, but I can go and get her.' However, Fotheringham suspected that the woman was trying to escape and pushed into the house instead.

Mary was found inside, upset and nearly naked. Fotheringham asked why she was in that state, and Park claimed that Mary's mother, a woman called Campbell, had handed the child into her care in that condition. Park was charged with child stealing and with stripping Mary and selling her pinafore, frock, shoes and stockings to two different pawnbrokers.

Park pleaded not guilty, but the jury had no difficulty deciding otherwise. Lord Moncrieff said it was a case of child theft, whereupon Lord Cockburn informed the court that he knew of three previous convictions for child theft, which carried a possible death penalty. Instead, Park was transported for fourteen years. She sailed for Van Diemen's Land on *Stately* the following year.

Park was fortunate. In 1808 another such case came before the Circuit Court in Glasgow. Rachel Wright was from Ireland, and on 8 July she saw a three-year-old girl called Flora Amos on her own in the streets of Glasgow. Grabbing Flora by the hand, Wright kidnapped her and fled on the coast road to Ireland. Either she looked suspicious or news of the theft was broadcast, but the keeper at the tollhouse at Prestwick in Ayrshire saw her and rescued young Flora. Wright pleaded guilty, and both Lord Henry Cockburn and the Lord Advocate proposed the death penalty, although there was some opposition. Nevertheless, Wright was condemned to death and hanged at Glasgow Tolbooth on Wednesday, 8 March 1809.

Child Stripping

A much more common crime was child stripping, when a woman lured a youngster into a dark or lonely place and stripped it to pawn the clothes. Some women made a career of stealing from children, such as Mrs Isabella Buchanan. She was already a four-times convicted thief when she appeared before the Circuit Court in September 1868 on a long list of charges of petty thefts from children. In one four-day spell in June she stole stockings and boots from five-year-old Euphemia Taylor in Trongate, seven shillings from nine-year-old Alexander Gavin in Green Street, a shawl from seven-year-old Magdalena Gardiner in Stevenson Street and a pair of boots from eleven-year-old Thomas Callaghan in Calton's Main Street. This time the judge made sure Buchanan would not be a menace to children for some time and awarded her ten years' penal servitude.

Equally unpleasant, if younger, was fourteen-year-old Elizabeth Valance, who spent three weeks in November 1871 terrorising helpless children. Acting with an accomplice, Valance scoured the streets of Glasgow for boys or girls on their own and robbed them of clothing, money or something their mother had sent them to buy. She was given five years' penal servitude in the 1872 Spring Court.

Child stripping was a fairly common offence, but it was unusual for a woman to strip the clothes from her own son. However, in Glasgow all things are possible, and in December 1850 Jane McDonald did just that. McDonald was a drunkard, and her sister had taken charge of her son and was looking after him. However, McDonald was unhappy at the situation and constantly arrived at her sister's house demanding the return of her son. On Christmas Day McDonald arrived again, but this time she succeeded in stealing away her son. Rather than take him home, she brought the boy to a dark close and stripped him of his trousers, which she pawned for 4d for whisky. She was given sixty days for her trouble.

Dens of Thieves

Children were not always the victims of crime; they could also be the perpetrators. When Dickens had Oliver Twist fall in with Fagan's den of thieves, he was not entirely relying on his imagination. Cities of the early nineteenth century were rife with tiny thieves, boys and girls who either stole on the orders of their adult masters, or through desperation in order to survive. Glasgow was no exception.

The Victorians were very aware of the Biblical quote that 'the poor are always with us', but some tried their best to alleviate the problem. Struggling with the concept of a *laissez-faire* economy, the philosophy of self-help and the attitudes that a man's money, like his personal life, was his own affair, there was still a strong streak of benevolence in society. There were a number of charities, one of which was the Industrial or Ragged School, which sought to take children from bad homes or the street, instil in them Christianity and the virtues of regular work, teach them a trade and prepare them for a useful life.

On Friday, 12 January 1849, two men of the Glasgow Industrial School found a boy lying on the pavement in Renfield Street, looking unwell and begging passers-by for money. The men found out he was Andrew Long, the son of two notorious drunkards. Rather than leave him there, they handed him over to the police night watchman and hunted out the parents.

Andrew's father was ensconced in one of the hundreds of Glasgow pubs, but the mother was arrested, taken to the Police Court and charged with allowing her children to beg on the streets.

It appeared Mrs Long had a number of boys in her care; some she trained to be thieves and others she sent out to beg, either by lying on the streets or by going from door to door. Bailie Smith sent Andrew to the Industrial School, and the mother to jail for sixty days.

'It Matters Not if the Prisoner is Nine or Sixty-Nine'

In December 1817 two minuscule thieves broke into John McIntyre's house at Bridgeton and stole a one-pound note and twenty shillings and sixpence in change. Their names were Hill Boyd Hay and Walter Turnbull, but rather than working for a crooked Fagan they were the sons of honest parents. When their fathers found them with the money they asked awkward questions, worked out that they had been stealing and handed the boys to the police. Perhaps they hoped only to scare them into the straight and narrow, but the police charged both with theft.

In May 1818 the case came to court. Both ten-year-old Turnbull and nine-year-old Hay were too small to be seen if they sat on the seat in the dock, so they stood on top, and still their heads just protruded above the dock. Not surprisingly, they were terrified and both cried nonstop as they faced the judge. When asked to plead, Hay admitted his guilt right away, while Turnbull had to be persuaded to plead guilty. The Advocate Depute displayed no sympathy at all and claimed that the case showed 'there was among the lower orders a looseness of principle and a tendency to commit crime' and that 'the present conviction will teach young persons . . . that if they commit a crime, it matters not if the prisoner is nine or sixty-nine'. Both children were sentenced to a year in jail, but the judge was sensible enough to order that they should be kept separate from other prisoners.

Not all children were so overawed by the judge. That same month three boys known only as Wilson, McDougall and Robertson were sent to the Circuit Court, but when Lord Pitmilly transported them for life as habitual thieves they laughed in his face after showing 'the utmost depravity' throughout the court proceedings.

Girls could also be offenders. At the Southern District Police Court on Friday, 27 August 1852, a young girl named Agnes Broadly stood in the dock accused of picking a lady's pocket in Bridge Street. The lady had been walking past the railway terminal when she thought somebody had touched her side. She looked down and saw Broadly's hand in her pocket, but before she could do anything the girl ran. However, another woman grabbed Broadly before she could escape. Broadly pleaded not guilty, but Bailie Mitchell sentenced her to sixty days. Broadly was a habitual thief who had recently been released from a four-month sentence.

Expert Child Thieves

Sometimes even experienced policemen could be astonished by the criminal aptitude of the young. In August 1845 a passing constable saw a faint light and heard suspicious noises in a confectionery shop in Argyle Street. He investigated and found five children sitting on the floor, busy munching their way through the stock. Juvenile thieves were nothing unusual, but when the constable investigated how they had entered the shop, he was amazed at their skill.

To get into the sweet shop, the children had snapped the lock on a wooden door to a neighbouring basement and entered a short passage. Their next trick was to break through a brick wall and enter the cellar next door, and then they forced open a padlocked trap door.

The Criminal Officers were impressed by the skill of these children, particularly as the oldest was only eleven, and the youngest a mere five years old, but despite their youth, Bailie Mackinlay had to pass them on to a higher court. Their crime was too serious to be tried in the Police Court.

The Other Side of the Coin

Despite the unremitting hardship of life at the bottom end of the social scale, and despite the poverty, the poor housing and the constant temptation to turn to crime, there was always a solid core of honest people. History seldom notices these decent men and women, for they just carry on with their lives, but just occasionally one or other of them does something that is recorded and remembered. These deeds are a testimony to the true people of Glasgow, and elsewhere.

Such a case occurred on Friday, 4 January 1850, when fifteen-year-old Walter McDonald was walking to his work as a painter and decorator. He was passing along Glassford Street when he saw a small parcel on the ground. He picked it up and found it was a bundle of banknotes all tied together. He thought it was around £30, a small fortune, far more than a year's wages. Many boys may have been tempted to hold on to the money, but instead McDonald handed it – unopened – to the police. When they checked, they found there was £150 in the bundle. They traced the owner, who handed McDonald a reward of £5.

Walter McDonald was only one honest boy among many. One child who made even more of an impression was a young boy named James Farrel, who lived in Jeffrey's Close, Goosedubbs, which in 1852 was one of the poorest closes in a locality famed for poverty and crime in the heart of old Glasgow.

Goosedubbs was a narrow street that stretched from Stockwell Street to Bridgegate, with cobbles under foot and a variety of buildings from tenements to low, crow-step gabled houses. Farrel had been in the close when he witnessed a pickpocket named David Moore grab a watch. The owner objected and chased the thief, who threw the watch away as he ran.

Young James Farrel picked up the watch and gave it to his mother, who told him to run to the police office and hand it in. James obeyed at once, and was summonsed to give evidence against Moore. He came to court in what were probably his best clothes and possibly his only clothes, but which the *Glasgow Herald* described as 'tattered garments that had originally been made for a man six feet high'.

The editors of the *Herald* were so impressed by Farrel's honesty that they raised a subscription for him, helped by Captain Smart of the police. The target was £5, but they raised £3 10/-, and an Edinburgh gentleman contributed a length of new cloth to make into clothes.

Captain Smart travelled to Goosedubbs in person to see Farrel. The boy was in a bad way, with a nasty dog bite on his leg, so Smart took the boy to the police surgeon and had the wound dressed, the lad washed and scrubbed and probably de-loused as well, then dressed him in a clean checked shirt and his first ever stockings and boots and a fine suit that the police tailor made with the Edinburgh broadcloth.

For all the child-related crime in Glasgow, the city was based on a solid core of decent people.

16

Riots

The nineteenth century was a time of contrasts. On the one hand, it was a time of great progress, with amazing strides forward in engineering and science, but on the other it was a time of shattered communities, massive emigration and social dislocation. In Glasgow, as in other major cities, people flooded in from the country in search of jobs and a home. Many of these people were uneducated and carried their ancient superstitions and fears with them. When relocated to an unfamiliar urban environment, the superstitions could blossom into mob violence.

The Glasgow Vampires

In February 1822 Glasgow was a burgeoning industrial centre. As well as being a centre of engineering, the city had a host of lesser industries. One was paint making. Charles Provand owned a small paint factory in Clyde Street, just to the east of the then hospital, and he lived on the premises. In every city of the period, there were crowds of children roaming the streets getting into mischief, snatching at opportunities to thieve, and watching everything that was happening. It was a pair of these children who saw strange events at Provand's factory and started a riot that did no credit to the city.

The children were looking idly through one of the windows of the factory when they saw a pile of clothes lying on the floor, stained with red paint. At about the same time they saw one of the workmen take his son into the building for some reason. Being youngsters and therefore endowed with wild imaginations, they put two and two together and came up with five. It was obvious to them what was happening: children were being inveigled into the factory to be murdered and their blood was being used as paint.

The children quickly spread the rumour, and Provand's factory became a place of horror to the young and the gullible. As well as those who believed the building was used to create pureed children, there were those who thought Provand was in league with body snatchers. At a time of deep concern about Resurrectionists, when Gothic fiction such as *Frankenstein* (1818) was appearing, such a belief was perhaps understandable.

On Sunday, 20 February 1822, a mob of children gathered outside the factory. They shouted at first and then began to throw stones, but Provand and some of his workers easily drove them away. They retreated, regrouped and tried again, with the same result. They tried a third and a fourth time, but the inhabitants of the factory were too old and too strong to back down from a gaggle of youngsters.

However, by four in the afternoon the mob had reformed and this time it was not merely composed of children. Youths and even adults had joined them and they advanced on the factory with great resolve, throwing barrages of stones in front of them. They rushed the building, smashed every pane of glass and erupted into the interior, tearing up the wooden doors and skirting boards and looting the contents, including even every piece of furniture in the place. Rather than keep or pawn what they had stolen, the mob threw their loot into the River Clyde; most of them were bent on destruction rather than profit.

For an hour the mob controlled the street. There was a brief stir when a party of police arrived and picked up a few prisoners from the fringes, but they could make no impression on the bulk of the crowd. There was another interruption when some local gentlemen believed they could persuade the mob back to order simply by force of their respectable characters. These hopeful gentlemen entered the house in safety, but the moment they started to speak, the mob turned on them in fire and fury. Some of the gentlemen escaped in a frantic scamper out of the house, but some retreated to the upper floor and barricaded themselves against the furore. One unfortunate gentleman tried to barge through the crowd and was chased to a house on Claremont Place. A crowd gathered outside and pelted the windows with stones.

The riot continued until five o'clock, at which time the master of police brought in a body of redcoats to quell the riot, followed shortly after by the Lord Provost, riding at the head of a jingling troop of cavalry. By the time the Lord Provost read out the Riot Act, the crowd had already subsided, and there was little resistance when six people were arrested. The cavalry remained on local patrol until midnight, while the police and some supporting infantry remained overnight.

Only when Provand searched his house next morning did he find that he had been robbed of his silver plate and his collection of antique coins. The Lord Provost announced a 200 guinea reward for anybody who pointed out leaders of the mob, and an ex-policeman named Richard Campbell was convicted and sentenced to be whipped though the town and transported for life.

Riots for Bread and the Charter

April 1848: Glasgow was festooned with placards for a mass meeting on Glasgow Green, with two agendas. The first was to support the People's Charter, which wanted political reform, and the second to call for a repeal of the Union between Great Britain and Ireland. There was also anger at the supposed stance taken by the government to stop the freedom of speech and the freedom of the press.

The authorities had their own agenda. They looked upon the Chartists as a danger to the peace of the city, if not to the realm, successors to the Radicals who had caused so much trouble in 1820 and first cousins to the revolutionaries who were spreading fire and blood across much of Europe. Chief Superintendent Miller did not expect serious trouble, but he prepared for any contingency by calling out every policeman and having them on duty in every part of the city.

The meeting itself was a relative success, as the different Chartist bodies rallied under their banners, 'The People's Charter in Defiance of the Dungeon', 'Taxation without representation is Robbery', together with navvies from the Caledonian Railway carrying hawthorn branches and a large number of the respectable middle and upper-middle classes. Of the estimated 40,000 people present, 10,000 were said to be women, and on this occasion there was not a hint of trouble.

'Now or Never, My Boys'

The situation was not repeated in May when around some 5,000 people rioted in the streets of Glasgow. The Chartists had gathered on the Green to ask for a wage of two shillings a day, but marched through the Gallowgate in a huge procession. Some carried weapons, and one man fired two shots into the air. Many of the city's bad characters joined the Chartists, not out of any feeling for political reform, but purely from a desire to create mayhem and plunder whatever they could. The riots lasted for two days, with the mob tearing up about thirty iron railings from around the Green, and around 500 at Monteith Row, to use as weapons. George Smith, one of the Chartist leaders, shouted out: 'Now or never, my boys; these are the ones we will easiest get.'

The Hungry Forties was a period of great distress and most of the mob would have been driven by hunger as much as any desire for reform. As they debouched into the city, the rioters smashed their way through the shutters desperate shopkeepers hoped would protect their property, and hurled stones and other missiles through the windows. They attacked the shopkeepers to the echoes of screaming women. Sometimes a host of rioters surged through the smashed window to loot a shop, then withdrew with their spoils and continued through the fearful streets. They looted their way through Wilson Street and Glassford Street, wrecking Stewart's victuallers and spirit shop, and William Dunn Caddie's spirit shop. They rampaged through Exchange Square, and one held a gun to Alexander Martin, while a howling mob looted his gun shop of sixty guns and nearly thirty pistols.

John Crossan, one of the leaders of the mob, reprimanded one of them for firing his pistol. 'Don't waste your powder,' he said. 'You'll have use for all you have before night is over.' They careered along Queen Street and smashed their way into William Lang's confectionery, looting the place bare as the proprietor ran out the back door.

Preceded by the clatter of a bell, a segment of the mob marched down Buchanan Street; a man smashed a rifle butt through the window of Finlay and Field's Jewellers and lifted over £1,600 of watches and chains. They swarmed around Robert Quin's cart and investigated the contents. 'Here's meal,' somebody said. One man thrust the barrel of a rifle between the wheel spokes, and as the cart abruptly halted, the horse tumbled to its knees. The mob sliced the harness and ripped into the meal sacks; some fired pistols into the air and others just shouted their defiance to the sky.

They rampaged along Trongate, threatened Duncan McLean with a pistol and robbed Musgrave's gun shop of sixty-eight guns, fifty-seven pairs of pistols and over 700 knives; threatened James Watson with a cutlass when he refused to hand over powder and shot but fled when the manager shouted out, 'The soldiers are coming!'

They robbed a spirit shop in Clyde Place and fired a shotgun at young Mr Morton, the proprietor's son. Morton grabbed a hatchet and came out to defend himself, but the mob crowded around the counter, smashed him with an iron bar and lifted everything in the till.

The violence was not all one-sided. The authorities had called up a large number of special constables to back up the police, while Bailie Orr led the cavalry. The combined force barged through a makeshift barricade of carts and planks at the head of the Saltmarket, scattering any serious resistance as the specials' long batons thumped on heads, backs and arms. Orr's army clattered down the Saltmarket and over Hutcheson Bridge; he confronted an armed crowd at the foot of Crown Street, and while Bailie Stewart balanced precariously on a cab and read the Riot Act, the cavalry charged. The mob ran. Stewart patrolled Gorbals for a while and returned to the city proper.

Just after five on the Saturday evening, Bailie Orr read the Riot Act again at Glasgow Cross, and then the Royal Scots arrived with red coats, crunching boots and glinting bayonets. The soldiers began to clear the streets, with the crowds gathering again the second they were gone. A cavalry officer found a horse for Bailie Orr, and he patrolled the city, the streets made gloomy after the rioters had stopped the gas supply to the city lamps.

There was a barricade to be removed in King Street, and outbreaks of stone throwing in Gallowgate and High Street, but the city quietened during the night and special constables replaced most of the soldiers. The authorities were sent to Edinburgh and Hamilton for more troops as the crackle of flames and clatter of breaking windows filled the night.

On the second day of rioting, a detachment of military pensioners opened fire on the largely unarmed mob and killed a few men. There was blood on the streets of Glasgow and mourning mothers and widows in the poverty-racked homes as the authorities regained control.

The courts handed out harsh sentences to those men who were arrested: John Crossan, who urged the Chartists to arm themselves, and encouraged them to loot, was given eighteen years' transportation; as was George Smith, guilty of mobbing, rioting and addressing the Chartist meeting on the Green. Hugh Barrons and Peter Keenan, James Campbell and John Gallagher, James Sloey, Charles O'Brien and John Lafferty all got ten years' transportation. Many others were given lesser terms of imprisonment.

Fishwives and Redcoats

Not all riots were political that turbulent year of 1848. It was the peak of the Hungry Forties, with famine and strife stalking Europe. With tempers and nerves on edge, it did not take much to escalate a minor occurrence into a major trouble, so when a drunken fishwife started shouting the odds near the Bridgegate on Saturday, 3 June, the police were quick to move in and try to arrest her. Unfortunately, a number of young Irish soldiers of the 27th Regiment of Foot sympathised with the fishwife and attacked the police.

The police called for reinforcements, but so did the army, and a general melee began around the Bridgegate, with police batons against the belts and boots of the soldiers and large numbers of the local populace joining in the fun. The police were getting the worst of it when Superintendents McKay and Cameron hurried up with two hundred men and spent the next hour cracking skulls and arresting drunken rioters. When an army lieutenant arrived with a picket, the remaining military outlaws withdrew back to barracks, although the police managed to arrest a solitary private and put one civilian in hospital.

The trouble was repeated on the Sunday, when crowds of civilians, stiffened by a number of the 27th Regiment of Foot, blocked the Saltmarket opposite the Bridgegate. No traffic could get through, and the crowd began to get restless. The police tried to clear the street, the crowd tried to clear the police and the town was ablaze again. In a carbon copy of the previous day, the crowd increased, with soldiers merging with the raucous rabble from the darkest closes until they overflowed from the Saltmarket to Bridgegate, Gallowgate, Trongate and the High Street. Indeed, the mob blocked all the main thoroughfares in the oldest part of Glasgow.

Not surprisingly, the respectable of the area contacted the police for more help. Once again McKay and Cameron gathered hundreds of officers and marched them across Glasgow to the trouble spot. They formed a firm line across the width of the Saltmarket and marched slowly against the mob. As they passed the openings of closes and streets, the mob dribbled away, losing cohesion with every few yards. But the police had to fight for their victory; there were bloody faces in the two hours it took to clear the streets, and fifteen men were arrested, including nine soldiers. The rioters were jailed for twenty to thirty days, and no doubt the army authorities added their own penalty on their return to the regiment.

Riots became less frequent as the century wore on, but the decent people of Glasgow lived with the knowledge that their streets could become a battleground at almost any time.

17

A Medley of Murders

One crime always stands head and shoulders above the rest for public interest and public horror. The crime is the most final of all: murder, the deliberate taking of a human life.

Death of a Soldier

On Friday, 25 February 1826, twenty-six-year-old Benjamin Lamont was returning to barracks in Glasgow after his furlough at home. He marched proudly in his tartan trews and red coat with the full feather bonnet balanced on his head, as befitted a soldier of the 78th (Highland) Regiment of Foot, the Ross-shire Buffs. However, even soldiers get thirsty, so he stopped at James Gray's public house in Parkhead and had a glass of something sensible and a pipe of tobacco. It was around nine in the evening when he emerged and walked until he was at Camlachie, a weaving and mining village then about a mile from Glasgow. Here he met three men and asked them the best way to the Duke Street Barracks in Glasgow.

When the men offered to take him there in person, Lamont agreed, and followed them along the road to a house called Haddo's Corner. From there they showed Lamont a shortcut through a series of fields called the Midpark. As they trudged through a ploughed field, Lamont asked if they were sure this was the best way, but two of his guides grabbed his arms and threw him to the ground, where he was robbed of five twenty-shilling banknotes, a red Morocco leather pocketbook, a regimental passport, a handkerchief and a linen shirt.

Lamont struggled to his feet, shouting, and one of his attackers levelled a pistol and said, 'Damn the bastard! He'll give information. Shoot him!' He fired into Lamont's thigh and then all three ran off.

Weak from shock and loss of blood, Lamont tried his best to crawl to the road. He shouted his loudest, and an Irishman ran up and helped him to the infirmary at the barracks. His wound was dressed, but he remained quite weak and very calm. He related exactly what had happened to him, languished for a few days, and on 15 March he died, quietly and without fuss.

The same night that Lamont was attacked, a gang of three men committed a robbery in the main street of Bridgeton, and there was speculation it may have been the same men. These three knocked a man down, robbed him of £2 10/-, then split up and ran away. When the victim called for help, a Calton police officer pursued and arrested one of his attackers. The man was Thomas Connor, a well-known bad man. However, it appeared that Connor was not involved in the murder of Lamont, and so the police began a search for the gang of three.

The police scoured the environs of the city and followed a trail that led right to Camlachie. In a classic late-morning raid, Sheriff Officer William Mckenzie, backed by Criminal Officers Christie, McLean, Stewart, Marshall and McGruer, arrested three men for the murder of Lamont. They were: Samuel McMenemy and Alexander McPhie from Parkhead, and Robert Hamilton from Calton. Two were weavers, all three had criminal records and one was a deserter from the 79th Regiment, the Cameron Highlanders.

Their trial took place in Edinburgh on 19 July, and all three pleaded not guilty. They provided alibis, with two claiming they had been at home in Parkhead, and the third saying he had been miles from the scene of the murder.

The evidence against the three men seemed overwhelming. Thomas Hamilton, a Parkhead weaver, had seen all three in the village the night of the murder and even described their clothes, with McPhie wearing a black coat and McMenemy a blue coat and light trousers.

Thomas Hamilton had been at a wedding in the village where, according to custom, there had been a number of celebratory pistol shots fired. Robert Hamilton carried a pistol, discharged it in the air and gathered a handful of small stones to use as ammunition. Thomas Hamilton said he saw the three speak to Lamont, and followed as they walked together into the field, but he kept some distance behind them. He knew that the three suspects had a bad reputation for causing trouble, and guessed they would attack the soldier.

When he met a man called Hamilton Cross coming from Camlachie, he happily told him, 'There's going to be a death tonight.' That phrase was not quite as ominous as it sounds, as 'death' was local slang for a brawl, but with the odds of three to one against him, the young soldier had little chance. The next man Thomas Hamilton met was his half-brother, George Hamilton. Thomas told him, 'I am just going to see what will happen.'

Thomas Hamilton followed them into the fields, and spotted Robert Hamilton on Lamont's left, McMenemy on his right and McPhie cutting off his escape. The moon dipped, but at that time of year there was still sufficient light for Hamilton to see what was happening. He heard McPhie say, 'Bugger of Hell', and then the whole party vanished in a fold of the ground, dipping toward the Camlachie Burn.

Rather than follow closely and probably be seen, Thomas Hamilton hung back, and a few minutes later he heard the sharp crack of a pistol. He ducked behind a bush; three men crashed back through the field and passed close by but without noticing him hiding there. He heard Lamont cry out 'Murder! Murder!', which was the recognised call for help at that period, but rather than attempt to assist, Thomas Hamilton took fright and ran home. He left Lamont, wounded and alone, in the middle of the field.

When the jury heard Thomas Hamilton's story, they must have thought there was no doubt the three suspects were guilty as charged. However, the defence were quick to put the record straight. First they highlighted the relationship between Thomas Hamilton and McPhie. The two were related by marriage, and there was bad blood between them. Thomas Hamilton had also spent six months in jail for embezzling equipment for a weaving web, so he was not the best character to rely on. Finally, although he claimed to have known more about the shooting than anybody apart from the principal antagonists, he did not immediately tell the police; he only turned informer after arguing with McPhie's uncle a few days later.

Despite the doubts about Thomas Hamilton's character, other witnesses appeared to corroborate his story. Hamilton Cross had also met the three accused with Lamont, and asked where they were going. When McPhie said they were going to Duke Street, Cross said it was a 'funny way to get to Duke Street'. He also heard the pistol shot and the cry of 'Murder', but unlike Thomas Hamilton, he immediately ran to help. Lamont had told him he had been robbed by three men. The defence highlighted the fact that Cross had also spent some time in Glasgow Jail, where he had been held as a witness.

The accused men relied heavily on other witnesses for their defence. Robert Hamilton freely admitted he had deserted from the 79th Highlanders in Campbeltown, but denied any part in the murder, while McMenemy and McPhie both produced witnesses who swore they were at home the night of the murder. The defence tactics worked. The jury were uncertain. Although the three suspects had been positively identified as being on the scene, the case was found not proven and all three walked free.

The murder of Private Lamont was a story of very unpleasant people, with Thomas Hamilton little better than the murderers. While the attackers were openly aggressive, he watched and did nothing to help, which may have contributed to the death of the soldier.

There were many other killings in nineteenth-century Glasgow.

Matricide

Crimes within the family always seem sadder than those between strangers, perhaps because the bonds are presumed to be stronger. Yet domestic disputes figure high on any list of murders. In the nineteenth century infanticide was probably second to wife beating, but there were also cases of husband beating and even children assaulting their parents. Matricide, however, where children actually killed their mother, was rare. Nevertheless, one such case occurred in Glasgow in May 1869.

Voices from the Clouds

Janet Hay was a sixty-year-old widow who lived with her thirty-seven-year-old, unmarried daughter Agnes at 36 South Coburg Street, Laurieston. Agnes was a slender, nervous woman who worked as a sewer in a muslin warehouse in Ingram Street, but she suffered from mental health problems. For months, perhaps years, she had heard voices from the clouds, but on 27 May they had been more threatening. The voices came to her at work and threatened to 'quarter her' if she did not do as they said. Not surprisingly, Agnes was scared, and hurried home to her mother, but the voices followed her.

Agnes hurried into the house but the voices would not leave her alone. They ordered her to murder her mother. She resisted, but the voices were insistent; they took control of her, so she grabbed her mother by the throat, threw her to the ground and began to throttle her. Janet Hay fought back, pleading with Agnes to let her go, but Agnes could not. As Janet held on to life, Agnes lifted a smoothing iron and smashed it against her mother's head, again and again until Janet Hay lay still and bloody on the floor.

Even with her mother undoubtedly dead, the voices did not disappear. Instead, they sneered at her for killing her mother, and then ordered her to murder a little boy who happened to be passing her house. Instead Agnes cleaned up the mess she had made in the house, washed the smoothing iron, hid it away behind a window shutter and walked across to her brother in Crown Street. After greeting everybody calmly, she told them she had murdered her mother.

Not surprisingly, Agnes's story caused pandemonium. Her brother rushed to inform the police, and Superintendent Robb and Dr Chalmers rushed down to South Coburg Street. They found Janet Hay with her neck severely bruised and crushed and a gaping hole in her head. Her skull was fractured and she was undoubtedly dead. The police had no hesitation in arresting Agnes, who confessed at once, but as the court believed her to be temporarily insane, she was not hanged. Other murderers were not so fortunate.

'Buchanan has Murdered Me'

The Bridgegate was the road to Glasgow's first bridge over the Clyde. At one time it was the home of the elite, but by the early nineteenth century that area did not always enjoy the brightest of reputations. Blackguards, villains and ladies of the night infested the closes and there were assaults, robberies and thefts enough to keep the police busy and newspaper editors happy. There was even the occasional murder. In October 1819 John Buchanan, a flesher, now more commonly known as a butcher, was charged with killing Jean Mackenzie.

As usual in murders, the case was sordid and fairly complex, with personal animosities seeking to twist the truth, and the past slithering up to spread old poison in the present. The first complication was in the name of the dead woman, for as well as being called Jean Mackenzie she was known as Ann Duff. On 13 October 1818, Mackenzie lodged in Bridgegate Street in the house of Isabel Mills. At about two in the morning the two women were sitting by the fire chatting with two men they knew when there was a knock at the door. Mills shouted out that she was not going to answer the door at that time, but a man's voice told her that if she did not open up they would kick the door down and come in anyway.

When Mills opened up, three young men barged in. She knew one of them, John Buchanan, but not the other two, James Nelson and Duncan Colquhoun. Her other male guests promptly left. Buchanan asked if there were any spirits in the house; Mills said no, so Colquhoun gave her a handful of coins and sent her and Nelson to buy some. It was just after two in the morning, so, not surprisingly, there were no shops open, and they returned after a fruitless scour of the streets of Glasgow.

In the meantime, Buchanan and Colquhoun became friendlier with Jean Mackenzie. Shortly after Mills returned, Buchanan invited Mackenzie to accompany him into a bed closet. Mackenzie agreed and they withdrew and closed the door. Their intention seemed obvious, but after a very few moments Mackenzie screamed out 'Murder!' in a hoarse voice. Mills rushed to the door to help, but Colquhoun and Nelson held her back. A few seconds later, Buchanan burst out of the room and hurried from the house, with Colquhoun and Nelson close behind. Mackenzie and Buchanan had only been in the bed closet for three minutes and when Mackenzie emerged, her face was bruised and swollen. She said, 'John Buchanan did it,' then ran to the window and called out 'Murder!' in the hope of alerting the police.

However efficient the Glasgow Police were, they were not fast enough that morning, and the three men got away. Mackenzie's face was bruised and swollen as she explained what had happened. The second the closet door closed, Buchanan had punched her, stabbed her on the breast and kicked her foully in the lower belly. Mills listened with growing malice. When she was sure the three men were out of the area, she left the house to fetch Mackenzie's half-sister, Marion Rankine, who lived close by. Rankine lived with her mother, who was lying sick with typhus but who had recognised her daughter's cries.

When Mills returned, Mackenzie was lying on the floor near the window, crying and bleeding from a small puncture wound in her chest.

She mentioned a pain in her heart, but at that time the other women thought the wound insignificant. For a while, Mackenzie was unable to speak, but after half an hour or so she asked for a drink of water. Mills and Rankine asked why Buchanan had attacked her, but Mackenzie gave only a vague answer that he disliked her because of some woman who had been banished from Glasgow. Rankine pressed for more information and found out that Mackenzie had given evidence at a court case where a girl named Mary Little had been jailed for stealing a shawl. According to Mackenzie, the second Buchanan had closed the closet door he had said, 'You bitch! You've sent Mary Little to Bridewell, but you'll put no more there!'

Then he had punched her and stabbed her with a fork.

The following day, Mills called in a trio of doctors, Dr Morrison, Dr Corkindale and Dr Watson. Eight days later, after complaining constantly of pain in her head, her heart and her belly, Mackenzie died. She had frequently asked for her mother during these days, and once said, 'John Buchanan has murdered me,' and when her mother arrived, Mackenzie threw her arms around her neck and said, 'Mother, although I never have another word to speak, Buchanan has murdered me.'

When Buchanan's case came to the Circuit Court in October 1819, Mr Jardine, the defence counsel, pointed out that Mackenzie had suffered from typhus about six months earlier. Jardine claimed that it was typhus rather than Buchanan that had killed her. Dr Corkindale and Dr Watson both inspected Mackenzie before she died. Corkindale prescribed castor oil and opium; he noticed the wounds on her breast but could not connect her symptoms of extreme pain in her belly with her apparent injuries. Watson also mentioned that Mackenzie complained of great pain in her belly but could not help.

The prosecution concentrated more on the evidence of the people present on the night of the assault. They called Duncan Colquhoun, another flesher, who confirmed that Mackenzie and Buchanan went into the closet together and Mackenzie called out 'Murder' shortly afterwards. He heard a noise like knocking on the partition wall, and then Buchanan emerged and boasted he 'had not missed her on the guts'. When the prosecution called Isabel Mills, Mr Jardine objected strongly, claiming Mills had often said she would hang Buchanan, 'even if she was hanging herself', so she was hardly an unbiased witness. The judge, Lord Meadowbank, overruled the objection and said that 'people in her situation were in the habit of using coarse and vulgar language to each other'.

The jury listened intently as Buchanan, a young, good-looking man, stood impassive. They found him guilty and the presiding judge, Lord Pitmilly, sentenced him to be fed on bread and water until 17 November, and then to be hanged. Furthermore, after death, Buchanan's corpse was to be handed over for public dissection. There was no reprieve.

18
Crimes of the Heart

With an avalanche of broken glass, the man burst out of the window and hurtled down the thirty-three feet to the stone-slabbed courtyard below. He landed with the sickening crack of breaking bones and a spatter of blood. Seconds later, a face appeared at the shattered window. Somebody screamed. Then a policeman walked quickly into the court, to be joined by a young man who had hurried down the stairs. The policeman looked up. 'He's dead,' he said. It was the early morning of 10 January 1880.

'Away Out of This with Your Fancy Man'

It had started a few days before, when Joseph Miller had moved in to the O'Neils' house as a paying sub-tenant. Miller was a respectable elderly man, a labourer and an ex-soldier. O'Neil was a cooper by trade, but since he had lost his sight he had become a hawker. Their house had one room and a kitchen, three stories up in an attic flat in Moodie's Court, off Argyle Street. As well as Miller and O'Neil, Mrs O'Neil and four sons shared the house in a happy congestion of bodies and noise. The fifth and eldest, Andrew, was a foundry worker who lived in Muirhead Street but spent that night with the rest of the family.

Until recently, Miller had lived with O'Neil's mother, but at the turn of the year he moved in with the body of the family. He was a generous man, quite happy to share his whisky with anybody, but particularly with Mrs O'Neil, which partially may have contributed to O'Neil's death. On the night before the tumble from the window, 9 January 1880, the O'Neil brothers, Andrew, James and Thomas, came home around nine o'clock, and Miller arrived about ten minutes later. Miller gave Mrs O'Neil a few shillings, and she went out for a mutchkin of whisky, which they knocked back within forty-five minutes, whereupon Mrs O'Neil and Miller went to a pawnshop, presumably to find some money. When they returned, O'Neil promptly ordered Miller out of his house.

There seemed no reason. There was no apparent disagreement, but Miller simply rose and left without any argument. Mrs O'Neil followed him, and after a while her husband began to cry. Miller and Mrs O'Neil came back about nine, singing their way up the stairs, and quite drunk.

O'Neil dried his eyes and looked up, 'Away out of this with your fancy man!' he said. Mrs O'Neil denied that Miller was her fancy man and tried to smooth things by dancing and singing with her husband. O'Neil seemed to have no objections, so the kitchen rattled to the sounds of drunken singing and unregulated dancing.

The McGees, next door neighbours, joined in, singing 'The Rocky Road to Dublin' as they danced, but after an hour or so they left. The younger O'Neils retired to bed, either in the kitchen or the other room as their parents and Miller smoked companionably together in the kitchen. The peace did not last long,

'I wish I was dead,' said O'Neil.

'You'll be dead soon enough,' Mrs O'Neil replied.

O'Neil raised his voice again. 'Away out of this, fancy man,' he said, but Miller denied he was a fancy man. There was a scuffle; O'Neil stood up and swung a punch, but Miller backed off into the adjoining room, only returning when O'Neil seemed to have calmed down. The O'Neils stood up and walked into the room Miller had just left. Mrs O'Neil was soon asleep. The sons looked at each other but – perhaps wisely – decided not to interfere. They knew that their father was a gentle man when sober, but when he was in drink he changed; he ground his teeth and sometimes grabbed his razor and threatened to cut his own wrists. He was not known to be violent toward anybody else.

Miller sat by the fire, brooding. Next door, O'Neil grabbed his wife's throat. She woke up with a start and screamed, 'What are you doing?'

O'Neil said, 'Nothing. Get out of here.'

Mrs O'Neil scrambled up and got quickly dressed. She ran through to the kitchen, crying, 'I'm being killed!' She turned to Miller. 'Go and calm him down, Joe,' she said.

Miller tried. He told O'Neil that if he was not going to sleep himself, at least he could keep quiet and let the boys sleep. Mrs O'Neil was distraught; two of the sons tried to calm her down, but she said she was going to find a constable and get her husband put in the police office until he sobered up. She fled outside the house but got no further than the stair head, where she stood until she composed herself. When she returned, she joined Miller beside the fire.

There was silence, broken only by O'Neil singing 'Auld Lang Syne' in a low, mournful tone. When he repeated the song again and again, Miller told him to be quiet or he would 'chuck him over the window'. O'Neil threatened to thump Miller for going out with his wife, and then returned to his song. Miller walked through to the other room. Nobody spoke. Miller returned. The singing began again. Miller went back through.

In the absence of a witness, nobody knows exactly what happened next. Miller gave his version of events, and the evidence of the sons in the kitchen added to that, but all that is certain was there was some sort of a scuffle and O'Neil was heard to say, 'Who's there?' One of the sons thought he heard O'Neil say, 'Let go my throat', but they were all aware of the crash of breaking glass. Miller came out of the room immediately afterward, shutting the door behind him. Mrs O'Neil shouted out, 'There's your father killed. He's out the window!' and as she yelled, Miller leaned on the mantelpiece, looking flustered, and then said quietly that O'Neil was over the window.

Andrew O'Neil was first to react. He ran downstairs and found his father lying senseless in a pool of his own blood and a policeman at his side. He returned to the house and told his mother. Bridget Mulroney, one of the neighbours, also saw O'Neil's body lying on the slabs. She met Miller at the door of O'Neil's house, and he told her to get back home, adding, 'You hear nothing and you see nothing.' It seemed clear that there had been a struggle, with the affections of Mrs O'Neil the underlying reason, although as so often, drink may have been the actual cause.

When the case came to court, Miller pleaded not guilty to murder. In his version of events, he claimed he had been in the kitchen when one of the boys told him their father had killed himself by jumping through the window. The jury, however, did not agree, and found Miller guilty of culpable homicide. He was sentenced to ten years' penal servitude.

Fraud on a Prospective Bride

All fraud is cruel, but some can verge on the sadistic. Such was the case on 10 February 1876, when young Flora McLeod sailed from her home in South Uist for Glasgow. Flora must have been excited, as she was going to meet her fiancé, a labourer who had moved to the city for work.

Flora sailed on *Dunara Castle*, a newly built MacCallum Orme 457-ton steamer that sailed every week from the Hebrides to the Broomielaw with cargo and forty-four passengers. While on the voyage she met a handsome young engineer named Hugh Brodie, with whom she got friendly. Indeed, they got more than friendly, and in the course of the short voyage Flora and Hugh got engaged. They stepped off the ship at Broomielaw arm in arm and very much in love, with Flora's labourer fiancé already consigned to history.

From the berth at the Broomielaw Flora and Hugh strolled to Dorset Street, where her friends waited for her. She introduced them to Hugh, and when her fiancé arrived to meet her, Flora threw him out without remorse. The speedy engagement continued, with Hugh expressing his undying love and Flora, the first time she had been away from the Isles, taking it all in. They arranged a further meeting in Glasgow Green, where they spoke of the practicalities: the banns, the ring and the ceremony. It was now that Hugh made a small confession. He wanted to hurry on with the wedding, but there was a slight difficulty: he had plenty money as engineers were well paid, but it was all tied up in the bank. Could Flora possibly lend him £2 and ten shillings?

Flora agreed immediately and parted with the money. And when Hugh asked for her golden earring as well, to pawn and raise money for the ring, she handed that over as well. And that was the last Flora saw of the charming Hugh. She had lost her fiancé, her money, her earring and her naivety all in the space of two days. Flora searched for Hugh and discovered he was no engineer but a much more prosaic fireman – a stoker – and she was not the first girl to fall for his charms. Hugh Brodie had a history of picking up unsophisticated girls from the Hebrides, promising marriage and leaving them with a broken heart and a depleted purse.

Other men also preferred multiple women.

Bigamy

Not yet twenty-one, Septimus Thorburn must have been quite a charmer. At least both his wives thought so. There was Elizabeth Trainer, whom he married on 19 December 1842, and no doubt to whom he swore his undying love. However, Helen Duffy also caught his attention, and on 17 November 1843, he tapped on the door of Hugh Hamilton in St Andrews Square and asked if they could get married, please?

Now Hugh Hamilton was a Justice of the Peace for the County of Lanark, and he was well known as a man who asked few questions in such circumstances. However, bigamy was a crime and Thorburn ended up in the jail for a year as a result of his romantic endeavours, but there is another angle to this story. Hugh Hamilton also married William Stewart to Barbara McBeth, which angered Stewart's other wife, Ann Williamson. She reported him to the authorities, who searched diligently for Stewart. They learned that he planned to abscond with his new wife to America, and swooped on the ship he was on as it lay in Gourock Bay. The police arrested Stewart, but if he expected support from his new wife, he was disappointed, as she remained on board and sailed alone to the United States.

Hugh Hamilton married up to three couples a week. He did not officially charge a fee, but occasionally he did accept half a crown as a token of appreciation. He had also been known to help celebrate the new unions with a dram or two of whisky, but on one memorable occasion he was paid a sovereign and a half. Hamilton had one golden rule: he never married a couple if they were drunk.

Although Hamilton was quite happy with this side business, it was illegal, and in 1844 Lord Cockburn, the Circuit judge, found out about it, quite by chance. In the Spring Circuit of 1844 Cockburn tried two cases of bigamy, both of which revolved around Hugh Hamilton. The JP's register showed over 1,200 such irregular marriages over the last decade, so if he was typical of the type it was no wonder that bigamy was such a major concern in the period. However, some hopeful grooms had other methods of achieving their objectives.

An Impoverished Sweetheart

William McMurray was a joiner with a problem. It was June 1862, and he was due to get married very shortly. Marriage meant certain outlays of money: to have the banns read, pay for the minister and even buy a wedding ring. McMurray had promised to pay for all these and then take his sweetheart as a wife, and then provide for her the rest of their lives. That was the arrangement, but there was a small hitch. McMurray did not have enough money to do any of that. Indeed, McMurray had barely enough money for the railway ticket he hoped would help him resolve his problem.

On 25 June, McMurray limped into the office of the Renfrewshire County Police. He was agitated and upset as he gabbled out his story to the duty officer. He had caught the Greenock train at Bridge Street and got off at Langbank. From there he walked by Drums, going toward Barrochan Mill, but three men approached him when he was half a mile from Hardgate Toll.

One of the men asked him the time. He said he did not know and walked a further few yards when there were footsteps behind him. Before he could turn somebody grabbed him, threw him on his back and wrapped a rope around his neck. One of the attackers was a bearded man about five foot seven inches tall, but he did not get a clear view of the others. He fought back as best he could, but he was choked into unconsciousness.

When he woke, McMurray checked his pockets and found he had been robbed. The three men had taken his new leather pocketbook with the £32 he had saved to pay for his wedding, as well as a passbook for the Union Bank.

At first the police believed McMurray's story. They sympathised with his loss, although they were surprised that there could be such a crime in what they knew to be a safe area. Officers scoured the countryside to make enquiries, but nobody had heard or seen anything. They called McMurray back, but when he altered his version of events they became suspicious.

After a while they realised McMurray's entire story had been a lie to hide his lack of money, but he was let off with a small fine. Given the right combination of circumstances, love was as capable of creating crime as hatred was.

19

A Rash of Robberies

The majority of crimes in Victorian Glasgow, as in most big cities, were irritating rather than dangerous. Drink-fuelled petty assault and opportunist theft were common, or squabbles between husband and wife, but the police were very aware of the presence of professional criminals, the men and women of the so-called criminal class, who lived by crime and nothing else. The Glasgow Police knew the names and faces of these habitual criminals and exchanged information with other forces throughout the country when the known names were on the move. Such a situation occurred in May 1856 when Glasgow was hit by a succession of burglaries that were marked by an unusual professionalism.

Burglars Abound

The burglars had an infallible technique. They usually worked on Sundays, when the respectable families were at church and their houses were empty, and they used false (or skeleton) keys to gain entry. They took only money, jewellery and items that were both easily portable and commanded a ready market, and they left without creating a disturbance.

From the fact that the burglaries had started at a given time, the police suspected the culprits to be returned convicts, perhaps ticket-of-leave men who had come back home to resume where they had left off. When Lieutenant Milligan of the Edinburgh Police contacted Mr Mackay, head of the Glasgow Criminal Department, on 6 May, that theory was virtually confirmed. Milligan said that two expert housebreakers had left Edinburgh some weeks before and were supposed to be operating in the Glasgow area. Their names were Campbell and Burns, and both had been transported for theft many years previously.

Mackay remembered Burns well. He had been a large-scale housebreaker, captured after making a huge haul of silver plate from a country house in Perthshire. John Robertson, of the firm of Maitland and Robertson, had actually arrested Burns, so Mackay knocked on his door and asked for his help in catching the thief a second time.

Robertson seems to have been a resourceful man; the following Saturday he saw two men in Argyle Street, one of them vaguely recognisable. At first he was not sure if he was correct in assuming it was Burns after the passage of time, so he followed the men around Glasgow for a few hours until he was certain. Burns and his companion entered the City Hall in the Candleriggs, a popular place for musical entertainment. They sat there and listened to a concert, with Robertson a few seats behind. When he saw the pair was quite settled, Robertson slipped out and informed the police, so three plainclothes officers accompanied him back to the hall. When the two suspects left, the police followed. They walked down Hutcheson Street, where the suspects split and walked in opposite directions.

The police continued to follow. One policeman traced Burns to 10 Coburg Street in the south side of Glasgow. The second man, who turned out to be Campbell, was followed to 30 King Street. The policeman waited outside, huddled in the doorway of a stair across the street. When Campbell left, the policeman followed across the Gorbals Suspension Bridge and on to Coburg Street, where he entered number 10, Burns' house. The officer remained outside, trying to be inconspicuous, and within ten minutes the suspects left, in the company of a third man.

They had changed from respectable clothes into scruffy, their hats had been replaced by caps and they moved with more caution than they had before.

Again the police followed, this time to a stair in Hospital Street. The suspects moved in cautiously, one at a time, and the police waited in the street outside. Half an hour passed, then an hour; occasionally one or other of the suspects would venture into the street and glance around, checking for police and returning, but without seeing the watchers.

Either the police grew careless, or they decided to hurry things along a little, but an officer blew his whistle and the three suspects exploded from the stair. They ran into Hospital Street, split up and fled in three different directions: it was a case of every thief for himself. However, the police expected that and chased after the running men. Campbell threw away a large bunch of skeleton keys and fought furiously for his freedom when the police caught him, but all three were carried to Gorbals Police Office.

When detectives searched the Coburg Street house they found nothing incriminating, but they had far more success at Campbell's house at 30 King Street. Campbell lived in the top flat, and when the police lifted the hearth stone they found a lovely little collection of the tools of the housebreaker's trade. There was a selection of files and beautifully crafted picklocks, a life preserver – better known as a skull-cracker – that was handy enough to fit up a sleeve or be concealed in a closed fist, but also heavy enough to kill. There was also a small 'dumb-craft', which was a mechanical device used for breaking open locks, and enough money to start a small bank. Campbell himself was a blacksmith by trade and an Edinburgh man. The mysterious third man was a Glasgow thief by the name of Ruth. It was a notable success for the police.

Robbery and theft were prevalent throughout the century, as they are now, and with an astounding variety of methods. Sometimes the thieves were ingenious, at others just brash and daring.

Brute Force

In autumn and early winter of 1852 a rash of housebreaking broke out in and around Glasgow. As most of the houses were robbed using the same procedure, the police surmised that it was a single gang of thieves. The method was very simple and lacked any pretence at subtlety, but was very effective. The thieves found out when a property was unoccupied then simply rammed themselves against the door until it collapsed, whereupon they swarmed in and ransacked the place. If the door proved too stout, the gang would smash in a panel, sneak in the smallest member to draw back the bolts and rob it the same way. They did not steal anything large but chose only the most portable of valuables, such as money or silver plate. When the police began increasing patrols and arresting every known thief on suspicion, the gang altered its base southward and began to operate in Ayrshire, first in Kilmarnock and then in Ayr.

On the night of Wednesday, 17 November 1852, the gang targeted the house of an Ayr merchant named Campbell Wright. They smashed open the door and pulled the house to pieces in their search for valuables, eventually breaking open a locked drawer and stealing £40, as well as some clothes and some silverware.

When the family returned they ran to the local police. Realising that the Glasgow gang was to blame, the police and sheriff officers watched the station of the Glasgow and Southwestern Railway, and Mr Christison, a sheriff officer, saw a pair of men he thought looked suspicious boarding the train to Glasgow. Christison whistled up the police and all the men in the carriage were arrested. When a Glasgow detective came down he identified them as William White, James Crawford, William McDonald and James Kean, all well-known thieves. It was a short and simple operation that ended the career of that particular gang.

Some thefts were even bolder.

The Maryhill Pirates

Hollywood and Robert Louis Stevenson have created the popular image of pirates. They tend to be specific to the seventeenth and eighteenth centuries, with elaborate costumes, tricorne hats and maybe an eye patch. However, pirates came in all shapes and sizes and haunted seas other than the Caribbean. In May 1856 there was even piracy on the Forth and Clyde Canal at Maryhill.

It is often forgotten that Scotland had its own canal network serving the major cities of the Central Belt. Of these, the Forth and Clyde was the principal artery. One basin of this canal was at Maryhill, then just north of Glasgow, and it was often busy with barges carrying coal for the shipping and the area's steam-powered mills.

On the evening of Thursday, 16 May 1856, one particular barge berthed in Swans Basin, opposite Swan's boatbuilding yard. The master was a cautious man, and rather than lie alongside, he anchored in the middle of the basin, for it was not unknown for thieves to creep on board at night to see what they could steal. That summer was particularly bad for theft, as the Coatbridge miners were on strike and men were desperate for anything to feed or shelter their families.

In the early hours of Friday morning, a group of miners appropriated a boat from the side of the basin and rowed silently to the barge. However quiet they were, they alerted the barge master, who ordered them off, only to be repelled with a volley of coal. Unable to resist against superior numbers, he ran to his cabin, allowing the miners free rein. They towed the barge to the bank and robbed her of ten tons of coal, while taking another five tons and about a ton of potatoes from other vessels. Once they were satisfied, the miners melted away with their spoils and were never caught.

Deepwater men were even more likely to be robbed than mariners on inland waterways.

Jack Ashore

With all the hazards of storm, shipwreck and icebergs, it is not surprising that many seamen lived for the periods when they were on shore. Sometimes, however, life on land could be as hazardous as it was on sea. In common with most sizeable ports, Glasgow had its predators, who viewed Jack ashore as a legitimate target. Some seamen had nothing but bad luck; one such was a Swede called Lars Pieterson from Stockholm, who caught a train from Liverpool to Glasgow in March 1854 in search of a berth.

While he was on the train, an American from Boston befriended him and helped him find a decent temperance hotel in Great Clyde Street. Pieterson left his luggage in the room. He tucked his kit under the bed, including some newly bought clothing and a red flannel shirt with 500 dollars carefully sewn inside. The pair thought the coffee house a little tame so hit the town in search of somewhere that sold alcohol. Many hours and many more drams later, a friendly young woman sidled up to Pieterson and kindly permitted him to take her to her room. She allowed him the brief pleasure of her body in exchange for the £15 in gold he had in his pockets, in addition to the few shillings she usually charged her clients.

At the same time as the prostitute was robbing him blind, his erstwhile companion returned to the temperance hotel and removed all Pieterson's clothes, including the red flannel shirt. When Pieterson returned to his hotel he realised he had been robbed of nearly all his money, and counted what he had left. He had a little over £4, which was plenty for him to forget all his troubles in a haze of alcohol. Unfortunately he was unable to do so, as no sooner had he left the hotel than he was nudged by a passer-by who also picked his pocket. The police never caught the Bostonian, and Pieterson presumably went back to sea a wiser and poorer man.

How to Break into a Business

The Victorians guarded their property in every conceivable manner. They had shutters and iron bars on the windows, bolts and chains on the doors, high walls topped with broken glass, guard dogs, private watchmen, ingenious safes and guns, but the thieves could be equally clever. In September 1851 the clothiers Donald and Company on the corner of Argyle Street and Miller Street were robbed after the proprietor took what he thought was every precaution against theft. They had moved into the premises three years earlier, after the previous occupiers had been robbed by thieves who had gained access by breaking through a brick partition in the cellar. Donald and Company removed the partition and built a two-foot thick stone wall in its place. They also supplemented their new strong lock on the cellar door with a six-inch thick block of wood.

All these precautions proved fruitless as on the night of Saturday, 19 September, three men robbed the premises. They wrenched off the staple that secured the new lock and forced aside the baulk of wood so they now faced a flight of steps that ended in the stone wall. They must have reconnoitred their target, for they carried pick-axes and hacked a man-sized hole through the wall and slid into the cellar beneath the furrier. The thieves had either come very prepared, or the proprietors had been careless, for they used a ladder to gain access to the ceiling of the cellar, where there was a hatch.

It took only a few moments to force it open, and the thieves pulled themselves through onto the floor of the clothiers. The shop was full of furs, satins and silks, but the thieves were after ready cash and opened all three desks. However they got only a few shillings there and although they tried to open the safe they failed. They did steal about £100 worth of various articles, which they may have thought a fitting reward for all their planning and effort.

While some robberies were never solved, there were also well known thieves who escaped justice.

Not Proven

Jane Faucit was a notorious thief with a string of convictions for theft, pocket-picking and general misbehaviour. Whenever there was a case of theft in the Trongate area, the police suspected Faucit and hauled her in for questioning. In April 1851 a man named John Brown was robbed in Trongate. A female had invited him into her house, and while inside somebody removed his watch and chain. However, when Faucit appeared before the Circuit Court in October that year, the jury did not think there was sufficient evidence and the case against her was found not proven. As soon as she walked free of the court, a crowd composed of scores of Glasgow's thieves, prostitutes and street-corner footpads cheered themselves hoarse and escorted her to a pub in Saltmarket Street.

Other thieves were anonymous, but with interesting techniques.

Stealing Change

On Saturday, 22 March 1826, Charles Harper was robbed. He ran a shop in Drygate Street and had ten shillings' worth of change spread out on the counter ready to give to a customer when he became aware of a boy hovering in the doorway. Before Harper could react, the boy had whacked down a long tar-smeared stick on top of the money, rolled it around so the coins stuck to the tar, lifted it free and ran. Too surprised to react, Harper could only stare as the boy ran, taking five shillings and sixpence with him.

Sometimes robberies could be very violent.

Stouthrife and Informers

Scotland has her own unique legal system that dates back to the Middle Ages. While there are elements that are similar to English Law, the civil law is based on Scots Common Law with an admixture of Roman Dutch Law. In criminal justice, the role of the public prosecutor is vital, with the Lord Advocate head of criminal prosecutions. Naturally in a system as old as Scottish Law, some of the terms will be unfamiliar to people from other countries, and indeed will be unknown even to indigenous Scots unless they have frequent dealings with legal matters. One such term is *Stouthrife*, which meant 'robbery with violence'. In the case, which occurred in Glasgow in April 1848, a house was broken into, the occupants terrified, the watchmen and owner assaulted and the owner robbed.

David Stirling lived in Hogganfield, at that time to the north-east of Glasgow. He was a successful businessman and owned a bleachfield, used for bleaching textiles, together with a warehouse and workshop for calendaring linen. He lived in an adjoining single-storey house and employed a resident maidservant and a private security guard, then known as a watchman. Late at night on Friday, 14 April 1848, the watchman, James Armstrong, was on his rounds when he saw two men prowling around the grounds of the house. Armstrong followed, and when he saw them attempting to break into the back window of the warehouse he shouted, 'Hey! What are you doing?' and they ran off. However, they did not run far. A few moments later they pounced on Armstrong as he walked past a pile of rocks; he heard the sound, but they jumped on him and knocked him down with a crowbar.

While one knelt on him, the other tied his hands behind his back with a length of tarred rope; one was wearing a mask, but Armstrong got a good look at the second. Once he was secured, the men ordered him to hand over the keys of the bleachfield counting house, where the money would be kept. Armstrong was a brave man and refused outright, so they held him firm and searched through his pockets, with one yanking free the key. Still dizzy from the attack, Armstrong could barely resist when the men dragged him upright. One man pulled a butcher's knife from inside his jacket and pressed the blade against his chest, so Armstrong cried, 'Are you going to murder me?'

But instead they ordered him to lead them to the counting house, saying, 'We will do no more to you if you don't speak above your breath', meaning just speak in a whisper, and added, 'But if you take one wrong step, we'll kill you.'

Armstrong had no choice but to comply. He took them through the boiler house to the counting house, where they again threw him to the floor. They struck a Lucifer match and lit a lantern. Armstrong expected their next order would be to show then where the money was held, but they saw a wooden desk and made their own judgement.

They did not waste time picking the lock but prised it open with the sharp end of the crowbar and emptied out the content. It was hardly worth their while: there was only six shillings in silver fourpenny pieces. As payday was looming, the robbers had hoped for the entire wages for the workforce. They cursed, pocketed what there was and grabbed the watchman once more, tied his ankles and pushed him callously to the floor with a final threat to remain silent or they would kill him. They left him there, walked away and locked the door behind them.

Perhaps the men were disappointed at the smallness of their haul, or maybe they had always intended a double-strike, but after leaving the watchman tied up in the counting house, they made for Stirling's house. For a moment they were frustrated by the locked door, but the smaller of the two swarmed up on to the roof, slithered down inside a chimney and opened the scullery door to let his companion in. They scraped a Lucifer and lit a coil of green wax taper, so the discoloured light pooled around them. After a quick look around they glided through the kitchen and checked the tiny kitchen in which the housekeeper slept.

Janet Anderson was curled up in a foetal ball and did not stir when they held the lantern close to her face. They nodded and moved on, silent and sinister in the echoing shadows. As soon as they left, the maid looked up; she had been awake all the time. She had heard the intruders come down the chimney. She thought it sounded like rats, then came the grating of the bar that secured the scullery door and the taller of the two men was over her bed.

Janet Anderson watched them cross a beam of moonlight that ghosted through the window; she thought the shorter man had his face darkened to disguise his appearance, while the taller man wore a moleskin jacket. She waited until they were past and then rose as quietly as she could, threw on her clothes and slipped out the back door to find Armstrong. However, as he was already tied up on the floor of the warehouse, she could not find him but blundered around in the dark for a few moments until fear took control and she hid herself, shaking, amongst the machinery in the warehouse. She waited there, crying, for some two hours until her courage returned and she emerged and knocked at the door of the carter and then the engineman. Both listened to her story, grabbed makeshift weapons and searched for Armstrong. They found him in the warehouse and released him.

As the servants played out their parts, the intruders opened the door to Stirling's bedroom. The noise wakened him and he stirred and sat up. He saw the two men rushing toward him, saw one with an upraised crowbar, and lifted an arm to protect himself. The pain was searing as the metal bar descended, breaking his arm. He fell back as they first punched him and then jerked him upright. He saw that both wore crepe masks, which they must have slipped on as they entered his room.

'What do you want here?' Stirling asked and added, 'What harm have I done you?'

'Whisht,' they said.

The demands were obvious. Where were the valuables? Hand over the keys for his chests and presses. The turned him to face the pillow and tied his hands behind his back, then twisted him the right way up again and said if he made a noise, they would kill him. When they lifted the crowbar again, Stirling gave them the keys and watched helplessly as they searched the house, crashing open all the drawers and the presses as they searched for anything valuable. There were some silver coins, but when they found a cask of whisky they stopped thieving and brought it straight into Stirling's bedroom. They had to ask Stirling's help to open it, but at last they worked out the secret, pulled out the bung, poured some of the contents into tumblers and drank while Stirling watched in suffering silence.

The two masked men seemed determined to drink themselves stupid and remained with the whisky for quite some time. When they rose they forgot to plunder the bedroom and grabbed only a couple of shirt stocks and some shirts and other articles of clothes. With this meagre plunder they left the house and returned to Glasgow, having only a few shillings profit and a deep drink of whisky for having injured two men and terrified a servant.

When the intruders had gone, Stirling searched for Armstrong. He could not find him, so ran instead to his neighbour, James Alexander, who accompanied him to the warehouse. At this stage Stirling believed that Janet Anderson had been an accomplice and had allowed the robbers in, as often happened with servants, but as time passed he realised she had not been involved. He was shaken and damaged, but the thieves had not gained much.

That same Saturday evening, a watchman in Bridgegate saw a man standing within a close. The man was swaying slightly, as if he had been drinking, his face was darkened with soot and he held a crowbar in his hand. Not surprisingly, the watchman questioned him, and when the answers were evasive, arrested him on suspicion. When the watchman searched him in the police office he found seven shillings and fourpence in silver fourpenny pieces and a few shirt stocks.

The suspect gave his name as John Ash, an Irishman from County Roscommon, who had lately been discharged from the 88th Regiment of Foot. The police later found his bonnet on top of the boiler in Stirling's scullery, while boot prints in Stirling's garden corresponded exactly to the sole of Ash's boots. As Ash went into custody, Stirling sent for Dr Easton, who found the crowbar had broken his arm cleanly, so it was easy to set.

Although Ash refused to name his accomplice, the police had a network of informers who fed them little titbits of information and this, augmented by the observations of the watchmen on the beat, gave them a good idea what was happening in the streets of Glasgow. Their chief suspect was a man named Daniel Cairns, a well-known thief. They learned he was hiding in Bridgegate, in a house in Merchants Lane, a narrow street of ancient houses with crow-stepped gables that ran up the eastern boundary of what historically had been the Merchants House.

Very early on the Monday morning, three officers strode up to the front door of the Merchants Lane house. However, the police were not the only people to have informants, and the inhabitants had made their own preparations. The police had to batter through the locked and barricaded front door, only to find their quarry had left his house, forced the door of a neighbour and slipped to freedom out of a back window.

Frustrated, the police searched the house and found treasure chests of stolen property hidden up the chimney and under the floorboards. Most of the items were clothes: high-quality items such as shawls and dress coats, together with a very ornate rifle. All these items were taken to the police office, from where notices were sent to search for the owners.

On Wednesday morning, a manufacturer from Paisley came to the police office and claimed all the stolen clothes. His house had been robbed on the Sunday evening, presumably by one or more of the people from the Merchants Lane house. The gun was not claimed, but the police suspected it had been stolen during the Chartist riots earlier that year.

The case came to the High Court in late May 1848. Both John Ash and Daniel Cairns were summoned to court, but Cairns did not appear. Ash was brought out of custody. He pleaded not guilty. The judge outlawed Cairns for his non-appearance, and Ash was transported for twenty-one years.

After the affair at Stirling's house a reward was offered for information that would lead to the capture of Cairns. He remained free for nearly a year and was only caught after a burglary at the shoe shop of Robert

Ramsay in Hamilton, south-east of Glasgow. This time Daniel Cairns had acted in concert with his brother William, and once again it was an informer who told the police where he was hiding.

On Tuesday, 27 February 1849, two detectives, then known as criminal officers, Patrick and McColl, raided a lodging house in Calton. They came without any warning, and so quietly the local criminal element had no time to issue a warning, and they left with both the Cairns brothers in handcuffs. The trial was held at the end of April, and the brothers were given ten years' transportation apiece.

Murder the Turnkey

David Stirling and the police may have thought that no more would be heard about Daniel Cairns, but there was one more shot in the Cairns' locker. The brothers were stuffed into the old prison at Hamilton while they awaited transportation to Australia. While English prisons used a combination of mind games, hard labour and idleness to break the will of the prisoner, Scottish prisons tended to be more progressive and often taught a trade or allowed the convict to pursue the same work as they had outside. However, this element of rehabilitation could also have its drawbacks.

Both the Cairns brothers were shoemakers. They continued this work, crammed three to a cell in the ancient jail of Hamilton. Shoemaking was a skilled trade that required hammers and knives, and in July 1849 the brothers devised a nasty plan to use their knives to murder the turnkey and Governor Ross, grab the keys and escape. However, they made the classic mistake of talking and trusting too much. They discussed their plans in front of the third inmate of the cell, and he informed the governor. He was quite a clever informant; Hamilton Jail had a system whereby Ross read all the mail the prisoners sent out, so rather than be seen talking to him, the third cellmate wrote a letter to Ross informing him what the brothers planned.

Governor Ross was equally clever. He gave no warning but pounced one night, grabbed the brothers and chained them securely in different cells. That was their last fling for freedom. Shortly after they were trundled to Leith and shipped south for onward transport to Australia on *Oriental Queen*. Maybe then Stirling could sleep in peace.

While these robbers went to great effort and gained little, others benefitted nothing at all.

Hiding a Hoard

In the eighteenth and nineteenth centuries, Glasgow was at the centre of a worldwide trading network. The wealth that flowed into the city was used to create some impressive architecture and financed merchant houses, shipping lines and new dynasties. The merchant families often built splendid mansions for themselves, and one such was Kenmure House in Bishopbriggs. The builder was Charles Stirling, a West India merchant, and it later became the home of William Stirling of the same family and firm.

Naturally such places were a tempting target for the thieves of Glasgow, and in January 1858 four men went on a housebreaking spree around Hillhead and Bishopbriggs. There was James McCabe, a man already convicted of theft; the others were Thomas Williams, William Thompson and William Johnston. First they hit Florentine Bank at Hillhead and came away with a silver tea caddy spoon and a silver-plated breadbasket. These were small, fairly valuable and easily portable items. Next they broke into a house called Huntershill at Bishopsbriggs, where they lifted a writing desk and five silver spoons. Their last stop was Kenmure House, where they made their largest haul: two crystal decanters, a mahogany tea caddy, a silver pepper pot, a crystal sugar bowl and a silver mustard spoon.

Overall, their gains were not enough to make them even moderately wealthy. A crooked pawnshop dealer or resetter would give them perhaps twenty pounds. Even so, they were fairly pleased with their night's work, as they carried their spoils along the banks of the Clyde. They knew that there would be an outcry after their exploits, so they decided to hide the goods and come back after the noise had died down. Shortly after eleven at night they passed the Dalmarnock Bridge, found a handy hedge they could use as a marker, dug a nice deep hole and stuffed in the spoil. After that they wandered off to celebrate in a pub.

Unfortunately for the housebreakers, they neglected to watch for witnesses. Their nocturnal activities had attracted the attention of a brace of boys, who followed to see what they were doing. They watched the thieves bury their loot, waited until the men had gone and promptly dug it up again. Rather than pawn it, the boys handed it into the Eastern Police Office. The police were quite happy; they replaced the silverware where it had been and set a watch. After a few days the four men returned and the police pounced. The four fought back, with Thompson producing a chisel and slashing Constable John McDonald on the thigh and the ear but the police were eventually successful and arrested them all.

McCabe, the old offender, was given six years' penal servitude, as was Thompson, while the other two were given four years each.

Other hoards remained hidden far longer.

Discovery

On Friday, 17 September 1875, a bunch of labourers were working in a brickfield to the north of London Road when one gave a sudden shout. 'What's this?' He scrabbled in the sand and hauled out something that gleamed golden. It was an expensive-looking but old-fashioned watch. The other workmen gathered around in amazement. The hole was about three feet deep and when they dug around they found another watch, then a third and a fourth. Not surprisingly, the men became quite excited; the noise they made attracted a crowd and a few stray hands sneaked in to lift whatever they could. The police were next and, unlike the labourers, they did not believe in the old adage of 'finders keepers'. Detective Campbell took charge of the case, and all the forty watches that had been unearthed.

The watches had been there for nearly thirty years. On Tuesday, 18 August 1846, there had been a break-in at the pawnshop of Adam Whyte in Orr Street, Calton, and over a hundred watches were stolen, along with a veteran's medal from the Sikh War. Captain Smart of the Calton Police searched for the thief, and arrested a returned convict. In October that year a cotton spinner named William Watson was digging for bait in a field near London Road and found a number of watches wrapped up in a handkerchief. The remainder of the robbery remained lost until that day in 1875.

A Slippery Customer

Sometimes thieves could be hard to catch and even harder to keep. Such a case happened in late August of 1868 when a thief snatched a gold watch and chain from a lady in King Street. The robbery happened so quickly that the lady could do nothing about it except give a description to the police. However, the Glasgow Police knew their criminals and the description matched a returned convict named Thomas Dunlop. They scoured the city, but Dunlop was not in any of his usual haunts. The police called in their informers, asked the right questions and discovered that Dunlop had caught the train to Edinburgh. They sent a description to the Edinburgh Police. Within a fortnight the Edinburgh Police had picked him up, and contacted their west coast colleagues.

The Glasgow authorities sent a sheriff officer named David Walker to bring Dunlop back to Glasgow, and that's where the trouble started. Dunlop was an experienced thief and seems to have also been glib with his tongue, for as soon as they got off the train in Glasgow, he persuaded the inexperienced Walker to take him for a quick dram in Princes Street before having him locked away in the police office. However, the publican was not keen to serve two men who were handcuffed together, and sent them on their way. Dunlop brushed fleetingly against Walker, and then led the way out the back door and pushed into a knot of men who were gathered in the close between the pub and the street.

No sooner had the crowd gathered around them than Dunlop cried, 'Now, lads!' and Walker found himself a target of half a dozen people, all intent on freeing Dunlop and getting a few good blows at Walker into the bargain. It was not hard to release Dunlop. In that brief contact in the pub he had picked Walker's pocket of the handcuff key, and while his friends enjoyed themselves in thumping the sheriff officer, Dunlop slipped away.

As Walker went down under a multitude of blows from the gang of men and women, he shouted for help. It was the old familiar cry of 'Murder! Police!' and as so often in nineteenth-century Glasgow, it worked. Two police hurried to the spot, in time to see Dunlop escaping and a blood-spattered Walker curled up on the ground. When the police grabbed Dunlop the crowd turned on them instead, and within seconds they were reeling under the assault. Once again Dunlop struggled his way free, and ran, leaving his companions to deal with the police. They did that so effectively that both constables were kicked nearly unconscious and Dunlop escaped.

The police were angered at this blatant affront to their dignity. The detectives in Central District turned all their resources on to the search for Dunlop. They checked all his known hideouts and pubs, put pressure on his known associates and gradually pushed him into a corner. They took a few days to trace him to the Trongate, but Dunlop did not intend to get caught. He ran. He ran up to the top of a stair, climbed into the attic and slipped through the skylight onto the roof, three stories above the corner of Saltmarket and Trongate. He hid there for a while, cowering behind the chimneys on the roof of blue-grey slates.

As the police tightened their net, Dunlop knew he would get caught unless he did something drastic. He stood up, poised, and was about to leap on to the next roof when the chimneystack gave way and he fell, first onto a single-storey building and then onto the ground far below. As bad luck would have it, he landed virtually uninjured, but right at the feet of Sub Inspector William Smith.

Dunlop shook himself, looked up and said, 'You neednae he feared, Willie. I'll no try and escape from you.' His brief freedom was over.

Bungling Thief

If somebody was to draw a caricature of a robbery at a jewellery shop, they might think of a man throwing a brick at a shop window on a dark winter evening. That is exactly what happened on 30 November 1864 in Gordon Street, Glasgow. It was six o'clock in the evening and a man carried a brick under his jacket, walked up to the jeweller's shop of Alexander and Son, took out the brick and threw it at the plate-glass window. His objective had been a case of diamond rings, but the brick did its work too well. It shattered the window very effectively, but landed on the glass shelf on which the rings sat and broke that as well. The rings tumbled down, too far out of reach for the man to pick up, so he snatched a gold guard chain worth a few pounds instead, but was soon arrested and jailed for a year. His clumsy attempt contrasted wildly with another type of thief.

Gentleman Thief

Glasgow was a rich city. She was one of the main powerhouses of the Empire, with a huge industrial base and magnates who were influential in Imperial and world circles, and as such she attracted attention from all across the globe. While most of the visitors came for legitimate business, others had their own ideas how to rake money from the city. One such was George de Fontenoy, alias Henry Edmund D'Orvil de Montenay, alias the Viscount Georges de Fontenoy, who arrived in Glasgow in July

1877. Fontenoy was a tall man in his mid-thirties. He spoke with a pronounced French accent, dressed immaculately and had impeccable manners as he took up residence in the Royal Hotel in George Square with all the appearance of nobility.

On 21 July 1877, Viscount Georges de Fontenoy called at the jewellery shop of Messrs James Muirhead & Sons of Buchanan Street. He was looking for a selection of diamonds for his wife, but only the finest would do. Could he see the best the shop had to offer? And would the shop be kind enough to bring them to his hotel so his wife could view them herself? In the nineteenth century, the aristocracy were viewed with an amazing degree of adulation, so of course the hotel fell over itself to oblige a viscount.

Helped by a willing assistant named John Fulton, Fontenoy looked over the best jewellery that Muirhead's had to offer and selected only the best of the best. He thought his wife might like a diamond necklace, particularly the one valued at £900, with forty-eight diamonds including a central stone of three carats. The stones reduced in size from the centre and had silver mountings and gold backs. The necklace was supported by a £400 diamond band bracelet consisting of seventeen joined squares, with a centrepiece of a cluster of small diamonds around a single large stone; and a £200 ring with two small diamonds set round a larger stone. Overall the three pieces carried a value of around £1,500. Fontenoy handed over his calling card, which had an impressive address of 12 Grosvenor Crescent, Belgrave Square, London, with the Royal Hotel, Glasgow, added in pencil, and acted like the French nobility he purported to be.

Fulton escorted Fontenoy to his rooms in the hotel. There was a parlour, with a dressing room off of it, in which Fontenoy's wife sat, waiting to view the diamonds so she could see if they were up to her high standard. Taking all three pieces of jewellery, Fontenoy carried them through to his wife. Fenton waited in the parlour. It may have seemed strange to him that Fontenoy's wife did not come through in person, but the ways of the aristocracy were weird and wonderful, and he waited patiently. After a few moments, Fulton looked up as his boss, James Muir-head, appeared.

Muirhead had learned that Fontenoy had approached other jewellers in Glasgow with the same request, but they had been less trusting than he. At least one jeweller had come to the hotel to check on the mysterious viscount and had not been impressed by the man's lack of luggage: two cases were hardly enough for an ordinary gentleman, let alone an aristocrat. With his suspicions awakened, Muirhead had rushed to the hotel. After the viscount had been missing for a lengthy period, Fulton had also worried and asked a helpful waiter if there were any other exits from Fontenoy's suite, and had been told there were not. All the same, when he and Muirhead tentatively opened the door of Fontenoy's dressing room, they found it empty of everything except a single leather bag and two empty jewellery boxes.

The waiter had been wrong. There was a second exit that led to a tiny room, which in turn opened to a narrow passage leading to a side entrance of the hotel. Fontenoy had grabbed the jewels and run, emerging into North Hanover Street. Despite all the efforts of the police and Muirhead's advertised reward of £300, Fontenoy got clean away. Muirhead sent out circulars with Fontenoy's description, while the police put details of the case in their own newspaper *Hue and Cry* and also spread the news to Europe. When Muirhead learned that a man of a similar description had used a similar technique to rob a jewellery shop in London, he may have felt slightly better, for he knew Fontenoy was a professional, but that did not bring back his diamonds.

The case slipped from memory and the police moved on to other things. Nearly two years later, in April 1879, Chief Constable Von Doneburgh of the Amsterdam police contacted Chief Constable McCall of Glasgow. Von Doneburgh informed McCall that the Dutch police had arrested a man who had sold a pair of very expensive earrings to a diamond dealer. When questioned he had given the name Henry D'Orvil de Montenay, and Von Doneburgh wondered if this could be the fellow McCall had been looking for some time ago? McCall asked for more details. When a photograph arrived he made a positive identification and obtained a warrant for Montenay's arrest, once the Dutch were finished with him.

It was another two years before Fontenoy had finished his time in the Dutch prison and the Amsterdam authorities contacted McCall to say he could have his man. Although he would not appreciate the honour, Fontenoy made history as the first criminal extradited from mainland Europe to Glasgow. Detective Hamilton and a sheriff officer named James Roden picked him up in the Netherlands. As Fontenoy had already twice attempted to escape in Amsterdam, the Dutch took no chances. They had roped his arms close to his sides and led him with a second rope around his waist, while policemen with naked swords marched all around him in case he slipped his bonds and dashed into the gaping crowd. As soon as they boarded the steamer *Seahorse* in Rotterdam, the Dutch police handed Fontenoy to the Glasgow authorities. Hamilton removed Fontenoy's bonds but watched him closely on the voyage to Hull, although apart from a desire to walk around the ship, Fontenoy gave no trouble at all.

On their arrival in Glasgow, a tired-looking Fontenoy was remitted to the sheriff and his history was gradually unravelled. He had been born in 1844 in Montreal, Canada, and was a native French speaker. He claimed to have a poor grasp of English, although he spoke other languages, but there was no doubting the strange life he had led. He had no fixed home and no means of income save his wits and his propensity to live the high life. Fontenoy appeared before the Circuit Court in August 1881, a year that the judges were escorted to the courthouse by cavalry rather than by the more normal police. If Fontenoy knew, he may have given a wry smile at this unconscious rendering of his own importance. He was not smiling when the judge gave him ten years' penal servitude, despite his obvious ill health.

Epilogue

With a city as dynamic as Glasgow, any book can only skim the surface of the crimes that were committed. Every day would bring its quota of thefts, assaults and drunken misbehaviour, but only a fragment would be recorded and even less would come to the courts. For every crime mentioned in this book, perhaps a thousand have been omitted; criminals and victims alike are anonymous in the murky morass of history.

The city has changed as well. Many of the bad areas were demolished in various improvements from the 1860s onwards, the worst of the tenements are merely memories and the old closes have been revamped. The old days of highwaymen and child strippers, garrotters and vitriol throwers are only a faded memory. Crowds no longer gather to gawp at the gallows fruit, there is little likelihood of a full-scale riot in the streets and steamships no longer race to the Broomielaw.

However, in many ways, Glasgow remains a city where crime is common. The annual report by Strathclyde Police in 2011/2012 stated that rape increased by 25 per cent, although violent crime fell. That year there were fifty-one murders with attempted murder falling from 278 to 209. Serious assault and assaults with intent to rob also diminished.

As this book is being written, the police force in Scotland is undergoing alterations, with a unified force planned for the whole country, a procedure that Chief Constable Smart contemplated at the height of the Victorian period. There is no knowing whether this initiative will succeed or fail, but there is no doubt that the Glasgow criminals will seek to exploit any weaknesses and the equally dedicated police officers will work hard to ensure there are few to exploit.

Overall, this small book can only give a hint of the crime that Glasgow experienced throughout the nineteenth century. It was intended to entertain as well as educate, but if it has raised some interest and brought even a slight measure of understanding to what was the Second City of the Empire and remains a fascinating place, then it has succeeded in its purpose.

Bibliography

Adshead, Joseph. *On juvenile criminals, reformatories, and the means of rendering the perishing and dangerous classes serviceable to the state* (1856) Knowsley Pamphlet Collection, University of Liverpool.

Armstrong, John. 'Transport and the Urban Environment,' in *The Cambridge Urban History of Britain, Volume III: 1840–1950* by Martin Daunton (Ed.) (2000) Cambridge.

Arscott, Caroline. 'The Representation of the City in the Visual Arts,' in *The Cambridge Urban History of Britain, Volume III: 1840–1950* by Martin Daunton (Ed.) (2000) Cambridge.

Barrie, David. *Police in the Age of Improvement: Police Development and the Civic Tradition in Scotland, 1775–1865* (2008) Devon.

Briggs, Asa. *Victorian Cities* (1963, 1968) London. *Caledonian Mercury.*

Cameron, Joy. *Prisons and Punishment in Scotland* (1983) Edinburgh.

Cochrane, Lord. *Circuit Journeys* (1888, 1983) Edinburgh, Hawick.

Cochrane, Lord. *Trials for Sedition in Scotland* (1888) Edinburgh.

Cochrane, Lord. *Memorials of his Time* (1856) Edinburgh.

Chesney, Kellow. *The Victorian Underworld* (1970) London.

Davis, John. 'Central Government and the Towns,' in *The Cambridge Urban History of Britain, Volume III: 1840–1950* by Martin Daunton (Ed.) (2000) Cambridge.

Donnelly, Daniel and Scott, Kenneth (Eds.). *Policing Scotland* (2005) Cullompton.

Dupree, Marguerite. 'The Provision of Social Services,' in *The Cambridge Urban History of Britain, Volume III: 1840–1950* by Martin Daunton (Ed.) (2000) Cambridge.

Ellis, Peter Berresford, and Seumas Mac a'Ghobhainn. *The Scottish Insurrection of 1820* (1970, 2001) Edinburgh.

Engels, Frederick. *The Condition of the Working Class in England* (1846, 1969) London.

Fraser, Derek. *Power and Authority in the Victorian City* (1979) Oxford. *General Police Act 1862.*

Fraser, W. Hamish. 'The Social Problems of the City,' in *Glasgow, Volume II: 1830–1912* by W. Hamish Fraser and Irene Maver (1996) Manchester.

—. 'The Working Class,' in *Glasgow, Volume II: 1830 to 1912* by W. Hamish Fraser and Irene Mayer (1996) Manchester.

—. Fraser, W. Hamish and Irene Mayer. 'Tackling the Problem,' in *Glasgow, Volume II: 1830 to 1912* by W. Hamish Fraser and Irene Mayer (1996) Manchester.

Godfrey, Barry and Paul Lawrence. *Crime and Justice 1750–1950* (2005) Cullompton.

Glasgow Herald.

Gordon, George. 'The Changing City,' in *Perspectives of the Scottish City* by George Gordon (Ed.) (1985) Aberdeen.

Gracy, Drew D. *London's Shadows: The Dark Side of the Victorian City* (2010) London.

Grimble, Ian. *Clans and Chiefs* (1980) London.

Hamilton, Judy. *Scottish Murders* (2006) New Lanark.

Harrison, Brian. 'Pubs,' in *The Victorian City: Images and Realities* by H. J. Dos and Michael Wolff (Eds.) (1973) London.

House, Jack. *The Heart of Glasgow* (1965, 2005) Glasgow.

Hughes, Robert. *The Fatal Shore* (1987) London.

Hunt, Tristam. *Building Jerusalem: The Rise and Fall of the Victorian City* (2004) London.

Jones, David. *Crime, Protest, Community and Police in Nineteenth-Century Britain* (1982) London.

Knepper, Paul. *Criminology and Social Policy* (2007) London.

Law, Alex; Gerry Mooney and Gesa Helms. 'Urban Disorders', 'Problem Places' and 'Criminal Justice in Scotland,' in *Criminal Justice in Scotland* by Hazel Croall *et al.* (2010) Abingdon.

Knight, Alanna. *Burke and Hare* (2007) Kew.

Livingstone, Sheila. *Confess and Be Hanged: Scottish Crime and Punishment Through the Ages* (2000) Edinburgh.

Luckin, Bill. 'Pollution in the City' in *The Cambridge Urban History of Britain, Volume III: 1840–1950* by Martin Daunton (Ed.) (2000) Cambridge.

Lyall, Heather F. C. *Vanishing Glasgow* (1991) Aberdeen.

McLaren, Duncan. *The Rise and Progress of Whisky Drinking in Scotland and the Working of the Public Houses (Scotland) Act, commonly called the Forbes McKenzie Act* (1858) Glasgow.

Massie, Allan; *Glasgow: Portraits of a City.* (1989) London.

Minto, C. S. *Victorian and Edwardian Scotland* (1970) London.

Morris, R. J. and Richard Rodger. 'An Introduction to British Urban History, 1820–1914,' in *The Victorian City: A Reader in British Urban History* by R.J. Morris and Richard Rodger (Eds.) (1993) London and New York.

Morris, R. J. 'Structure, Culture and Society in British Towns,' in *The Cambridge Urban History of Britain, Volume III: 1840–1950* by Martin Daunton (Ed.) (2000) Cambridge.

Murray, Patrick Joseph. *Not so bad as they seem: The transportation, ticket-of-leave, and penal servitude questions* (1857) Knowsley Pamphlet Collection.

Palmer, Sarah. 'Ports,' in *The Cambridge Urban History of Britain, Volume III: 1840–1950* by Martin Daunton (Ed.) (2000) Cambridge.

Pooley, Colin G. 'Patterns on the Ground: Urban Form, Residential Structure and the Social Construction of Space,' in *The Cambridge Urban*

History of Britain, Volume III: 1840–1950 by Martin Daunton (Ed.) (2000) Cambridge.

Rafter, Nicole Hahn. *The Origins of Criminology: A Reader* (2009) Oxford.

Rafter, Nicole Hahn, and Mary Gibson (translators). *Criminal Woman, the Prostitute, and the Normal Woman* by Cesare Lombroso and Ferrero Guglielmo (2004) Durham and London.

Rodger, Richard. 'Employment, Wages and Poverty in the Scottish Cities,' in *The Victorian City: A Reader in British Urban History 1820–1914.* by R.J. Morris and Richard Rodger (Eds.) (1993) London and New York.

Saul, S. B. 'Britain and World Trade 1870–1914,' in *The Economic History Review, New Series* Vol. 7, No. 1 (1954)

Smout, T. C. *A Century of the Scottish People 1830–1950* (1987) London.

—. *A History of the Scottish People 1560–1830* (1969) London.

Tobias, J. *Nineteenth Century Crime, Prevention and Punishment* (1972) London.

Trainor, Richard H. 'The Elite,' in *Glasgow, Volume II: 1830 to 1912* by W. Hamish Fraser and Irene Mayer (1996) Manchester, Manchester University Press.

'The Moral Effects of Machinery on the Population,' in the *Dublin Penny Journal* Vol. 2, No. 53 (July 6, 1833).

Watson, John. *Once Upon a Time in Glasgow* (2003) Glasgow.

Whitmore, Richard. *Victorian and Edwardian Crime and Punishment* (1978) London.

WEBSITES

Convict Transportation Registers Database. < http://www.slq.qld.gov.au/resources/family-history/info-guides/convicts   >

Early Clyde Steamers. < http://www.paddlesteamers.info/EarlyClyde Steamers.htm >

National Library of Scotland Digital Gallery. < http://digital.nls.uk >

Old Glasgow Pubs and Publicans. < http://www.oldglasgowpubs.co.uk >

University of Glasgow. Manuscripts: Special Collections. < http://special.lib.gla.ac.uk/manuscripts/ >